High Yield Investments, Hard Assets and Asset Protection Strategies

BILL BODRI

Top Shape Publishing, LLC
1135 Terminal Way Suite 209
Reno, NV 89502

ISBN-10: 0-9989764-7-3
ISBN-13: 978-0-9980764-7-8
Library of Congress Control Number: 2018900460

DISCLAIMER

CONTENTS

PREFACE

Many investors are seeking higher yield investments for their portfolios, but don't know about the many alternatives available that are not interest rate instruments. If you use the right instruments, you can create a continuous cash compounding machine that will automatically reinvest your yields and grow your capital substantially larger. At the same time, many investors currently fear investing in any types of interest rate or other fiat paper instruments, and are instead seeking hard assets such as gold bullion as insurance against financial calamity. Yet other investors are simply interested in ways to protect any of the financial assets they have. This collection of reports from the *Income&Assets* newsletters introduces the many different types of high yield investment instruments available to the public, as well as the hard assets currently favored by sophisticated investors and various ways to protect your portfolios and preserve your wealth in periods of economic breakdown and government confiscations.

INTRODUCTION

With interest rates at historic lows due to the Federal Reserve's zero interest rate policies along with the negative interest rate policies of other central banks, yield investors are starved of income and being forced into higher risk investments.

At the same time, there is a global movement away from both the U.S. dollar and fiat paper investments, precisely the bonds and stocks that might prove of interest, and into hard assets such as gold and silver, oil or gas wells and farmland real estate. Some give off income and others do not. Many people want to protect their portfolios by investing in hard assets, but which do you choose?

Lastly, how do you protect your assets in this new world where your bank deposits are considered unsecured credit loans to the banks, where governments can confiscate your assets or outlaw them overnight (ex. Bitcoin), and where central bank risk is actually a real thing?

The past issues of the *Income&Assets* newsletter, published by John Newtson and Bill Bodri, went deeply into these issues. Here now is a summary of the best high yield and hard asset investment ideas pulled from past issues of *Income&Assets* and edited for book format.

Through these explanatory chapters on various high yield investments, hard assets and asset protection strategies you will quickly gain insight into the various types of investments available, especially for those seeking to create an automatic compounding machine of high yield assets, and will know what to do to protect your wealth portfolio.

CHAPTER 1:
A TALE OF TWO INVESTORS

The Wall Street Journal, in order to sell subscriptions, for years would mail out a two page solicitation letter that has been called "the greatest direct mail sales letter of all time." Perhaps you've seen this letter that ran continuously with minor changes from 1975 to 2003. It was sent to millions of people and produced a billion dollars in subscription revenues. It is believed to have worked longer and better than any other direct mail piece in history.

This sales letter, written by Martin Conwoy, was the workhorse circulation builder for *The Wall Street Journal.* The beauty of the letter was its simplicity. Written in plain language, it told the story of two young men who were very much alike at the start of their careers, but whose fortunes diverged because over time one consistently read *The Wall Street Journal* while the other did not. That, of course, is what the letter was designed to make you believe since it was selling *The Wall Street Journal* subscriptions.

First the letter sold you on the premise that knowledge equals success and then the idea that *The Wall Street Journal* possessed this "success knowledge." Finally it sold you on a subscription. See for yourself the beauty of this letter:

> On a beautiful late spring afternoon, twenty-five years ago, two young men graduated from the same college. They were very much alike, these two young men. Both had been better than average students, both were personable and both – as young college graduates are – were filled with ambitious dreams for the future.
>
> Recently, these men returned to their college for their 25th reunion.
>
> They were very much alike. Both were happily married. Both had three children. And both, it turned out, had gone to work for the same Midwestern manufacturing company, and were still there.
>
> But there was a difference. One of the men was manager of a small department of that company. The other was its president.

What Made The Difference

Have you ever wondered, as I have, what makes this kind of difference in people's lives? It isn't always a native intelligence or talent or dedication. It isn't that one person wants success and the other doesn't. The difference lies in what each person knows and how he or she makes use of that knowledge.

And that is why I am writing to you and to people like you about The Wall Street Journal. For that is the whole purpose of the Journal: To give its readers knowledge – knowledge that they can use in business.

A Publication Unlike Any Other

You see, The Wall Street Journal is a unique publication. It's the country's only national business daily. Each business day, it is put together by the world's largest staff of business-news experts.

Each business day, The Journal's pages include a broad range of information of interest and significance to business-minded people, no matter where it comes from. *Not just stocks and finance*, but anything and everything in the whole, fast-moving world of business... The Wall Street Journal gives you all the business you need - when you need it.

Knowledge is Power

Right now, I am reading page one of The Journal, the best-read front page in America. It combines all the important news of the day with in-depth feature reporting. Every phase of business news is covered. I see articles on new inflation, wholesale prices, car prices, tax incentives for industries to major developments in Washington, and elsewhere.

And there is page after page inside The Journal filled with fascinating and significant information that's useful to you. The Marketplace section gives you insights into how consumers are thinking and spending. How companies compete for market share. There is daily coverage of law, technology, media and marketing. Plus daily features on the challenges of managing smaller companies.

The Journal is also the single best source for news and statistics about your money. In the Money & Investing section there are helpful charts, easy-o-scan market quotations, plus "Abreast of the Market," "Heard on the Street" and "Your Money Matters," three of America's most influential and carefully read investment columns.

If you have never read The Wall Street Journal, you cannot imagine how useful it can be to you.

A Money-Saving Subscription

Put our statements to the proof by subscribing for the next 13 weeks just for just $44. This is among the shortest subscription terms we offer – and a perfect way to get acquired with The Journal.

Or you may prefer to take advantage of our *better buy* – one year for $149. You save over $40 off the cover price of The Journal.

Simply fill out the enclosed order card and mail it in the postage-paid envelope provided. And here's The Journal's guarantee: Should the Journal not measure up to your expectations, you may cancel this arrangement at any point and receive a refund for the undelivered portion of your subscription.

If you feel as we do that this is a fair and reasonable proposition, then you will want to find out without delay if The Wall Street Journal can do for you what it is doing for millions of readers. So please mail the enclosed order card now, and we will start serving you immediately.

About those two college graduates I mentioned in the beginning of this letter: They were graduated from the same college together and together got started in the business world. So what made their lives in business different?

Knowledge. Useful knowledge. And its application.

An Investment in Success

I cannot promise you that success will be instantly yours if you start reading The Wall Street Journal. But I can guarantee that you will find The Journal always interesting, always reliable, and always useful.

Sincerely,

Peter R. Kann Publisher

P.S. It's important to note that The Journal's subscription price may be tax deductible. Ask your tax advisor.

Of course I take it that you are smart enough to realize that becoming successful at investing or becoming wealthy does not hinge on whether or not you read *The Wall Street Journal*. Let's get that notion out of the way from the start. The proper path is to identify the few important successful investment principles to follow that, over the course of years, will make a giant difference in your investment outcomes. What sound investment rules or principles, when regularly followed, will separate you from the pack of average or even losing investors? That is the question we can see that this letter raises. In other words, what are the few rules in the world of investing that, when consistently followed, will truly differentiate between retiring rich or poor?

The equivalent investing parable to Martin Conwoy's sales letter would be "a tale of two investors." It would tell how the net worth of two men diverged over the course of decades because one consistently applied sound investment principles and the other did not. Just as we can say that a man will develop a good character over time because he lives his life following the principles of good conduct whereas hardened criminals will not, the results of the two investors will diverge over time because one consistently follows proven investment principles while the other does not.

The story will go that each of two investors had from the start enjoyed the same educational advantages, had the same starting capital and were exposed to the same opportunities. As far as anyone could judge, their prospects for investment success were therefore equally good. However, at the end of two decades one was substantially richer than the other, financially independent, while the second had very little savings at all and still had to depend on a salary for his living.

What are the key differences that can produce such a result ... the key principles that you would like your own children to know from an early age so that they, too, can follow a sure road that accumulates wealth enough over time to make them financially independent?

If you want to accumulate the wealth that produces financial independence, or want to go a step further and produce a financial legacy that can be passed onto the next generation, this takes more than just access to the knowledge that newspapers or websites can provide. It takes more than learning about some new market indicator, knowing where the Dow Jones average is headed, or understanding how global economic factors will affect some particular segment of the market. It takes more than learning some new trick to trade futures, options or stocks and bonds.

In my book *Super Investing* I discuss ten ways whereby people typically become rich, and if you are one of the wealthy who has followed one of these paths (start a business, marry rich, become a celebrity, invent a perennial revenue stream, etc.) then you probably don't have to know much about the markets at all. But those fortunes are rare indeed and that fate is probably out of reach except to a very few.

While Get Rich Quick schemes are popular with the ordinary public, they rarely if ever make anyone rich. The real truth is that the average Joe has to create a prosperous future himself through the consistency of smart private actions that can compound into a great result over time. Plenty of people have done this using investments as their road to riches, but you must have realistic expectations and discipline along the way. The secret isn't accurate forecasting about the market or good stock-picking but about making a plan, staying the course by sticking to that plan, eliminating unnecessary risks, and keeping your costs low. Luck can help amplify your results to the upside, but the basic principles of success and prudence are what will clearly separate the financial winners from the losers.

History clearly proves that average individuals can become wealthy if they prudently follow a proven model of successful investing. This is what everyone is looking for – a proven path for financial success. There is no escaping risk on any such pathway because there is no wealth without risk, but you can certainly minimize that risk by disciplining your actions along a set of proven wealth principles that are forged into a plan.

That's what this is all about.

All approaches to financial independence rely on religiously following a small set of principles that as a general model have consistently produced large income and even generational wealth for others. If you are disciplined enough along these lines, and your children also follow the same rules, a family can accumulate the beginnings of a great legacy that can greatly benefit society. On the other hand, if you don't save and invest then you will end up with nothing by your retirement years. That seems to be the most common outcome of the average Joe who is looking to get wealthy through investments, but who doesn't know how to properly take action.

If you are interested in the quest to become wealthy through investing, here are some of the proven principles you need to follow for the path of success.

Rule 1 – First and Foremost Don't Lose Money

When Warren Buffett was asked about his number one investment rule he replied, "First, don't lose money." When asked about his second most important investment rule he responded, "See rule #1."

If you lose 10% of your money then you must then make 11% to get back to even again. If you lose 20% then you need to make 25% to get back to par. At a 50% loss you actually need to double your money – in other words make 100% - to once again get back to even.

If you thought making 50% in the markets was difficult then think how difficult it is to have to double your money because you let your loss go too far. It is certainly far harder to make money than it is to lose it.

This arithmetic clearly shows the advantage of using stops to get out of bad investments so that you avoid even larger losses. While losses may be unavoidable in the field of investments because you cannot eliminate risks entirely (and no one is infallible with their investment choices either), they can certainly help protect us by preventing losses from going too far.

This rule is the reason why famous value investor Benjamin Graham said you must buy stocks whose price offers a wide margin of safety, which is because that margin of safety can help protect you from ruin. Your first concern with investing it to therefore avoid the loss of your capital by preferring *quality* assets that offer a margin of safety.

Bad loans, gambling, options and futures, fad collectibles and just plain stupid investments are some of the ways we mindlessly throw away money that could be earning us rates of return we could be compounding into yet more money over time. As Buffett says, don't lose money. If we avoid losses or cut them short, we both protect our initial capital and all the extra capital it could earn us over time due to investment diligence.

Rule 2 – Trust to the Magic of Compounding

Einstein said that the magic of compound interest was one of the wonders of the world. When you hold assets that throw off dividends, royalties or interest and which also appreciate in value, and when you reinvest those returns in yet more of such assets, that is making use of the magic of compounding. All great investors will tell you that this is the basic road to riches.

In other words, as an investor you have two roads in front of you. You can try to select and then invest in assets that will appreciate in value or buy assets that will throw off a yield. Then you must reinvest that yield in other such opportunities to see increasing returns over time.

On the road of compounding, time is your friend. To get the greatest possible returns through compounding on the "easy millionaire" road you must start early, stick to an investment and reinvestment plan of the highest (but safest) yields possible that you must compound as often as possible, and ignore the chatter of the day that might distract you off this proven path.

You don't have to be rich to make compound interest work for you, but it does require that you save and sacrifice today in order to reap a windfall tomorrow. Don't spend more than you make, but instead save and invest those savings in compounding investments such as high yield interest rate instruments and income-producing securities. Compounding only works through time, so it doesn't matter how much you start with as long as you do start. Just start doing it and let the miracle of compound interest work for you!

Richard Russell, editor of the *Dow Theory Letters,* often drew attention to extraordinary study, courtesy of *Market Logic,* of Ft. Lauderdale, FL 33306, that explained the magic of compounding. Paraphrasing the study he wrote,

> In this study we assume that investor (B) opens an IRA at age 19. For seven consecutive periods he puts $2,000 in his IRA at an average growth rate of 10% (7% interest plus growth). After seven years this fellow makes NO MORE contributions – he's finished.
>
> A second investor (A) makes no contributions until age 26 (this is the age when investor B was finished with his contributions). Then A continues faithfully to contribute $2,000 every year until he's 65 (at the same theoretical 10% rate).
>
> Now study the incredible results. B, who made his contributions earlier and who made only seven contributions, ends up with MORE money than A, who made 40 contributions but at a LATER TIME. The difference in the two is simply that B *had seven more early years of compounding than A.* Those seven early years were worth more than all of A's 33 additional contributions.
>
> This is a study that I suggest you show to your kids. It's a study I've lived by and I can tell you, "It works." You can work your compounding with muni-bonds, with a good money market fund, with T-bills, T-notes, P2P lending loans or Oil and Gas Royalty Trust income. There are lots of high yield alternatives that can be put to use.
>
> At age 65 we will find that investor (A), who put in a total of $80,000, made $893,704 for a 11-fold increase in their wealth. On the other hand, wise investor (B) who started earlier and only put in $14,000 ended up with $930,641 in earnings for a 66-fold increase! That's the power of compounding early.

Rule 3 – Avoid or Defer Taxes and Fees

One of the commonest traits of the rich is that they are very sensitive to avoiding taxes. The smartest structure their investments to minimize taxes, which is something you absolutely must do, too, if you want to be able to maximize your wealth. Basically, you must figure out ways to make your investments tax efficient.

Always follow the law, but never pay taxes if you can avoid or defer them. There is nothing so painful as working hard to make a buck and then having Uncle Sam come and take away a large portion of your sweat labor. Not only are you poorer for the taking, but now you no longer have that capital available that you might use to compound into a larger fortune. By deferring taxes you are able to use your money for extra periods of profitable compounding.

The same story goes for minimizing investment fees. After all, you cannot compound money that went to pay an investment manager. John Bogle, founder of The Vanguard Group of mutual funds, pointed out that the wonderful magic of compounding returns can easily be overwhelmed by the powerful tyranny of compounding fees and costs, so you must minimize fees.

In Bogle's 2009 book, *Enough: True Measures of Money, Business, and Life*, he explained how fees, taxes and frictional costs can harm an investor's total returns.

> Let's start with the costs, where it is easiest to see through the haze. Over the past 50 years, the (nominal) *gross* return on stocks has averaged 11 percent per year, so $1,000 invested in stocks at the outset would today have a value of $184,600. Not bad, right? But it costs money for individuals to own stocks-brokerage commissions, management fees, sales loads, advisory fees, the costs of all that advertising, lawyers' fees, and so on. A good estimate of these costs is at least 2 percent per year. When we take out those assumed investment expenses, even at the rate of only 2 percent, the historic rate of *net* return would drop to 9 percent, and the final value would drop by more than one-half-to just $74,400. If we assume that as little as 1.5 percent is paid by taxable investors to cover income taxes and capital gain taxes on that return, the after tax-rate of return would fall to 7.5 percent, and the final wealth accumulation would plummet by *another* one-half, to $37,000. Clearly, the wonderful magic of compounding *returns* has been overwhelmed by the powerful tyranny of compounding *costs. Some 80 percent of what we might have expected to earn has vanished into thin air.*

As Bogle advised, you should minimize the "croupier's" take because minimizing fees will flat out increase your returns. The hole in the bucket you should plug also includes the drain of taxes and other associated costs that chip away at your investment capital. While the magic of compounding increases your returns, you must remember that this magic doesn't work as well when you end up compounding a lower net due to high fees and drainage costs over time.

Rule 4 – Put Faith in Value Investing and Momentum Investing

After computer analyzing hundreds of different types of investment strategies to determine their risks and profitability, super stock analyst Wesley Gray concluded that there are really only two basic investment strategies that have historically worked over the long run and which will most probably work far into the future:

> In the end, when you really want to be intellectually honest about it and

you throw as many grenades as you can at these different "alpha systems" it really boils down to two strategies that have worked for the last hundred years and they're probably going to work for the next hundred years. One is value-based strategies where we're buying cheap stocks. The other one is momentum-based strategies, buying securities that have had strong relative strength relative to other securities in the market at a given point in time. Those two systems, those core algorithms however expressed ... as long as you're in those two veins you're probably good. Everything else I would say is questionable at best and data mining at worst.

Value investing is fundamentally about buying good stocks when there is overreaction to bad news. The key to value investing is to buy a valuable (and hopefully income producing) asset when the price is at a bargain, but only those underpriced quality assets that are fundamentally sound and just mispriced at the moment. In short, in value investing you focus on buying the cheapest, most out of favor but *quality* stocks to beat the market.

In his book on the secrets to becoming rich, J. Paul Getty said that all you have to do to get rich is buy assets for less than they are worth. The market or another buyer will one day recognize the mispricing and then you have made a profit. Value investor Warren Buffett had a favorite phrase that expressed this same idea, which is that you should look for investment opportunities where you are buying dollars for pennies.

This is the gist of value investing, which is searching for great assets that are underpriced, buying them at a steep discount, and then waiting to sell them when they return to fair value or boast an over-optimistic premium.

The simple fact is that situations change, eventually the market will recognize any mispricings and low prices will eventually be bid back up to what is fair value once again. Thus this process of buying good assets on the cheap has a *strong tendency* to produce profits rather than losses. If like a contrarian you can go against the crowd and buy these situations when everyone else is a naysayer, this is how you can make extraordinary profits via yet another proven path to riches.

If an investment throws off net income during your holding period, then that's even better than paying for an asset's upkeep while you wait. Hence by investing in stocks, real estate and even businesses that temporarily hit hard times and decline in price but are still strong enough to survive and pay their own way, you can in time become much richer. Whenever you can find assets selling for pennies on the dollar that can easily be resold later for fair value when times spring afresh, then dig in.

In momentum investing, on the other hand, you basically want to invest in securities that have had consistently strong performance over a certain period of time and the evaluations about "strong performance" must be performed on a regularly scheduled basis using consistent measuring rules. In order for momentum systems to work you have to trade securities a lot so you need frequent rebalancing. And because of the churn, once again you have to be very sensitive to slippage, taxes and volatility.

If you have a long enough time horizon and can handle the volatility and tax problems then momentum investing is the clear winner between these two basic strategies. It typically makes 7-8% more than the market's return while systematic value investing typically produces a 3-4% alpha. Momentum investors want to be invested in slow grind, clean, smooth momentum stocks that continue to grind into the future instead of jerky, crazy momentum stocks that jump all over the place. If you employ automatic selection systems, trading rules and algorithms to trade stocks in a risk-adjusted momentum fashion then you're going to grow your wealth in the fastest, safest and most profitable way I know.

Rule 5 – Start Small But Work Towards the Diversification of Multiple Streams of Income

Many years ago Robert Allen wrote *Multiple Streams of Income.* This book etched out what is now the dream of most investors and business people alike, which is to own multiple streams of uncorrelated income so that you can become financially independent and never have to work in the future.

The best scenario for an investor is that he doesn't need "to play" the markets at all because he already has plenty of assets and all these independent, steady streams of income. He is diversified and owns income-producing real estate, interest paying bonds, T-bills and CDs, dividend paying stocks, oil and gas trust royalties, P2P lending income, shares in profitable businesses, and a wealth portfolio diversified by country and contents.

You can only build up this type of portfolio over time. It is not something that you can put together in a single day. The biggest challenge for those starting from scratch is to save enough money to become able to invest in any of these avenues. This usually means that you must sacrifice your current consumption to save. Without large funds at the start you have to start small, and if you start out with little capital then this means sacrificing for the final goal. In any case, you just have to get started.

There is no arguing that this is the way the world works, but most people are unwilling to just get started without waiting for things to be perfect in their lives. Wherever he is now in life, the little guy must adopt the policy of avoiding debt, bettering his credit score (so as to cut debt charges when he finally needs it), never spending more than he makes, increasing his savings and then compounding it through wise investments that throw off income and which he can, in turn, invest in more investments that throw off yet more income.

From money the opportunities for making more money arise, so in time, by following this path he can create multiple streams of larger and larger income just like the rich man. As stated, you just have to decide to get started and then get started. P2P lending, for instance, starts with as little as a $25 investment.

As Robert Kiyosaki revealed in *Rich Man, Poor Man,* a typical problem is that small investors mistake liabilities for assets along this route. They want to buy expensive cars, boats, houses or delve into hobbies that require continual cash upkeep rather than invest in items that instead throw off income and will increase in value.

If you truly want a future life of financial wealth and leisure, the planning starts now at day one. Take inventory of your expenses and cut out the frivolous. Don't spend more than you make. Cut down your credit card debt and try to improve your credit score. Get rid of what is costing you money rather than making you money. Look at the income producing possibilities in front of you based on your resources, however minor they might be, and start trusting to the road of compounding. In time by using this route you can become a financial winner.

Rule 6 – "Beware the Texas Oil Well Being Sold in New York"

"Beware of Trojans bearing gifts" has an analogy in the field of investments: beware the Texas oil well that is being sold in New York ... or Tokyo or Shanghai or wherever. If that oil investment were a good deal then the local Texans, who are experts at oil deals, would have already snapped it up. Doesn't that make sense? Always ask yourself this question: "Why are *you* so lucky to be given this 'great' opportunity?"

Whenever you are given an opportunity like this, including the chance to invest in foreign real estate, the fact that we are talking about a foreign location should give you pause for thought. If the deal is so good then why haven't the locals scooped it up? This should always be the question to consider because scams and scoundrels abound in the world of money always searching for unaware people they can pilfer.

Furthermore, beware the "limited" investment opportunity made open to you at last moment's notice. It is rarely an opportunity, and most likely a bad deal where you aren't given enough time to clear your head and think through the possible faults. As Warren Buffett and Fidelity's Peter Lynch pointed out, *only invest in what you understand.* That, rather than a special deal you can't comprehend, is enough to bring you riches over the long run. Special deals, while exciting your feelings of privilege, status, or advantage, more often than not fail to deliver the dreams they conjure up.

Therefore, be simple when investing. Avoid complication. Financial institutions typically sell complicated products that charge high fees but which usually don't deliver any kind of outperformance. So don't fall for the rosy scenarios offered by the hucksters of complication. You can avoid complicated products that few understand and still outperform the market by using very simple strategies that involve no exotic promises.

Depend on the 80/20 Pareto principle for your investments and only focus on the things that matter. Your goal is to minimize complexity because in general, complexity offers too many ways in which something can go wrong and usually does. It is usually just a sales pitch to justify higher fees when a simple system would work much better.

In short, be simple and you will sleep well at night. Your worries will be less and your returns will be higher.

Along these lines in the best of all worlds you want to be invested in liquid assets that always give you access to your money, rather than always having it tied up, so that you can have your money when you need it. Maintain your liquidity as much as possible because if all your money gets locked up you often end up getting screwed in life. It's usually locked up when you either need it the most, when that particular investment is crashing, or when opportunities offering much better returns are out there.

Rule 7 – Be Patient and Don't Succumb to Pressure

Over the years one of the greatest burdens I've seen on investors is the pressure to make money during hard times when there are very few good returns available. Feeling the pressure "to make money" they therefore delve into exotic or lower class investments that lose money when they could have just accepted the discomfort of lower returns and preserved all their capital instead.

The wise investor waits for his chance. He never feels pressured to "make money" in the market. He knows that a realistic expectation for equities is to make 7-8% per year and there will be some years when you suffer losses. This is the way of the world, so you need to manage your risks so that you can stay the course and sit through the drawdowns without abandoning a good strategy.

As a contrarian at heart, the wise investor is never swayed by the crowd and suckered into investments because of the clamor and glamour. He waits until the price is just right to guarantee him the return he wants. Perhaps he stores his unallocated wealth in a cash account or simple S&P500 index fund while waiting for opportunities, but he readily reapportions parts of it when any good opportunity arises.

By investing in an index fund, for instance, he stays invested in a low cost way and eliminates the pressure of having to decide what to do next. Automation of the investment process, through rules developed by historical testing, also eliminates the pressure of decision making and the burden of having to decide what to invest in.

Unfortunately, the small investor tends to be impatient and pursues Get Rich Quick schemes that can never pan out. In the end, he wastes his money chasing one new stock market idea after the other, or sees his wealth disappear through a variety of senseless schemes that lack any fundamental value. Feeling the pressure to make money and beat the rat race in the quickest way possible, he basically becomes a gambler rather than investor, and the odds at winning through speculation are never good.

The rich investor, on the other hand, patiently holds his course on the road of pursuing value – cheap quality value. As a contrarian, he waits for a chance to buy things when they are temporarily cheap and sells them when they become overextended while the public is losing its head with the belief that the current uptrend will go on forever. Remember that no stock rises forever because after all the buyers are in there is no one left to buy, and then the price must turn down. In buying and selling, the wise investor sets things up so that he feels no undue pressure.

The biggest successes of the wise investor therefore come from being an expert on values because he will score when he buys great assets at suppressed prices before those prices bounce back. If there aren't any good value opportunities, he simply doesn't feel any pressure to invest but simply waits. He keeps his maintenance costs low, avoids speculation, stays out of debt and simply waits for value to appear that he can pounce on. In the meantime he depends on the laws of compounding and like *Rich Dad, Poor Dad* avoids assets that are really liabilities.

Rule 8 – Establish Avenues of Financial Insurance

During the course of a lifetime of seventy or eighty years, you are likely to see one or more of the following national calamities: a banking collapse, bond market collapse, currency devaluation, currency controls, tremendously higher taxation, a cut in social welfare spending, high unemployment rates, hyperinflation, deflation, 50% stock market decline, the unavailability of food, price controls, a severe decline in national exports, political upheaval, popular uprisings, civil war or external war, and technological or other changes that totally eviscerate entire sections of the national economy.

The three most common ways to protect yourself from some of these domestic risks are by owning a *foreign bank account* denominated in the world's safest currency, holding physical gold and silver in a way that is out of the reach of the government, and owning income producing assets that can provide both food and income during a crisis.

Over the last several thousand years of history, privately owning physical gold or silver has been the safest and surest way to protect one's wealth during crisis and calamity. The precious metals have no counterparty risk so they maintain their value across borders and are easily sold to others wherever you are in the world. They are also highly portable and easy to hide. Your best insurance against the possibilities of domestic disaster is not only holding a second passport and having worldwide relationships, but setting up contingency arrangements along these lines.

A second passport is something you absolutely must consider since it allows you to avoid the blowback of your country's foreign policy when it runs amuck. It helps you to escape any government measures for people control, gives you extra financial options and mobility, and allows you to pass on multiple citizenships to your future children and grandchildren.

Summary

If you follow these few rules then you are on your way to achieving financial wealth, or even generational wealth. Much of the story behind the financial success of the wealthy is about avoiding what is wrong rather than doing what is right, such as avoiding losses by refusing to get into bad investments in the first place. Remember that if you weed a garden then you can often forego the fertilizer because with the weeds removed the crops will take care of themselves. So learn to avoid bad investments in the first place. Learning how to take small losses quickly, such as by setting stop-losses on securities purchases, is also a habit that the financially savvy always master.

While we have been discussing the means to grow your wealth, the last point to remember is that your real wealth is your health, your relationships, and ultimately your own spiritual development. Without health your money and possessions are not enjoyable. Without relationships there is no one to enjoy them with. And without a spiritual path the protoplasm of life has no higher purpose or ideal other than just to exist.

Wealth can and should be used to enrich your life, and it also has the great power to help others. Once you achieve the objective of making more money won't you also consider using it to help ennoble people and benefit society? This will ultimately make the pursuit of wealth a higher calling than just remain a desire for a more opulent road of consumption. The objective of leaving behind a legacy of charity is one of the finest gifts one can give to mankind. For a richer life, please think about this option both at the end of the game and along the way.

CHAPTER 2:
DIVIDEND GROWTH INVESTING

The topic of income investing, and especially high yield investing and its re-compounding, should definitely include dividend stock strategies. Given enough time, investing in the right dividend stocks and compounding the dividend cash thrown off by those stocks can become a powerful road to riches. For a careful investor, this can definitely serve as a cornerstone to building wealth over time.

There are several forms of dividend investing and many books have been written about it. In my personal opinion, most of them do not provide us with very good investment systems. However, I want to introduce a very sound form of dividend investing, out of the many systems suggested, that matches quite nicely with the wealth building strategies of Warren Buffett.

Just as you might want to teach your children the principles within *Rich Dad, Poor Dad,* this dividend stock approach embodies a particularly useful long-term investment philosophy that you might want to share with your children. A fundamental key is that it requires diversification. I know of many individuals who got tremendously hurt in the 2008 market crash because they followed this strategy without following the principle of diversification. For instance, many people put their retirement funds into "safe" Citibank stock that crashed and which has never recovered since (just as many got suckered with Enron). Many are the stories I have of individuals whose wealth got destroyed because they put most of their money into one basket.

An inherent idea behind high yield investments is to create multiple streams of passive income for your wealth portfolio, but not to become dependent on any single source for your revenue. You are looking for the safety of revenues and the risks entailed require diversification. Unforeseen disaster can strike any form of asset and income plan, and thus there is always the need to be prepared against adverse risks. The average millionaire has about seven streams of income feeding their fortune and I hope that over time you can slowly set up something similar with the information within.

I believe that you should never pursue stock trading as a source of excitement, but should only pursue stocks as a *potential source of asset accumulation and income.* Furthermore, you should also avoid trading and investing if you are not willing to learn emotional control and self-discipline. Basically, if you are not willing to work on yourself to develop self-control then you should not take up trading and investments. You should just invest in mutual funds instead. In this case, just give your funds over to professional investment managers who manage hedge funds, mutual funds or index funds.

To master trading takes training and discipline. For instance, you must learn a particular trading method, style or technique that is suited to your personality. You must master that method and then learn how to skillfully apply it. Trading also requires that you learn how to control your emotions, such as patience, in order to minimize risks and manage your trades.

Basically, the process of learning the skill of trading or investing is a process of constant self-development, and if you are not willing to submit yourself to the road of self-improvement that will break bad habits and instill new good habits then you should forego trading and/or investing and let other people manage your funds for you.

My own philosophy is as follows: Trading the markets is done to make money, but the process of learning trading - with all its requirements of study, preparation, risk management, execution and so on – is so demanding that it should always be viewed as a form of personal self-improvement. Since your wealth is at stake, on which depends your future, a commitment to self-improvement and self-correction goes hand in hand with the desire to increase one's net worth through investments.

You should try to diversify any wealth-building program to prevent it from relying on any one single thing. You should consider various asset accumulation and passive income strategies for your portfolio so that you are not chained to just one method of wealth generation, especially if it requires a lot of time, energy and commitment. Even the most profitable of stock, options, forex or futures traders have bad spells, and therefore they need some diversified means of steady income generation during those periods.

As a believer in multiple streams of income, I want you to consider as a foundation stone the dependable strategy of compounding high yield returns over time. As I discussed in my book *Super Investing* and revealed in *Breakthrough Strategies of Wall Street Traders*, this is one of the sure roads to wealth that has been used by many people in the past.

The Single Best Investment Strategy

For this topic of dividend stock investing, I want to introduce the work of Lowell Miller, author of *The Single Best Investment: Creating Wealth With Dividend Growth*. Miller is the founder and chief investment officer of Miller/Howard Investments and has been a proponent of dividend-focused investment strategies for decades. His book is important because of the wealth program it espouses using dividend stocks.

Most dividend stock strategies suffer from one flaw or another. There is not just the problem of dividends being cut, but the problem of poor stock selection from the start. With dividend stocks, if you invest in a declining stock then you will lose part of your capital even though it pays dividends, which also can be reduced or terminated without notice. Furthermore, if a stock is not purchased with the intent to hold it forever, this means that the stock eventually must be sold. That being the case, by what criteria do you decide it is time to sell a dividend stock? Most dividend stock strategies need proven ways to sufficiently protect assets from these downside risks.

Miller's dividend stock methodology addresses some of the most common problems with these strategies. His basic philosophy is that financially strong companies with rising dividends offer the most consistent performance as well as the highest added value for your portfolio. The problem arises in selecting a quality company that is "financially strong" so that its stock continues paying dividends and does not need to be sold because it goes into a decline.

In *Super Investing*, I pointed out that one of the core components of Warren Buffett's investment strategy was to buy good companies that throw off cash so that he could then invest that cash in more good companies that also threw off cash, and so on *ad infinitum*. Buffett doesn't use just one investment strategy to guide his investment decisions. He uses many strategies. However one of the glues that holds them together is his desire for cash-compounding. He is looking for cash and ways for that cash to safely compound. He is on record saying, Buffett has said,

> Our acquisition preferences run toward businesses that generate cash, not those that consume it [...] however attractive the earnings numbers, we remain leery of businesses that never seem able to convert such pretty numbers into no-strings-attached cash.

Warren Buffett is *an investor rather than a trader*, so he wants to buy companies that will keep thriving over the long term and keep throwing off cash that he can then, in turn, use to make other investments that will also generate cash. That is how he grows his portfolio's wealth rather than through the pursuit of trading profits.

The cornerstone to his overall wealth generation process is that *he wants to create a cash-compounding machine*. Bill Spetrino, author of *The Great American Dividend Machine*, essentially says the same thing as well. Howard Miller's basic idea is that you must also create this very same mechanism.

Most people are confused about how Warren Buffett selects stocks because they think Buffett is primarily all about picking "moat" companies (businesses with sustainable competitive advantages that can fend off competition and earn high returns on capital for many years to come). They forget to remember that this cash-compounding strategy is the reason he wants to pick moat companies.

For a company to keep throwing off cash it needs to (1) survive and (2) keep making money. Therefore Buffett wants *good or great* companies whose "goodness" means that their survival is not at risk during bad economic periods. "Good" to Buffett means safety of his capital. However, it is not that these stocks will simply survive and/or go up in price. Buffett wants that, too, but the issue is that they will survive and *keep generating the cash he wants*. You can buy a stock either for yield or because you think something will appreciate in value, and Buffett wants both.

Buffett always wants to avoid losing any of his initial capital investment. Since he never wants to lose money, his stock selection process is first and foremost about minimizing stock selection risk so that he never loses any money. This is why he won't even enter into an investment if he doesn't think it will make at least 15% during the very first year of his investment.

In effect, this means that his purchase price must be excellent. Therefore he tries to buy every stock at a discount so the yield is as high as possible and his bargain price somewhat protects him on the downside. The way to get these bargains is to buy stocks during a crisis situation or buy on imaginary fear.

Warren Buffett's strategy means that he doesn't look for high-flyer stocks. He doesn't invest in companies he cannot understand. He doesn't rely on earnings forecasts either but looks for solid businesses that have a solid history of throwing off cash and are throwing off cash *now*. He also chooses companies that he thinks, from just some simple principles, will continue to thrive into the future. He doesn't make his analysis overly complicated. Buffett also always looks for some protections when making his initial investments because a margin of safety helps to insure this rosy future. These are all concerns that play a role in his stock selection.

There are many ways people can look at Buffett's investment strategy, and I'm just mentioning a few aspects without going into the many dimensions of his overall philosophy. You can view Buffett's strategy in many ways and this is simply one way of looking at it. A firm called AQR reverse engineered Buffett's strategy, which they revealed in a paper called "Buffett's Alpha," and came to a different conclusion that he basically bought cheap high quality firms and used some leverage. He buys companies that are cheap first, and then quality is a secondary consideration after price. AQR said "Buffett's returns appear to be neither luck nor magic, but, rather, reward for the use of leverage combined with a focus on cheap, safe, quality stocks."

What I'm most interested in pointing out, on the order of *Rich Dad, Poor Dad* type philosophies, is that it would serve you well to view Buffett's portfolio as a whole whose parts are designed to service an internal compounding machine. That is the message I want to convey, namely how to create a perennial cash-compounding machine by investing in the right type of dividend stocks that are purchased with judicious timing (meaning a bargain price).

Buffett wants to invest in good businesses that will continue to throw off cash. The more cash they throw off due to rising earnings, the higher their stock prices will go. The cash thrown off by these businesses can in turn be reinvested in other income-producing vehicles to provide a further boost to his portfolio's ability to compound itself. Buffett wants cash streams, and more importantly steadily increasing cash streams and the reinvestment of that cash to build increased value through further compounding. That's the basis of a dividend machine.

In your investment portfolio you can also choose to the do the same thing. You can especially do this through your own approach to dividend investing.

Here is the basic wealth compounding formula: invest in solid businesses (so you don't have to worry about potential bankruptcy and the loss of your investment principal) that will generate cash, and then reinvest that cash in more businesses that will likewise throw off cash so that you can continue compounding forever. Make sure that the yield when you buy is attractive, and keep doing this over time.

It takes time, but *the law of compounding definitely builds fortunes*. It has done so in the past and will always do so in the future because of the laws of compound interest.

The more money you compound and the longer you compound, the more your wealth will grow. The growth of wealth along these lines is sometimes boring and slow, but it is sure and sound. This is a simple strategy for building a retirement fortune when you have enough time ahead of you. While you can never predict that any particular long-term stock investment will do anything for you in terms of building up your retirement assets (since the stock might eventually crash one day) you can definitely depend on these cash-compounding principles to build a large nest egg over time. All you must do is get all the components right. That of course is the challenge with any investment strategy. If you do it right then you are a hero and if not you can lose money just like anything else in the field of trading and investments.

In terms of dividend stocks, the dividends from dividend stocks can be reinvested in yet more dividend-producing stocks in order to generate yet more dividends, and those new additional dividends can then also be reinvested in yet more dividend-producing stocks to produce even more cash dividends, and so on the compounding can go. This formula, which you should now know by heart, always holds.

This is the basic wealth generation process, but few actually think about it deeply enough to try to institute it. They trade stocks in a flippant fashion of quick buys and sales hoping to make money, or they buy stocks as longer term investments (after much careful analysis and consideration) hoping they will go up in value. Rarely does anyone think of building a continuous cash-compounding machine. That commitment takes discipline.

Two key principles always need to be kept in mind to institute this strategy: (1) never lose your investment principal (so protect it on the downside), and (2) you must seek secure streams of *increasing* dividends rather than steady or decreasing dividends. Unfortunately a stream of increasing dividends cannot be assured. What you can insure is that your initial dividend yield is as high as possible at the time of your purchase.

If you select stocks that won't fall in value and whose dividend streams will increase rather than just stay constant then anyone can see that you have a powerful formula for building wealth. It's not the *only formula* for wealth creation out there, but it is a solid "get rich slowly" formula that has been responsible for many family fortunes over the years.

It is not the only formula that I recommend to families which want to become wealthy, but it is a major one that I want you to consider because it works so well and is just that simple. You have to use a strategy that appeals to you and works, and this one may appeal to certain types of people.

Howard Miller's investment philosophy is based on this same idea of continuous compounding that he tries to achieve through the astute selection of dividend stocks. His often quoted investment formula for picking stocks is:

"High Quality + High Yield + Growth of Yield = High Total Returns"

Miller wants to invest in stocks that will remain dividend performers for years. Like Buffett, he therefore needs good companies in his portfolio that will both retain their value and continue to do well over time. Both he and Buffett therefore recommend selecting stocks with good managements and good business models because that translates into staying power.

Traders are different from investors and don't think this way. What is common is for traders to jump from stock A to B, B to C, and then C to D so that they never really give the process of compounding a chance to work. They are looking for *trading gains* (and sometimes just excitement) rather than the fulfilling the objective of building an automatic compounding machine.

Income compounders must act like investors rather than traders. They need to view companies as potentially steady economic entities which either can or cannot throw off cash they can then use to buy more companies satisfying the same criteria. Hence, company/business selection is paramount from the get-go.

Even if you fill your portfolio with great stocks, nothing lasts forever. Markets turn down and good companies often go bad simply because situations change. Therefore investors still need to know *when to sell their stocks*, and for this they can always turn to the field of technical analysis tools and techniques. Investors must rely on fundamental analysis to evaluate the stocks they want to buy and hold for long periods of time, but they can also always benefit from the trader's toolbox of technical analysis.

Dividend investors especially need to look for companies with excellent management teams. A management team helps to maintain a company's profitability through many different kinds of economic circumstances. Without good management a company will not be able to survive or deliver steady or increasing earnings growth even in the best of conditions.

Buffett wants to insure against stupid managements so he always looks for stocks with business model moats. Those moats help to keep the businesses alive even if management turns incompetent. This is one of his key considerations. As he once said, "I try to buy stock in businesses that are so wonderful that an idiot can run them, because sooner or later, one will."

Miller has a comparative approach to selecting dividend stocks, which is that he looks for quality companies that are durable businesses. Mirroring Buffett's criteria, they must have a business model that is durable enough to survive and that durability mimics Buffett's idea of a moat. Both Buffett and Miller agree that the businesses they normally seek will not be the glamorous, sexy high flyers in the news.

In essence, for a dividend compounding strategy that produces a high yield investment strategy you want to invest in companies with dependable business models throughout all types of economic environments. Generally, the business model dependables which satisfy these criteria will be companies providing the necessities of life like utilities, banks, insurance companies, food companies, or drug companies … companies where you pay for their products on a daily or regular basis. They are usually big, financially strong companies, but you must buy them at a discount.

Miller's basic dividend-reinvestment philosophy is that the key to large investment returns over time is not to figure out which stock market sector will outperform, which investment style will perform best over the next several years, or even which country will outperform. Rather, his basic philosophy is that the big driver of wealth accumulation *is income from dependable companies and the reinvestment of the income that they throw off.*

Here are the astounding mathematical facts behind his conclusions that corroborate this entire idea of building a continuous dividend-compounding machine ...

When you take a look at the stock market over a rolling 5-year period, you will find that 43% of your return is based on dividend income; over a rolling 25-year period you will find that 63% of your total return is based on dividend income and the reinvestment of that income; and over an 80-year period, more than 95% of the total return is based on dividend income and its reinvestment. Over the long run the greatest part of the return in the stock market is *due to dividends and the reinvestment of those dividends.*

In short, your dividend income can be channeled to buy more stock and the additional shares that you buy can in turn generate yet more dividend income and so on. If the stock market keeps going up so that your share prices rise along with it, and if your stocks keep producing dividends that you reinvest then you have a perfectly reinforcing compounding machine. You have a well-proven formula for accumulating wealth over the long run.

Naturally this formula depends on selecting the right stocks because you want them to (1) currently pay a high yield in dividends (2) be increasing their dividends over time and (3) be increasing in share price as well. That's the basis of Miller's formula: "High quality + High yield + Growth of yield = High total returns."

If you follow this strategy then you don't have to worry about what's the "next big thing" or finding the "next hot area" in the stock market. You don't have to be chasing the next stock mentioned on CNN. You don't have to be forecasting the stock market, and can stop worrying about all its gyrations up and down.

You just have to keep applying this basic strategy *over and over and over again* to see your wealth grow through time. You can actually retire from using such a strategy when consistently applied over the long run.

According to Ibbotson's most recent yearbook that traces asset class returns (published by Morningstar), starting in 1926 a single dollar invested in large company stocks would have grown to $144 at present. However, if in addition to the capital appreciation you included the receipt and reinvestment of dividends then that $1 would have risen to $4,676.

In other words, dividends and the reinvestment of dividends accounted for a whopping 97% of total returns!

Ibbotson's study clearly shows that *over very long periods of time* the price of stocks alone is responsible for only 5% of the total return, which is why many people base their entire retirement strategy on an investment philosophy of reinvestment compounding. If you wisely reinvest the income from investments while you're building your assets then come retirement time you will have that income to spend.

This is a tremendous lesson to teach your children! Over the long term, there is a tremendous multiplier effect from investing in stocks that pay dividends and then reinvesting that income in more of the same. Even if you don't want to use it yourself, this is a dependable wealth formula to teach your children. Sit them down and pass on the knowledge so that they don't have to figure this out.

For long-term *investment* strategies, including this one, the general rule is that you don't want to be juggling stocks in and out of your portfolio all the time. While in "trading" you normally jump from stock A to B to C to D, "investing" means that you usually stick with shares for a longer time period. Therefore with investing you have to pick higher quality companies overall.

To ensure this, you will need a more stringent set of buying criteria to help pick the stocks that are most likely to retain their value over your holding period. As Buffett demonstrates with his own portfolio, the selection preference should then veer towards companies whose products and business models are natural survivors. For instance, many consumer stocks are safer than high tech stocks because they are harder to self-destruct. If the businesses thrive, the earnings and cash flow they throw off can then produce a commensurate increase in the value of the underlying equities, all other things being equal. You will then have both capital gains and increasing income from your investment over time.

This same basic principle is found in the field of real estate investing. For instance, real estate investment properties normally produce rental income. Investment properties are also valued in large part based on their cash flow from that rental income. If the rental income from the property increases then the value of the property should also increase as well. A wise property investor therefore benefits by both the property appreciation and higher income. As long as a property continues to be rented the cash flow can keep coming in indefinitely.

When you buy a stock rather than property it will also throw off cash, but you then have the additional benefit that you can avoid all the problems involved with managing real estate on your own such as fixing toilets, roofs and so on.

The same goes for buying Oil and Gas Royalty Trusts. When you purchase an Oil and Gas Royalty Trust you can then own an oil or gas well (or part of an oil or gas field) for the income it generates and avoid all of the troubles involved in having to manage and operate the wells yourself.

In other words, the stock market gives you an opportunity for creating a cash-compounding machine without requiring that you get involved with the management of the companies you buy. With real estate investing you have the same opportunity of creating cash compounding, but you have the potential headache of managing the properties you buy. One expects that both the stocks and properties will go up in value after you buy them (otherwise you wouldn't buy them), but holding stocks is always easier to manage.

Bonds as Investments Versus Dividend Stocks

Now because they also throw off cash and similarly don't have to be managed, investors often raise the idea of buying bonds to build a high yield compounding machine instead of buying dividend stocks, oil and gas wells and real estate. There are some problems with this strategy you should note.

One of the beauties of real estate, over bonds, is the fact your income from rental properties can rise over the years to match the inflation rate. The same can be said for the revenues from oil wells or dividend stocks. Yes, there are risks to the downside when you buy these types of assets, but if you buy bonds instead then *your returns are fixed and cannot rise to match inflation.*

Howard Miller said that he spent quite a bit of time studying fixed income and came to the conclusion that bonds are not a very good investment over the long term. This was the same conclusion that famed value investor Walter Schloss also arrived at.

Schloss liked the strategy of buying undervalued stocks with dividends to pursue this very same strategy of creating a long-term wealth-compounding machine. He preferred to buy many undervalued assets because the large scale diversification of holding many issues – along with undervalued prices - lowered his chances of losses. He specifically chose this particular strategy of buying many stocks, rather than Buffett's strategy of buying just a few good businesses, in order to reduce his risks. The compounding strategy was similar to Buffett's but the implementation of the idea was different.

As to bonds, Schloss also said, "Prefer stocks over bonds. Bonds will limit your gains and inflation will reduce your purchasing power."

The point is this: bonds can serve to diversify a portfolio by dampening its volatility but they are not a very good investment for long periods of time because they actually give you a negative return after you adjust for inflation.

Which Dividend Stocks?

If you are sold on this idea of building an automatic compounding machine as a means to wealth, the next question is, "Which dividend stocks should you buy?" We know what Buffett thinks, but what are Miller's thoughts on choosing dividend stocks?

Miller's basic rule is: "High quality + High yield + Growth of yield = High total returns" so he likes sectors in the market that offer high yields, consistent earnings, and which have generated consistent dividends and consistent dividend growth.

In this formula, Miller chooses "high yield" to normally mean that the stock is in the top four deciles of yield in the universe of stocks, where 10 represents the highest yield stock decile (many of which are pass-through investments such as REITs and MLPs). Miller's dividend-growth investment strategy tends to concentrate in the 7th, 8th and 9th deciles of yield income with pass-through stocks focused in the 10th decile.

Several academic studies have found that selecting U.S. stocks based solely on their dividend yield is a better strategy than selecting them based on their dividend growth rates. The primary reason is that in order for a company to pay dividends the company's management has to adopt a discipline of investing only in the most profitable projects. If you buy stocks that already have a high dividend yield then the shares are also attractive in the sense that you also avoid having to wait a long time for dividends to grow into a substantial income stream.

On the other hand, selecting stocks based solely on the fact that they were high dividend growers was not as good for growing a portfolio as selecting stocks based on high yields. The reason is because high dividend growth rates can disappear.

Investors pressure such companies to continue growing dividends at a high rate that is unrealistic and they ultimately suffer from underperformance when high dividend growth rates revert to normal.

How about the earnings growth, balance sheet, cash flow and other such criteria for picking high quality dividend stocks?

For a "quality stock," Miller normally wants a company's interest obligations to be reliably covered by the cash flow it generates. He wants its cash flow to cover the interest obligations by a magnitude of at least three to four times, and he prefers two times the cash flow coverage of dividends. In general the better the coverage, the higher the quality the stock.

The basic idea behind these coverage ratios is that he wants businesses that are financially strong and robust enough to both survive *and* thrive. If a company has no debt then that is the best situation of all. If a company has debt, you do not want it to be choking on its debt payment obligations when times become tight, and you don't want it to be so cash tight that it cannot possibly raise its dividend consistently.

Here is a larger list of Miller's basic dividend stock selection rules for building a basic dividend compounding machine:

- In terms of "high quality," the company must be financially strong. Miller says that if the company's bonds are investment grade (S&P ratings of BBB+ or better) then that satisfies this criteria.

- Seek a relatively "high current yield," typically twice that of the overall market and never less than 1.5x of the S&P500 yield.

- Be sure that the company's "earnings growth" will support dividend growth. An earnings growth rate of between 7% to 10% is sustainable for a large company.

- Look for good valuations because that will help protect you somewhat on the downside. Seek a Price/Sales ratio of 1.5 or better with a P/E ratio and a Price/Book ratio below that of the market. Cash growth is a big plus.

- Use charts to buy stocks, but not to sell them (because you should be willing to hold them through their ups and downs as long as they remain high dividend paying viable businesses). For a buy signal, look for signs of rising relative strength after at least six months of underperformance.

- As to "dividends," sell whenever the dividend is in doubt, when it has not been increased in the last year (i.e., twelve months) or when the story has changed.

- Diversify extensively. Invest using equal dollar amounts for each stock.

Utility Stocks

One particular stock sector that Miller favors for his dividend growth reinvestment strategy is utility stocks. As a source of passive income, utility stocks definitely deserve careful consideration because of their stable operations. In fact, when people think of safe dividend investing the utility stocks are normally the first thing that comes to their minds.

In *The Single Best Investment,* Miller wrote that he "conducted the only long-term study that exists of utilities as a class." He found that the total returns from utility stocks dwarfed that of bonds and that the sector was even competitive with the average of industrial stocks. Over long periods of time utility stocks provided almost as much total return as the S&P 500, but experienced half the volatility while generating twice the income!

This is an incredible finding. After he adjusted for inflation, we discovered that they provided eight times the return of bonds over the same period.

> For the period of our study, 1945-1990, Dow Jones Utilities Index average annualized return was 11.75%, or 7.50%, after adjusting for inflation, which averaged 4.7% during those years … During the same time frame, long-term bonds returned 5.60%, or a paltry 0.85% after adjusting for inflation … The S&P500 returned slightly more than the utilities at 12.25%, but the S&P500 was almost twice as volatile as the utilities or, as the consultants like to say, twice as risky. In other words, on a risk-adjusted basis, the utilities were almost twice as attractive as the overall market. …"

What this all means is that the right utility stocks can definitely become a key part of a cash-compounding formula. You do not need a portfolio to be primarily composed of consumer goods companies, but can also buy utility issues if you use judicious timing to buy them when they represent a bargain.

Remember the Basic Strategy

Lowell Miller reminds us that there is a larger picture concerning a dividend reinvestment strategy that investors should always keep in mind. He says,

> Remember, we are not trying to *beat the market* here, nor are we even seeking what others might call the *best* stocks. We're trying to create a compounding machine that will be robust and durable for at least an entire investing life, one that will provide equity-like returns with some measure of reliability and predictability over time, one whose income will rise. And because its income rises, the investment will also rise in market value.

It is hard to pick the right trading style or long-term investment strategy, which is why we need t learn about different cash cornerstone strategies and investments. Like exercise, there is no one "best" trading or investing technique, strategy or style that fits all. The "best one" is the *one you do* rather than the "theoretically best exercise" that you won't ever do at all. Like a membership to a gym that you never visit, *if you cannot keep to the plan then the best of strategies is useless.*

Many are the roads to wealth, so it is up to you in life to decide which trading style and/or investment style you ultimately want to master. You need to therefore know all your highest probability options for success. After knowing your options then it is easier to choose a plan based on your deepest interests. The strategy, technique, style or plan that best matches your strengths and interests is the one you are likely to master and keep following with the discipline required for ultimate success.

Now let's put this short discussion about the possible roads to wealth aside. As either an active trader or less active investor, you should try to use strategies and techniques that are historically tested and/or have successful real time track records. If some other trader has mastered a technique that has led him from rags to riches, you should learn as much as possible from that method and see if there is something beneficial within it that you can master. The same goes for the slower field of long-term investing. With this in mind, whether you are an investor or trader you must always remember that the strategy of creating a cash-compounding machine works in spades!

Dividend growth investment strategies are one of those strategies that you should consider for the passive growth side of your portfolio. You can essentially compound the dividend returns from safe cash flow stocks by investing in yet more cash cornerstone stocks so that slowly, over time, the compounding increases your wealth.

Investing in undervalued (underpriced) large companies that not only consistently pay dividends, but which consistently increase them over time sounds very boring. However, the idea of doing this to create a "compounding machine" that will relentlessly grind out income and capital appreciation over the long-term is a philosophy to study and even teach to your children.

I want to emphasize that over and over again because you should always pass on your knowledge to the next generation so that it can be successful, too, and avoid the difficult and painful learning curve that we ourselves have had to tread. While you might not want to use this particular wealth-building strategy, it might be perfect for someone you know.

This type of strategy is so robust that it will still work fifty or one hundred years from now just as it does today. You can use it for real estate, for high yield investments, and for dividend stocks just as we are discussing. It is best when the underlying asset holds its value over time and keeps rising to match the pace of inflation. That's the basic strategy in a nutshell, and the reason we are discussing this single philosophy.

There will always be ups and downs in the stock market that can unseat the profitability of traders and automatic trading systems for awhile, but you can always temper your trading risks during those up and down periods if you devote a portion of your portfolio to the principle of cash-compounding.

For many people a "compounding machine" income strategy using dividend stocks will seem too slow to grow their wealth, but for others it may be just the perfect thing they can manage to build the stream of income they want for their retirement. It is a sensible plan based on real financial facts rather than a fad or a method that depends on guessing market movements. This long-term strategy can guide investors toward creating stock portfolios that will produce consistent returns without having to play the market, which is advice that Warren Buffett often emphasized.

CHAPTER 3:
TOOLS FOR INCOME INVESTING

If you asked what stocks are guaranteed to grow over the next coming years, no one could tell you. If you asked which ones will probably go up in price, analysts could make an educated guess, but couldn't tell you that for certain either.

As a point of fact, no one can even guarantee that a company like Apple Computer will be around in ten or fifteen years time or that it will even remain a market leader. It most likely will still be here, but as to its long-term position in the marketplace we have to remember the lesson of the Dow Jones Industrial Averages whose composition of "market leaders" has changed fifty-one times since its inception in 1896. No company stays a leader forever!

This touches upon one of the many reasons why most mutual funds have a hard time beating the market. Fund managers typically try to pick high flying momentum stocks or "market leaders" they believe will rise in price far into the future. They are looking for price appreciation rather than yield. All of their intellectual power is dedicated towards a quest for outperformance. Even so, Vanguard Funds founder John Bogle pointed out that the net performance of the stock picking prowess of fund managers is so dismal as compared to the performance of the market indices that investors might as well save the fund management fees and buy index funds instead. You will probably get a better return that way, he says, instead of buying mutual funds or even by picking stocks on your own.

Most academics tend to agree.

As Warren Buffett's history shows, spectacular performance doesn't have to come from picking "hot" stocks. Buffett has always adhered to the discipline of value investing rather than momentum investing and goes about trying to "buy dollars for pennies." He has many strategies he uses for trying to do so rather than just one.

Primarily, Buffett wants to buy quality companies at a discount with the term "quality" representing a judgment (which incorporates a margin of safety) that the business will both survive and continue to make money going into the future. He also adheres to basic and time-tested principles of wealth compounding, namely the idea of buying assets that will throw off cash that he can then invest that cash in yet more assets that will throw off yet even more cash, and then continue compounding in this way so on *ad infinitum*.

You will be hard-pressed to find fund managers who can actually do this successfully and achieve long-term track records of 20% or more per year like Warren Buffett. Those managers, especially those managing several billion dollars, are few and far between.

Now because of this lack of performance and for many other reasons as well, you will often find investors choosing to do stock selection on their own. It is only through research that they can build a diversified portfolio of stocks which have the special criteria they seek, so the question arises as to which software screens or packages will help them do the required research.

There are many stock screeners out there, and the top rated ones you might investigate include Zack's stock screener (Zacks.com), the Finiv stock screener (Finiv.com), Google Finance's stock screener, the Motley Fool stock screener, the Uncle Stock screener (UncleStock.com), ChartMill.com, StockFetcher.com, PastStat.com, the Yahoo! Finance screener, Trade-Ideas.com, and the Prophets screener from the ThinkorSwim.com trading platform. There are also website software platforms such as the Morningstar stock screener, Marketwatch screener, DripInvesting.com, MeetInvest.com, CEFConnect.com, EquityClock.com for seasonality screening, StockScreen123.com, ETFscreen.com, ETFdb.com, and the SmartMoney Select Stock Screener.

The internet is filled with investment information sites, and we particularly like the insights from SeekingAlpha.com and ZeroHedge.com. Of course there are many others, too, as everyone has their favorite site for analysis as well as for charting purposes. For charting I personally like the ThinkorSwim.com software platform.

There are also two "non-profit" investor-education organizations that you might consider for learning more about picking stocks: AAII and BetterInvesting.

BetterInvesting (www.betterinvesting.org), formerly the National Association of Investors Corp. BetterInvesting, has been around since 1951. It is basically an umbrella group for over 10,000 local investment clubs.

AAII, or the American Association of Individual Investors (www.aaii.com) is an investor-education group founded in 1978 with a current membership of around 150,000 members, which speaks to its popularity. The unique approach of AAII (other than its educational articles) centers around its stock screener that can provide you with the track records of a wide range of stock selection strategies and investment approaches.

In other words, AAII periodically computes the relative performance of various popular investment strategies – according to its interpretation of their rules – which can then help you separate the wheat from the chaff as far as outperformance claims go. This monitoring of performance covers many popular investment strategies such as the Dogs of the Dow, Magic Formula, CAN SLIM variations, O'Shaughnessy VALUE STOCK screens and so on.

The idea of showing the real time historical performance of such strategies, and which stocks are selected by those strategies, is to allow investors the chance to outperform both the market indices and most mutual funds. If you pick a strategy that has historically outperformed the market and continue to invest in the stocks selected by that strategy (as identified by the rules used in the AAII screener) then you just might have a chance of truly outperforming the market. In other words, the screener is a way of helping you grow and protect your assets.

If you want to do fundamental analysis of stocks you now have a short list of websites you might try first for screeners. No one can guarantee that you will become a better investor by using these tools just as no one can guarantee you will become a better driver because you own a high performance Ferrari.

What you need to first and foremost do is educate yourself as to basic investment principles, and additionally find a historically tested investment strategy that you are willing to continuously, religiously follow. This comes down to doing historical research as to what really works and knowing yourself as to whether you will continue to use that methodology.

As to executing your investment plan and staying true to the course, this comes down to mastering your emotions. This is because it is your personality and emotions that will usually stand in the way of instituting the very rules that you have historically tested and found will give you the greatest chances at investing success. Unless you turn over the process to a computer, which most people do not want to do, outperforming the market will come down to following the rules of a tested strategy you have selected when it seems hardest to do.

That is about the gist of it. First, do research to find an investing technique that has worked over the long-term and will likely continue doing so into the future. You will no doubt find several such possibilities. Pick the one that you are most likely to use, the methodology or investment technique that matches with your views, habits and personality and therefore the one whose rules you will adhere to following. It is said that you cannot get well from medicine you don't take, and so at the end of the day successful investment management comes down to following your investment system in a disciplined fashion.

CHAPTER 4:
FINANCIAL INDICATORS

We are almost done with reviewing various ways to monitor stocks and financial conditions in order to protect your portfolio. To best protect your stock portfolio you need to know a few economic indicators that will give the most accurate pulse of the economy's health. As examples, investors typically await reports on the GDP growth rate, unemployment rate or inflation rate in order to make trading or investment decisions. Such numbers are important because "as the economy goes, so goes the stock market" and accordingly the health of your investments. However, they are not the very best indicators to monitor.

If you know in which direction the economy is headed because you monitor the *proper* economic statistics, you can make adjustments to help protect the value of your portfolio. Certain economic indicators can clearly reveal how the economy presently stands and where it is headed, but these are the ones that few people use.

If you want to better protect your assets using economic statistics you therefore need to know about a few very special but relatively unknown indicators. While there are countless economic indicators that commentators talk about in the investment field very few will truly give you an honest handle on the economy or paint an accurate outlook for the stock market. In fact, many excellent indicators (food stamps, student loans, health insurance costs, labor force participation rate, median family income, worker's share of the economy, tax payments, electricity usage, etc.) are commonly ignored because they tell a tale that the government would not like the public to comprehend.

The indicators I recommend that you monitor can help you gain an idea of where the economy is going even though most of them are statistics that few people have heard about. That is probably the most interesting thing about these indicators, which is that despite their great forecasting power most people have never even heard of them, including many financial professionals!

Once you understand these indicators and what they stand for, however, you will have a far better handle on comprehending the state of the economy than from looking at nearly anything else available to you. Furthermore, you will be equipped to ignore the nonsense spit out by Wall Street spinsters trying to unload shares when they are trying to make you bullish during an obviously bearish scenario. You will also become somewhat protected from the fantasy story promoted by the federal government through its various mathematical manipulations of government statistics (such as seasonal and statistical adjustments or redefinitions) to make those statistics tell a story it wishes to tell. Do governments fudge economic statistics? Yes, they lie all the time.

So let's begin …

Warren Buffett's "Desert-Island Indicator"

In 2009 Warren Buffett was being interviewed by CNBC reporter Becky Quick and was asked which single economic indicator he would want available if he were stranded on a desert island and had access to one and only one number.

Before you read ahead, ask yourself what that one indicator would be? What one economic statistic would you want in your hands in order to get an accurate pulse on the financial markets and future health of the nation?

Buffett's response took nearly everyone by surprise. What one indicator did he favor? He actually mentioned two that encapsulated the same notion - "freight car loadings" and "truck traffic" data.

Let's keep it simple and focus on just freight-car loadings to understand this unexpected answer. The freight-car loadings "desert island indicator" has become famous because few people had ever considered it before Buffett mentioned it. Until that interview no one had ever heard this statistic mentioned by TV commentators, analysts or the large investment houses and yet this is the single most important indicator that Buffett, one of the best investors in the world, would want to follow! While most people are following interest rates, stock prices, GNP, unemployment and the like in order to get an idea of the state of the economy, Buffett said that this one statistic was the best way to feel the pulse of the American economy.

Here's why.

Freight car loadings is a figure produced by the Association of American Railroads (AAR), which publishes this weekly figure every Thursday morning. It reveals the number of railroad cars loaded each week and thus shows the volume of raw materials and industrial supplies being moved by rail around the country. The idea is that more industrial production activity in the country equals more freight traffic, and so an increasing or decreasing number tells the tale of the nation's economic activity in real time.

It therefore makes sense to get a bead on the strength of an economy through railway traffic volume. Furthermore, the figure comes from a party that has no reason to fudge the statistic. Their trustworthiness is the same reason why most analysts use railway figures and electricity consumption (power production) figures when they want to get a feel for the pulse of China's economy, which is because these numbers are also far more trustworthy than any other statistics put out by the · Chinese government.

The freight car loadings index is tremendously useful as an economic indicator because it shows the real demand for a certain proportion of the economy but becomes a pulse rate for the health of the economy overall. It shows the quantity of raw materials and finished products being shipped by rail, which is still the most cost-effective way of shipping in the United States, and thus serves as a measure of economic activity. Buffett prepared this one number over all others as the single best way to judge how the economy was doing.

Think of it in this way. All the materials that are being transported by America's railways will at some stage get used in some way. The materials will either be processed into finished goods for sale or stored as inventory that is pressed into service at a later date.

When manufacturers need to make products they must order raw materials that are usually transported by rail, and those shipments are measured by freight car loadings. When inventory levels drop, raw materials are also commonly ordered by manufacturers as a precursor to manufacturing and this is reflected in freight car loading figures as well.

In other words, freight car loadings offer a very accurate early warning sign of the future direction of the U.S. economy. Coal shipments are skewing the indicator right now because there is currently a switch to natural gas underway that has a disproportionate effect on this figure. Nevertheless, when the indicator is booming and trending upwards the general rule is that you can expect good times ahead because the trend suggests that the economy is improving.

In short, this is one way to get a good bead on the direction of the American economy. If you want to see if the economy is moving forwards, you might turn to this figure instead of GDP, which is subject to many statistical manipulations to paint a picture that the government wants to portray.

The corresponding index for trucking, rather than railroads, is the American Trucking Association's For-Hire Truck Tonnage Index. This too gives an indication of what is being shipped across America's roadways and hence is also a sign of an economic boom or bust. Together with the freight index, tonnage currently shipped by railroad and/or roads gives a very direct indication of American economic activity. This most likely works for other countries as well.

The Baltic Dry Index

So now we have two land-based economic measures, which cannot be easily fudged by the government but give a clear direction of the U.S. economy.

The good news is that there is also an ocean going equivalent for the health of the world economy. This is the Baltic Dry shipping rate index, also known as the Baltic Dry Index or BDI, which can be used to keep an eye on the world economy as a whole. It is a number issued daily by the Baltic Exchange in London, and it traces its roots all the way back to 1744.

Every day hundreds of ship brokers from around the world are canvassed for the current freight cost on twenty-three global shipping routes for various types of cargo. We are talking about transporting dry freight such as coal, cement, metal ores, building materials and grain such as a 100,000 ton shipment of iron ore from Australia to China. The cargo can be transported on four different sizes of oceangoing dry bulk vessels and this is reflected in the BDI.

The shipping routes selected for the BDI are meant to represent the entire shipping market, meaning that the cargo on these lanes is large enough in volume to matter for the overall market.

All this data is collected and then combined into creating one single number, the

BDI, that is then made electronically available.

Since the BDI provides an indication of the price for moving the major raw materials by sea, it serves as a basic barometer of the volume of world trade. In other words, the index gives us an idea of the global demand for raw materials because it measures the global supply and demand for the commodities shipped aboard dry bulk carriers. If you are a manufacturer you must buy raw materials whenever you want to start building more finished goods or infrastructure projects—things like automobiles, machinery, roads, buildings and so on. Producers stop buying raw materials when demand slows down, when they have excess inventory, or when infrastructure projects stop, too. A low BDI thus indicates a slowing of the world economy.

The BDI certainly has some flaws (which we'll get into), but it can serve as a leading economic indicator for future economic growth and production. It is a very practical economic indicator for demand on a global scale. It is a more objective measure than most government statistics because the prices it tracks are not subject to speculative manipulation by investors or government agents. It is compiled from real data that is difficult to massage or distort. It is developed to reflect the clear forces of supply and demand and the index is not subject to revisions. If you want a clear reading on the state of the world economy, or a relatively accurate predictor of the global economy, as a first step you can certainly turn to this index.

Remember that the BDI doesn't deal with container ships carrying finished goods. It measures ocean freight costs for the raw material precursors to production and infrastructure demand. This makes the BDI a leading economic indicator that predicts future economic activity. It basically tracks the earliest stages of global commodity chains.

If you are interested in the world demand for finished goods, you need to look at an index constructed from the container rates for shipping those types of products (container rates for the individual containers loaded onto ships). Harper Peterson & Co., a global leading chartering agent, has been tabulating an index like this called the HARPEX (Harper container index) for years.

The HARPEX index measures the rates of moving mostly finished goods globally, which makes it an excellent indicator of global *consumer activity*. While the Baltic Dry Index tracks freight costs for dry bulk ships that usually carry bulk cargoes and raw materials, the HARPEX tracks changes in freight rates for several types of container ships over broader categories. By tracking container shipping rates, the HARPEX index is considered a suitable indicator of global economic fleet shipping activity.

The HARPEX index usually shows the same forecast as the BDI, but is more of a coincident index rather than leading index. The Baltic Index tends to forecast movements in the global economy and usually precedes movements in global stock markets. The BDI also tends to presage higher interest rates because when more materials are being shipped around the world they need to be financed. That greater demand for credit tends to raise interest rates. The Baltic Dry Index thus has a habit of foreshadowing major turns in the economy and stock market usually by about 3 to 6 months.

Let's see how investors can interpret the BDI. Typically, the demand for commodities and raw goods increases when global economies are growing. For investors, knowing when the global economy is growing is helpful because that means stock prices, commodity prices and the value of commodity-based currencies should be increasing.

Conversely, the demand for commodities and raw goods decreases when global economies are stalling or contracting. For investors, knowing when the global economy is contracting is helpful because that means stock prices, commodity prices and the value of commodity-based currencies should be decreasing.

The BDI is a measure of the supply/demand mismatch *at the moment*, and can change drastically on a dime. It is little else beyond this.

Here is how to interpret the BDI when it is moving up:

- Global economy is growing
- Commodity prices should increase (due to increased demand)
- Companies should continue to grow
- Stock prices should increase (because of higher profits)
- Commodity currencies (Canadian dollar, Australian dollar, New Zealand dollar) should start to increase in value

Here is how to interpret the BDI when it is moving down:

- Global economy is contracting or slowing down
- Commodity prices should decrease
- Companies are starting to contract
- Stock prices should decease
- The value of commodity currencies should decline

A sharp move up in the BDI means global trade is increasing. Conversely, a sharp move down means it is decreasing. Any sudden or sharp decline of the BDI is likely to happen before a recession since producers will have substantially curtailed their demand, thus causing shippers to substantially reduce their rates in an attempt to attract cargo.

These interpretations are not foolproof but are just general principles, so you should not immediately jump to conclusions when the BDI starts trending upwards or downwards. You must be wary of making quick conclusions.

Let's see why …

For instance, the BDI could go up (a positive sign) in an environment where the demand for commodities was shrinking (a negative sign) if the supply of ships was shrinking even faster. Inversely, the addition of new shipping capacity might trigger a decline of the BDI if shipping demand was not expected to change significantly in light of this new supply.

The BDI's value is also not solely driven by the underlying demand for commodities transported by sea but by changes in the supply of shipping as well. As an example, when a large supply of new cargo ships hits the market, this oversupply changes shipping rates and cause them to fall. The BDI could also fall simply because there was an increase in the number of ships available to carry dry commodities.

While the supply of ships available to move materials around the globe can distort the BDI, in general it is difficult to distort this supply because it takes years to build a new ship that could be put into service (to increase supply). Also, it would cost far too much to leave ships empty in an attempt to decrease supply.

The demand that affects the BDI comes from commodity buyers who need raw goods for production. It is difficult to manipulate this demand because it is calculated as a result of someone placing orders to have raw materials shipped, and no one is going to pay to book a cargo ship without actually using it (unless for nefarious reasons some powerful group decides to buy up as much cargo space as possible, without actually using it, in order to create an artificial shortage of some regularly ocean shipped-commodity in order to drive up world prices).

Because the supply of shipping is very tight and highly inelastic, small fluctuations in shipping prices are easily observed in the movements of the index. Thus, marginal increases in demand can push the index higher rather quickly, and marginal decreases in demand can cause the index to fall quite rapidly. Hence, you cannot just jump to conclusions for every wiggle upwards or downwards in the index.

The BDI can also be distorted by changes in the cost of fuel and insurance, temporary port closures, and many other factors. Bunker fuel, for instance, accounts for about 40% of a vessel's operating costs. When oil prices rise this increase is incorporated into higher shipping rates. Thus the costs of fuel can change the index.

Some ports, especially during particular seasons, can also become congested and tie up the ships within them, which will also boost shipping rates until the ships are released. Furthermore, there might also be higher geopolitical risks (political instability or risk of war) for some shipping locations, which would in turn boost insurance rates and consequently shipping rates. Lastly, there is also significant seasonality in the demand for some commodities (such as grain and coal) that will create fluctuations in the BDI when the transport of these commodities is in high or low demand.

Thus the various ways for interpreting the BDI are just simplifications of general tendencies. You certainly can have situations where there is a weaker BDI, for instance, while the underlying commodity demand and emerging market growth could be strong. Nonetheless the BDI can still tell us something about global demand and trade, and thus the world economy, regardless of noise issuing due to the seasonality of shipping patterns, changing costs, the supply of ships, geopolitical tensions and factors unique to each country.

Overvalued or Undervalued?

What other indicators might be important to an investor?

How about something that measures whether the stock market is under or overvalued? This would be extremely useful! Typically I would recommend the valuations created by John Hussman, but Warren Buffett offers something easier.

In two separate interviews in 1999 and 2001 Warren Buffett explained to Carol Loomis of *Fortune* magazine that determining whether the stock market is expensive and over-priced or cheap and undervalued doesn't have to be complicated. He uses a very simple calculation to get at the answer, and once again the simplicity of his approach surprised everyone reading the interview.

Basically, value investor Buffett divides the total market capitalization of the U.S. stock market by the gross national product, or GNP, to determine whether stock prices are cheap or too expensive. In other words, he looks at the market value of all publicly traded securities as a percentage of the country's business.

In this calculation Buffett uses the GNP gross national product rather than gross domestic product, or GDP. The gross national product measures the value of goods and services that a country's citizens produce *regardless of where they live* so it includes what American companies produce abroad. It is therefore a very large measure of national productivity.

Now this ratio has certain limitations, but it is a very simple measure of where stock valuations stand at any given moment in time. With it you can get a good feel for whether the stock market is expensive at any particular moment. Buffett explained: "If the percentage relationship falls to the 70% or 80% area, buying stocks is likely to work very well for you. If the ratio approaches 200% - as it did in 1999 and a part of 2000 - you are playing with fire."

To compute this number we can do the following. If we want to calculate the market value of all publicly traded securities we can add the total market capitalization of the New York Stock Exchange to the total market capitalization of the NASDAQ stock exchange. Or, we can simply use a monthly figure supplied by the World Federation of Exchanges, which reports the market capitalization of various world stock markets. To find GNP you can turn to the website of the Federal Reserve Bank of St. Louis, which features most U.S. economic data.

Dividing the total market capitalization by GNP then gives us a percentage that can easily be interpreted as undervalued or overvalued. It's an alternative to more complicated valuation measures such as the Shiller P/E or Tobin's Q (market capitalization / corporate net worth) and is a nice way to see if the market is over or undervalued in aggregate. That's a nice statistic to have.

The Velocity of Money

There is yet another powerful indicator largely ignored by mainstream analysts, which is the velocity of money. Hardly anyone ever discusses it but you will see how useful it is for cutting through all the propaganda about an economy being or not being in a recession.

What is it and why is it important? It is particularly relevant because it is presently broadcasting a "canary in the coal mine" warning about the health of the U.S. financial system despite all the ZIRP and QE efforts that have been in effect for the past few years.

Technically, the velocity of money is *the frequency at which one unit of currency is used to purchase domestically produced goods and services within a given time period*. In other words, it is the number of times one dollar is spent to buy goods and services per unit of time.

If the velocity of money is increasing, then more transactions are occurring between individuals in an economy. The result, in this scenario, should be that growth (as measured in GDP) should be rising. Unless, of course, that the number is at some extreme indicating an economic disaster such as hyperinflation.

Right now the velocity of money is declining and the rate is so bad that it has broken lows set fifty years ago! It is continuing to fall rapidly in both the U.S. Economy and that of Canada, the EU and Japan, thus indicating a failure in the monetary policy that is trying to stimulate these economies. According to this number the entire global economy is in recession; the recession of 2007-08 never ended. The pathogenesis is being shared globally due to a commonly wrong approach to monetary policy, namely the QE, ZIRP and NIRP monetary policies of the world's central banks.

Basically, a declining velocity of money means that fewer transactions are occurring in an economy and a recession is indicated. It means that money is not moving in the body economic. Such is the present case despite all attempts by the Federal Reserve to hide this fact and to create an economic stimulus through ZIRP interest rate and QE money printing policies.

Despite low interest rate returns in their bank accounts, consumers and businesses are simply holding firm to their money rather than investing it, and that's largely because they see poor prospects for any new investment projects. Very little new capital formation is therefore occurring inside the U.S. economy, which is exactly the opposite situation that the world's central bankers want to see. In fact capital destruction is what is actually happening because of their misguided monetary policies.

How so? Debts are being dissolved through various defaults and deflationary actions and market liquidity is collapsing. The money velocity is declining as businesses are ruined along these lines. The statistic is a clear indicator that the economy is going to mush, and you should keep an eye on it to know whether you are headed for a recession or even the other extreme, which is hyperinflation. If ever the velocity of money were to briskly rise to new heights it would indicate that consumers were immediately using any money they had to buy goods and services, which is a situation that often happens in rampant cases of inflation or hyperinflation (where people act to buy real goods and services as stores of wealth rather than paper money).

ShadowStats.com for Consistent Government Indicators

Lastly, I wish to introduce an exceedingly trustworthy source for economic statistics that are much more realistic than the numbers put out by the U.S. government. That is the website www.ShadowStats.com run by John Williams.

Many analysts have claimed that important economic numbers, such as GDP or the unemployment rate, are routinely mathematically manipulated by government for the objective of cutting its costs or instilling higher confidence in the economy. Unfortunately, that manipulation is telegraphing wrong messages about the U.S. economy, rendering the numbers useless as reliable forecasting aids or price discovery tools for industrialists, investors and financers alike.

There is no doubt that in order to make things look better than they really are, important U.S. government statistics are periodically being redefined, seasonally adjusted or subjected to a variety of other mathematical manipulations that serve to understate negative changes that might "spook the market" or cause mandated government and corporate labor payments to increase within the economy. In other words, we are being lied to because we are being given fake statistics.

Let's take just one statistic as an example.

Of particular interest is the inflation rate number (monthly CPI report) put out by the government since many of us know from personal experience that the government is vastly underreporting the current rate of inflation. The government has a particular interest in reporting a number as low as possible because it can thereby keep low the annual cost of living adjustments to Social Security and other government benefits while over-estimating the true level of GDP. According to the U.S. Census Bureau (Jan 2013), nearly half of Americans receive benefits from some type of government program, and most of these programs have payments that are tied to the CPI in some way. The government therefore has a vested interest in suppressing CPI figures.

The manipulation to report the CPI lower than it actually is allows the government to pay out less to these programs and also allows U.S. corporations to keep employee wage increases low, which increases their profits and enhances their competitiveness. Under-reporting the true level of inflation also allows the Federal Reserve to keep its discount rate far lower than it would be, too.

This CPI inaccuracy all started back in 1983 during a time of rapidly increasing inflation. At that time the U.S. Bureau of Labor Statistics (BLS) began to alter its calculations in order to curb the increases it had to pay in Social Security and federal pension payments. Mike Bryan, a vice president and senior economist in the Atlanta Fed's research department has publicly confirmed that there have been times when the way that inflation has been calculated has changed on a monthly basis.

Basically a lower-than-true reported CPI rate benefits many vested interests, and so there is a definite incentive to "cook the books." For instance, if the government was to admit that inflation is rising right now, the Fed would be pressured to raise interest rates, which would be unacceptable to its current ZIRP policy that is necessary to keep the U.S. financial system solvent. In reporting a realistic number it turns out that banker bonuses, corporate stock options, corporate salaries, retirement benefits and politician elections also become at stake. Therefore over the past few years, and especially since 2008, the CPI inflation rate has become a heavily manipulated number through academic theories of readjustment that are used as a cover to systematically under-report its true level.

In order to provided a CPI measurement that is consistent over time, John Williams at ShadowStats.com publishes two alternate CPI estimates: one based on the pre-1990 official methodology for computing the CPI-U, and the other based on the methodology which was employed prior to 1980. When looking for accurate figures of the inflation rate, GDP growth rate, or unemployment rate of the country you should turn to Williams' figures first. However, Williams is not the only one with an alternative CPI figure. If you are interested in the true level of inflation in America you might also consider the Chapwood Index compiled by Ed Butowsky since 2008.

Back in 2008, Ed Butowsky realized that it was simply a myth that the government CPI figure accurately represented the increase in the average American's true cost of living. He therefore set out to compute a better number. Using social media, he surveyed his friends across the country to see what they purchased with their after-tax income and narrowed the list down to the most frequent 500 items. Then he asked people in America's 50 largest cities to check the prices on those items periodically. The result became the Chapwood Index of inflation. While Williams keeps the computation methodology of inflation consistent over time, the Chapwood index strikes at the very heart of matters by measuring what Americans truly buy without any seasonal adjustments or substitution assumptions such as those incorporated into the BLS calculations. It is released only twice a year and uses just *real prices* rather than prices adjusted due to some type of theory.

The list of components within the Chapwood Index includes rent, mortgage, home repairs, electricity, car loans and leases, oil changes, parking meters, Starbucks coffee, People magazine, Advil, postage and envelopes, insurance, gasoline, sales and income taxes, tolls, fast food restaurants, toothpaste, car washes, pizza, Verizon FIOS, Dish TV, iPhone service, dry cleaning, movie tickets, cosmetics, water delivery, newspaper delivery, dish towels, gym memberships, piano lessons, laundry detergent, light bulbs, school supplies, pet food, underwear, plumbing emergencies and health insurance. In other words, the Chapwood Index reports the unadjusted actual cost and price fluctuation of the top 500 items on which Americans spend their after-tax dollars in the 50 largest cities in the nation. If you want a true rate for inflation in America then this number reflects the true cost-of-living increase in America. For the true rate of inflation forget the government statistics and turn to this.

Now the reason all these numbers are relevant is because they will give you a better handle on what is happening in the economy than you can get with the equivalent government statistics. All these numbers I've reported on are more accurate, less likely to be fudged, and more useful, too.

If you want to make certain decisions about your investments you should rely on accurate rather than inaccurate data in your decision process. I thought it prudent that you should have this data available for your asset protection responsibilities rather than be at the mercy of government data releases, which many analysts state are being increasingly manipulated so that they are useless.

If you want an indication of economic activity in the U.S. then I suggest you look at freight car loadings and the velocity of money.

If you want an indication of world economic activity then look at the Baltic Dry Index.

If you want to know whether the stock market is over or undervalued then you can look at Warren Buffett's formula of dividing the total market capitalization of U.S. stocks by GNP. A second choice are the valuation indicators produced by John Hussman of the Hussman Funds.

If you truly want to rely just on government statistics then use those put out by ShadowStats.com because these numbers are more reliable than government released figures. For the best bead on the inflation rate turn to the Chapwood Index.

If you have good data you'll make better decisions. These sources will certainly help lead you to better investment and asset protection decisions.

CHAPTER 5:
P2P LENDING

In today's low interest environment, are you satisfied with the amount of interest you are currently earning on your bank account? If not, there is a way to make a lot more.

Instead of parking your money in a CD or interest bearing bank account that might pay you a paltry 1% this year, why not flip things around? Why not become a bank yourself and start making loans to individuals who will pay *you* a much higher interest rate than that 1%? In today's internet world, that can now be done.

A new type of online financial intermediary, which is not a bank, does all the difficult work of matching borrowers to investor-lenders like you to make this all possible. If you lend your money carefully, the interest you earn on your loans can amount to many times more than you could possibly receive from bank accounts, CDs, bonds or even dividend stocks!

The way to start earning more money this way is to get into "peer-to-peer" or "person-to-person" lending. It's also called "P2P lending," direct lending or crowdfunding. This is a fast growing asset class largely ignored by financial advisors, but which gives you yet another option for long-term wealth accumulation.

Using the internet, P2P lending basically gives *you* (a private investor with money) a way to make loans to perfect strangers ("peers" or borrowers) who possess sufficient creditworthiness. Because you actually make an entire loan or part of a loan to an approved borrower, you are entitled to the returns earned by the loan.

In P2P lending, the matching of borrowers and lenders is made possible through online lending platforms. The platforms function as intermediaries to the borrowing-loaning process and are the center of the fast growing P2P financial industry.

Here's the kicker! The P2P companies that own and manage the online lending platforms are *not banks*. They are companies producing competition for banks. They use your funds to make loans, and you collect part of the interest earned in return. The P2P companies collect credit criteria from potential borrowers, verify it, evaluate their creditworthiness, arrange for the loans to the borrowers, carry the loans on their books, collect repayments and pursue defaulters. Your involvement is simply being an investor who chooses which loans you want to make.

P2P companies do not have banking licenses so they must use real banks to make the actual loans. Then they sell pieces of those loans to investors like you through the online portals they manage. Investors simply browse and then select the loans they want to fund after the borrowers have been vetted by the P2P companies and been assigned a level of creditworthiness.

In short, P2P lending enables willing borrowers and lenders to connect with each other through a single online platform that bypasses traditional banks, and which thereby offers substantial financial advantages to both parties. Borrowers get loans at better rates and lenders get to keep the interest on the loans just like a bank would. As a lender you can make fractional loans to borrowers and thereby diversify your risks from putting all your money in just one loan.

All borrowers must meet certain credit qualification criteria, such as a minimum FICO score, before they are allowed to apply for online loans. Once approved, their loan is added to the online lending platform, investor-lenders can then find and then fund the loan, and then borrowers start to repay their loan automatically online. P2P loans are set up to be repaid automatically by debiting the borrower's bank account via automated check handling (ACH) payments.

As an investor, you can open a P2P investment account and then immediately connect with potential borrowers through the online platform. You can browse the loans on the platform, select the ones you want to fund, and then start earning money on the loan portfolio you build up. The loan requests usually range between $2,000 and $35,000 in value and are charged varying interest rates based on someone's creditworthiness.

You can make a "fractional loan" that invests as little as $25 in part of a larger loan or make a "whole loan" that funds one in its entirety. This means that multiple investors are often taking share in the same loan to a borrower, thus lower their overall risks if that borrower defaults.

In P2P parlance, each fractional portion of a loan is called a "Note," and the *smartest investors build a widely diversified portfolio of many different Notes*. Because even the best of loans can default, they never concentrate their investments in just a few Notes because it is far too risky. In this way they spread their risk among many different loans instead of risking all their money on just a few.

As stated, before a loan request is listed on the lending platform, P2P companies will perform some level of verification on every borrower. Some of the data that potential borrowers need to supply, such as monthly income, is self-declared and cannot be systematically verified. After the evaluation process, borrowers are then also given a grading of creditworthiness. Each P2P firm has a different way of grading borrowers and giving them a final credit rating.

On average, about 90% of potential borrowers are rejected in the application process, usually because of poor credit scores or because their credit histories cannot be verified. This is in your favor. If a borrower passes the verification process, then their loan request becomes approved for investors.

Investors can select to fund a loan while it is going through the verification process, but the loan will not be issued if the borrower fails verification. If that happens, the loan's listing will be deleted from the online P2P platform and all the money that has been pledged to fund it will be returned to the potential investors. Once funded, a loan will also be removed from the P2P platform.

Borrowers whose loans were approved and then funded by investors will receive their money (less an origination fee that goes to the P2P company) in just a few days once funding is complete, and then must begin making repayments within 30 days. Loans are usually made for either 3-year or 5-year terms at fixed interest rates. The monthly loan repayments will follow a standard amortization schedule for principal plus interest.

It is quite common for many skilled P2P investors, who learn how to intelligently select loans and manage their risks through ample diversification, to earn nearly 10% per year on these Note investments. That rate of return is much higher than what you can receive on your bank account or CD.

With such returns possible, this new form of income generation has been rapidly growing in popularity among knowledgeable investors, especially when they see the extremely low yields on alternative interest rate investments. You might even consider P2P lending a new "mega-trend" because the volume of loans has been growing at far more than 100% per year.

When the economy is getting better and unemployment is falling, this can be a very profitable form of investing that may offer a much better yield than bonds or CDs. On the other hand, when the economy turns bad your P2P lending could produce losses because of higher loan default risks, so if you don't manage this form of investing carefully you can certainly lose money. Even so, to lose 5% on your money in a year is a far lesser amount than a 20% decline in the stock market.

P2P lending is not a sure thing, but it certainly makes it possible to earn much more income than many other interest rate alternatives. You are really investing in consumer credit, just like a bank, with the caveat that your loans are not being backed by any borrower-pledged collateral.

The bright point is that *consumer credit is traditionally a low risk, high yield asset class if you make consumer loans in a scientific way just like a bank does.* With P2P lending, the actual track record indeed shows that you can definitely create a steady cash flow from a well-diversified pool of high quality loans! The key principle to remember is that safety in P2P lending comes from investing in a large number of diversified loans.

The gist is that you should not consider yourself a "saver" when getting into P2P lending. The proper mindset to cultivate is that you are an *investor* who faces risks, but who is willing to shoulder those risks, like a bank, for a higher rate of return than what can normally be earned on a CD, savings deposit or riskier bond investment.

Before we discuss many of the risks you must consider for this new asset class, let's discuss why borrowers are now turning to P2P loans rather than bank loans.

Why are P2P Loans Growing in Popularity?

One of the biggest reasons behind the growing trend toward P2P loans is the fact that many banks have cut back on their lending. While banks don't seem to be lending anymore, as long as your credit is good enough you can easily obtain a P2P loan for paying off credit cards, debt consolidation, home improvement, or even small business! The only big question will be the interest rate you will pay on the loan.

Borrowers typically prefer the P2P lending process because it is quicker and much easier than going to a bank. Since the entire P2P transaction process takes place online, it can be done in a fraction of the time it usually takes for a bank loan to be approved. Potential borrowers appreciate that they can instantly access the online P2P lending platforms through their smartphones and laptops rather than have to line up at a brick-and-mortar bank for a prolonged visit. They want to save time and avoid the inconvenience of banking interviews and delays.

Yet another big benefit to borrowers is the financial savings. P2P loans are potentially cheaper than bank loans. They usually have low fixed rates, no hidden fees, and are not burdened with prepayment penalties. In other words, when you receive a P2P loan you know exactly what you are getting into.

The P2P lending platforms also have lower overhead than traditional banks. Most of their service architecture is automated so that they are free of a large banking bureaucracy. With less costs to cover, they can provide cheaper loans to borrowers than the higher interest rates charged by traditional banks to maintain their profitability. Operating on lower costs, the P2P lending platforms can then pass those savings onto borrowers.

Their lower costs and online operations also makes it easier for the P2P platforms to grow without requiring a lot of extra capital. They can easily attract borrowers utilizing online ads, social media and through the type of traditional direct mail campaigns typically used for credit card marketing.

At the same time they charge less to borrowers, the efficiencies of the P2P companies give investor-lenders the chance to earn high yield returns, too. The P2P industry basically gives investors such as you *a way to participate in the consumer credit debt market whose lucrative returns were previously only available to the banks and credit card companies.*

Basically, both borrowers and investor-lenders are benefitting from the P2P revolution. Lender-investors who invest responsibly are presently earning a higher return on their money than what is traditionally available from a bank savings account or CD. Borrowers are also winning with P2P loans because they are paying a lower interest rate than what banks would charge for credit card advances or consumer bank loans. *If you want to pay off some credit card debt, you should definitely look into a P2P loan!*

If a borrower takes out a P2P loan whose interest rate is less than their credit card rate, they can use those funds to immediately pay off their credit card debt and realize a savings of several percentage points per year. These savings may be very substantial in the case of a credit card borrower who has a very good credit rating because they would likely be able to secure a loan at the low end of the interest rates charged on the platforms. Right now, P2P interest rates are typically ranging between 6% and 25% on new loans in the United States. The interest rate borrowers must pay depends upon their credit standing and their loan's duration.

The loans you make through the P2P system are typically unsecured by any collateral, and the money investors loan isn't protected by any government guarantees either. However, you can still earn great returns if you manage the expected loan default rates and returns.

Loan default rates, which are the key concern of lender-investors, differ by the risk class and vary from about 2% to 12% depending upon that risk level. This means that you can expect a certain proportion of P2P loans to definitely default at some time during their lifetime. Investors must understand that it is not a matter of *if* it will happen, but *when*. If you make lots of loans you will most probably end up investing in some loans that will default. That is the nature of P2P investing. Nonetheless, great returns are possible. Even with unavoidable default rates, the track record demonstrates that the return available for investor-lenders who fund a well-diversified portfolio of loans is typically in the range of 6% to 12% per annum.

Some investors can earn more, even after taking into account the defaults from borrowers who fail to repay their loans. So even with the typical default rates, which are common fare in the consumer loan market, you can still earn substantial returns if your P2P Notes are chosen in a favorable fashion. That is the most important lesson for P2P investing - to make money in this new asset class, the key is to rely on diversification and the law of large numbers to protect yourself from the inevitable defaults.

Because borrowers can always default, investors must carefully select the loans they choose to participate in. They must only invest in those with the highest likelihood of repayment and must also diversify across a large number of such loans. Following these rules, there is ample money to be made if you do this right. It is actually a great way for those of mathematical bent to beat the bankers and earn fantastic returns, so let's talk a little about the P2P lending companies themselves to get a better feel for the options available to you.

Prosper and Lending Club

The entire field of P2P lending was initially started in England by a company called Zopa, which is the world's oldest and Europe's largest peer-to-peer lender. Zopa stands for "zone of possible agreement," referring to the fact that borrowers and lenders are looking to be matched with one another and reach agreement on loan rates.

Funding Circle and Ratesetter are other competitor platforms that operate in the U.K. while SocietyOne is Australia's leading P2P platform. Many countries across the world also have P2P lending services, too.

In the United States, the two largest peer-to-peer lending institutions are Lending Club and Prosper. Both of these companies were launched by successful technology entrepreneurs and are based in San Francisco. They are the only two U.S. firms you should initially consider when you are just getting started with P2P lending. Because these lending platforms do not have banking licenses, they use WebBank, a bank in Salt Lake City, Utah, to make the actual loans to borrowers. Their online platforms then sell pieces of those loans to investors, who can use whatever criteria they like to select the loans they want to finance.

Each state in the U.S. has different rules for P2P borrowers and lenders. Currently, residents of 47 states can apply for Prosper loans, and residents in 44 states can apply for Lending Club loans. For investors, 30 states allow their residents to invest in Prosper loans while only 26 states are open to Lending Club. Borrowers need a minimum FICO credit score of 660 to borrow from Lending Club and 640 to borrow from Prosper.

Both Lending Club and Prosper earn their profits by charging borrowers and lenders certain fees. In addition to paying the interest rate on their loan, borrowers are charged between 1% and 5% of the loan amount as a one-time origination fee. Investor-lenders are charged an annual loan servicing fee of 1% for all the work that the P2P firms do in matching borrowers and investors, carrying the loans on their books, collecting repayments and pursuing defaulters. The P2P firms are profitable with these fees, which still allow investors to make 6-12% per annum returns.

While this rate of return may seem high, that is so only in the light of the currently low interest rate environment that has been artificially produced by the money-printing actions of the central banks. If governments were not interfering with the natural cost of money in the marketplace, 6% to 12% per annum would probably represent the historical true value of money under normal circumstances.

This calls into question whether you should become a P2P lender if, say, the interest rates on government guaranteed CDs were to rise to 6% and you were only making 8% on your money while shouldering the extra risks involved with P2P lending. For now interest rates are being kept artificially low, but you must keep this issue in mind should interest rates rise in the future.

Now let's take a look both of these platforms where you might become an investor-lender to earn great returns like a bank.

Lending Club (LendingClub.com)

As of 2015, Lending Club is the larger of the two American P2P firms, and since 2007 has now facilitated more than $6 billion in loans. Over 72,500 investors have used Lending Club to fund these loans and participate in their returns. The average borrower at Lending Club has a 770 FICO score, 16.6% ratio of debt-to-income, 15.5 years of credit history, and personal income of around $72,000.

Lending Club categorizes borrowers into seven different loan grades: A through G. The A Notes represent the "lowest risk" borrowers seeking loans whereas the G Notes represent the "highest risk" borrowers. The highest risk borrowers are charged the highest interest rates. Each loan grade is further partitioned into five sub-grades. The seven loan grades therefore turn into a total of 35 separate grades for borrowers classified as A1 down to G5. The most important factor for determining someone's loan grading is the data in their credit report. Those with the best credit history receive the A1 grade, which carries the lowest interest rate.

The average interest rate for a Lending Club loan is currently around 14-15%, and the average loan size is approximately $14,000 on this P2P platform. The Lending Club site reports that 83% of Lending Club borrowers use their loans to refinance existing debt such as by paying off their credit cards.

To become a Lending Club investor-lender, you can open an account online if you meet a number of eligibility requirements. Because these eligibility rules change from time to time, you should check the Lending Club website for the latest qualification rules. A primary rule is that you must be at least 18 years old to become a Notes investor.

Currently, Lending Club Notes can only be sold to residents of California, Colorado, Connecticut, Delaware, Florida, Georgia, Hawaii, Idaho, Illinois, Kentucky, Louisiana, Minnesota, Mississippi, Missouri, Montana, Nevada, New Hampshire, New York, Rhode Island, South Dakota, Utah, Virginia, Washington, West Virginia, Wisconsin, and Wyoming. They are not presently being offered or sold to residents of any other state, the District of Columbia, any other territory or possession of the United States, or any foreign country. Some states have a net worth or gross income eligibility requirements that residents must meet to qualify for Notes investments. Typically you are only allowed to purchase Notes up to 10% of your net worth.

Prosper (Prosper.Com)

Prosper Marketplace was the initial pioneering P2P lender in the U.S., but is smaller than Lending Club because of some early missteps in its business model. Nonetheless it has issued over $1 billion in P2P loans since it began operations in February 2006 and like Lending Club is growing extremely fast.

Prosper Notes are categorized by seven loan grades called Prosper Ratings: AA, A, B, C, D, E and HR. AA Notes represent the highest level of borrower creditworthiness whereas HR Notes stand for the highest risk borrowers. Prosper also differs from Lending Club in that it uses more than just a loan grade to rank borrowers. Each borrower is also assigned a proprietary Prosper Score ranging from 1-11. This internal scoring system was developed after Prosper analyzed the payment history of actual borrowers on their platform.

Prosper uses both the Prosper score and a borrower's credit information to determine the interest rate to be charged and to estimate the default probability for every loan. The average loan size is around $10,000 on the Prosper P2P Platform and the interest rates are roughly the same as for Lending Club.

Investors in the following states can invest in Prosper Notes: Alaska, California, Colorado, Connecticut, Delaware, District of Columbia, Florida, Georgia, Hawaii, Idaho, Illinois, Louisiana, Maine, Michigan, Minnesota, Mississippi, Missouri, Montana, Nevada, New Hampshire, New York, Oregon, Rhode Island, South Carolina, South Dakota, Utah, Virginia, Washington, West Virginia, Wisconsin and Wyoming. As with Lending Club, there are various net worth requirements to become a lender-investor which are listed on the Prosper website.

The U.S. Marketplace

Borrowers who want to pay off credit card debt or consolidate other debts constitute the largest source of loan demand since these borrowers typically find that their credit card interest rate can be substantially reduced with a P2P loan. This is a good space for lending since the Federal Reserve Board reports that credit card lending has not had an unprofitable quarter, even after loan defaults, for the past 20 years. During this time the credit card companies and banks have consistently earned an annualized compound return of approximately 11% on consumer debt, and *this is the marketplace that you are essentially tapping into with P2P loans.*

The reason banks remain highly profitable with this business is that *they rely on the law of large numbers when making loans* and expect that a highly diversified pool of credit card receivables will have a predictable, stable rate of defaults and delinquencies that is within their band of risk tolerance. Now that many of the early kinks have been worked out of the Prosper and Lending Club systems, that also happens to be the case with their platform lending records.

This is yet another reason why interest in P2P lending is growing among investors. The returns are so predictable and profitable, when Note investments are made in a disciplined fashion, that big money has entered this arena. Hedge funds have become avid investors in P2P loans because there is now a sufficiently large steady stream of new loans that can supply the volume necessary to build and manage an institutional portfolio.

In short, P2P originated loans are fast becoming an institutionally accepted asset class. In May 2013, for instance, Google purchased a $125 million stake in Lending Club, thus proving institutional interest in this new field of investing. Executives from traditional financial institutions are also joining the peer-to-peer companies as board members, lenders and investors, indicating that this new financing model has established itself in the mainstream.

The success of personal P2P lending has effectively validated the crowdfinancing model for the financial industry, even compelling the financial establishment to enter the field. In time we may even see large P2P funds marketed by Wall Street, or collateralized P2P loan portfolios, but until then you must invest your money in P2P loans by yourself.

What are the Risks?

It is an iron-clad rule that every investor should consider all the risks of any investment before committing their money. P2P lending definitely has a number of risks you must consider before you get involved with this type of investment, as follows:

Default Risk - The primary risk to P2P lending is that borrowers will default on their loans. Most P2P loans are unsecured, meaning that they are not backed by any collateral. Unsecured consumer lending is always considered risky, so when borrowers fail to pay, their loans have to be sent for collection. Both Prosper and Lending Club list the average default rates for loans, by credit ratings, on their websites.

Remember when making loans that any money you invest in Notes (loans) is *not protected* by any government guarantees, so there is no protection against losses other than good risk control and money management on your part. Of course, that is the case with most investments. What you must understand is that losses *will definitely occur* so you just have to develop the mindset to accept them.

A study by Nickel Steamroller has found that the vast majority of defaults occur in the first 18 months of a loan, with the largest proportion occurring between the 6th and 11th months. Once you get near the two-year mark of a three-year loan, there tend to be very few defaults even for the higher risk loans.

The good news for investors, as with bankers, is that each time that they receive a payment for one of their loans, the amount of their money at risk is reduced significantly. This is because they will have received interest for that period and will have also been repaid a fraction of their loan principal as well. The basic rules to remember for lowering your default risk is that you must carefully choose which borrowers to lend to, diversify your investments across different borrowers, and always invest in fractional parts of loans.

Once again, you must be perfectly clear that many of the P2P loans you will make *absolutely will default*. You will also definitely find that certain categories of loans (such as educational loans or small business loans) will be riskier than others (such as credit card or car loans) in terms of their default rates. In aggregate, loan performance will not just differ because of a loan's credit grading but because of other differentiating criteria as well.

The only reason P2P lending becomes steadily profitable is when you can do it in large enough scale were the default rates become accurately predictable across different loan categories and criteria, and the impact of those defaults does not hurt your overall rate of return on the money you have invested.

Poor Loan Diversification – Many new investors in P2P loans make the mistake of having too little diversification in their accounts. They do not take advantage of the $25 minimum investment size available for loans, but instead make the mistake of concentrating their money in just a few large loans.

Consider this for an investor with $2,500: if you invest in 25 loans at $100 each you are running a much higher risk than if you invest in 100 loans at $25. With only 25 loans in your portfolio, two defaults could wipe out 8% of your gains ($200/$2500)!

The great advantage to P2P Notes is precisely the fact that they offer you easy diversification *through very small investment amounts*. For instance, if you were to purchase a bond then you might be paying around $1,000, but you can put as little as $25 into a lending Note. While $10,000 could buy 10 different bonds, the same amount could be turned into 400 different P2P loans. Thus you can enjoy a much greater degree of diversification that makes it safer for you to invest in riskier but higher yielding loans.

The P2P Platform Risk – A rarely considered risk to this new asset class is that the firms owning and managing the P2P platforms could possibly go bankrupt. Of all the risks, this is probably the least likely to happen because the P2P firms are extremely profitable and sufficiently capitalized at this time.

If there ever were to be a bankruptcy, the P2P firms also have legal agreements with backup loan servicers who will take over servicing the loans. Nonetheless, you would probably suffer some disruption in service if a P2P intermediary went bankrupt and could possibly lose some principal if this ever occurred.

There is also the chance that P2P lending could be legislated out of existence, and there is little you can do about potential changes to the regulatory environment. Furthermore, a loss of electricity and internet access could jeopardize the platform as well.

Interest Rate Risk – Almost all P2P loans in the U.S. currently have a term of three or five years, which is a long time to hold an unsecured loan. During this time, national interest rates could increase substantially, meaning that money you loaned at a lower interest rate faces an opportunity cost since it might have been parked elsewhere with a lower risk.

Therefore you must consider the interest rate risk for this type of investment: if an FDIC insured investment is paying 6%, investing in a lending Note paying 7% is not necessarily a wise decision for the risks you are taking.

Liquidity Risk – A big drawback to P2P lending, compared to interest paying bonds, is their lack of liquidity. There is a growing secondary market where P2P Notes can be sold, called the FOLIO Investing marketplace, that is available to the holders of both Prosper and Lending Club Notes.

To access this alternative trading marketplace (aka ATS), you must open a brokerage account with FOLIO Investing. Afterwards you can sell or purchase existing Notes on the exchange to manage your liquidity needs. FOLIO Investing charges users 1% of the face amount of a Note as a transaction fee for providing the ATS service.

Unfortunately, even with this secondary marketplace, selling your Notes can be a long drawn out process. You may have to lower the price of your Notes substantially if you want to sell them quickly. It makes sense to familiarize yourself with various strategies for how to sell your loans in the Folio Investing marketplace if you need liquidity (or want to maximize your returns).

The secondary marketplace is still in its infancy, so the truth of the matter is that it is not very easy to quickly resell Notes you no longer want, or necessarily sell them at their true value.

If you therefore need to liquidate your entire investment in P2P Notes you will likely lose some principal in the process. Since most loans are held for three or five years, as a P2P investor you should develop the mindset that your Note investments will be locked up for that time horizon.

To reduce this liquidity problem, you might consider concentrating in just three-year Notes rather than the five-year loans. Since every monthly loan repayment recovers a fractional part of your principal, holding three-year loans is less risky than five-year loans on a comparative basis.

The Track Record

When Prosper initially started, most early lenders lost money investing in its P2P Notes because the loan default rates were too high. The company had not yet developed a winning formula for weeding out the highest default risks. In fact, nearly 40% of loans issued in 2006-2007 defaulted at Prosper, and the early Lending Club numbers were not very good either. Since then, both Prosper and Lending Club have refined their criteria for loan qualification as well as their borrower grading systems. In consequence, the average default rates for their various loan grades has plummeted.

As to current investor returns, most P2P investors are earning more than 6% on either platform but not more than 10%. While many who are careful with their loan selection process are averaging at least a 10% annualized return, by no means are these returns typical or assured. Investing in P2P loans has risks and is *not* a guaranteed way to make a specific interest rate return that you desire.

Once again, the key to profitability as a Notes investor is to diversify your investments. Both Prosper and Lending Club emphasize the fact that diversification is a key component to a successful lending strategy.

Lending Club states that owning at least 100 Notes reduces the risk in your returns, meaning that nearly all investors with at least 100 Notes have experienced a positive return. On its website, Prosper states that "For Notes purchased since July 2009, every Prosper investor with 100 or more Notes has experienced positive returns."

Prosper also states that investors with at least 150 Notes have over a 97% chance of making a 7%+ return. Furthermore, statistics show that those investing in 200+ Notes have only a 4.8% chance of an annualized return less than 6%. Those who have invested in 400 or more Notes have only a 1.1% chance of annualized returns less than 6%.

What this all means is that diversifying across multiple Notes and ratings and doing so over time will tend to increase your safety and returns in this new asset class of consumer loans. For example, the statistics show that investors with 400 Prosper Notes (which can be obtained with a minimum investment of $10,000) are nearly 24 times more likely to see an annualized return over 6% than those who only invest in 25 Notes.

The reason you should *invest in many Notes across many borrowers* is because if you put all your money into one loan and that borrower defaults, you potentially lose 100% of your total investment. Thanks to the law of large numbers, spreading your investable money over hundreds of quality loans enables you to significantly reduce your risks.

Unless a large portion of your loan portfolio's performance is correlated - as happened with the housing crash (and which will likely happen if unemployment rises everywhere such as during a recession) - with enough diversification the volatility of your returns will be low enough to produce stable positive results. The default rate on loans should therefore be a predictable problem that careful investors can handle.

The statistics show that if the average borrower pays an interest rate of approximately 13%, then even after deducting 3-4% losses for defaults and any service fees charged by the platforms, this can still leave a typical return of 8% to 12% to holders of broadly diversified portfolios of P2P loans on Lending Club or

Prosper. The final rate of return, or ROI that you will ultimately earn on your investments will depend upon the size of your loan portfolio and the various types of loans you invest in.

Selecting Profitable Notes for Investment

After you open up an account with Lending Club or Prosper, you will certainly need some disciplined way to choose which loans to invest in from the hundreds of Notes available. There are several ways to do this.

One way is to select an automated investment plan, administered by either Prosper or Lending Club, where your money will be allocated automatically among many different loans. For instance, you can build a customized plan at Prosper based on your own loan selection criteria, or let Prosper automatically invest in Notes for you based on a credit risk you select. Prosper has an automated system, where you set it and forget it, called "Automated Quick Invest." Lending Club also has an automated system where you can invest your money with just a few clicks. Lending Club allows you to select an automated investment plan based on an average interest rate, or you can choose from one of their automated investment options that focus on low, medium or high risk Notes.

Other third party firms, such as LendingRobot, can also automate the loan selection process for you while only costing a very small fee. They allow you to "set it and forget it" to handle your P2P investing. For instance, LendingRobot can automatically select loans for you based on its own historically backtested criteria, or you can automate your own selection criteria in its purchase order system. Once you open an account, LendingRobot will use its API to automatically notify the P2P platforms of any purchase orders on your behalf that are selected by your loan criteria.

Since many of the "best loans" are quickly snapped up by sophisticated investors using highly researched rating algorithms, LendingRobot will even allow you the option of piggybacking their decisions too. LendingRobot can determine the most popular loan investments within the first five seconds after new loans are introduced on the P2P platforms, and put in orders for you to participate in those same investments.

The assumption is that these fast movers are somehow being rated favorably by aggressive hedge funds and other financial parties who are using advanced mathematics to select the very best Notes, and so LendingRobot gives you the ability to capitalize on their research and invest alongside them.

This type of automated approach may be a very wise strategy for beginning investors. As this asset class has matured and larger institutional investors have entered the market, the speed at which loans are fully funded on the P2P platforms has increased dramatically. As more sophisticated investors have entered this marketplace, the length of time to fully fund a loan has gone down from two weeks to a matter of minutes or less for the loans with the most attractive characteristics. Sophisticated investors, such as hedge funds, are now analyzing available loans as they are published and instantly making buy decisions for those Notes automatically.

Of course you can always select loans individually, one-by-one, on your own rather than have Prosper, Lending Club or some other firm select them for you automatically. This route typically appeals to those who like to do mathematical analysis. In this way you might create a widely diversified portfolio of different loan grades, or you can also just focus on one particular set of loan criteria.

If you are going to pick Notes yourself then it still means that you will have to select from hundreds of possible loans. You will still need some way to narrow down your selections. Lending Club and Prosper both provide filters for manually browsing through their loan portfolios, and you can select loans by certain criteria that are available on these filters. It is possible to download the CSV file of all available loans and filter them in Excel or some other software program to come up with a set of criteria you can use when making these investments.

My advice is that no one should try to pick loans themselves until after they have done some historical analysis of the loan history at Prosper or Lending Club and found an investment strategy that has performed well in the past. Whatever you discover that differentiates good performing loans from bad loans can become part of a set of selection criteria for selecting loans.

As an example, you might partition the loan history into borrowers who were home owners or not to investigate whether there were any differences in default rates and net returns based on this criteria. Another popular strategy is to segment borrowers into those who have and have not been shopping around for more credit over the past six months, which means their "credit inquiries = 0." Once you develop an overall strategy from this type of analysis, then you can apply that same strategy consistently into the future.

There is no guarantee that any historically backtested strategy like this will continue to perform the same way in the future, but this type of "deep dive analysis" will help prevent you from investing blindly. It will give you the best chances of avoiding losses and maximizing your returns.

Taking the long view, you want to train yourself over time to become a much better investor for both assets and income. You want to develop the right habits that will bring prosperity to yourself and your family. One of the best success habits for wealth accumulation is that you should always try to perform some type of non-superficial analysis on whatever investment opportunity you are considering. If you adopt this habit of studious analysis, it will help you move forwards on the road of wealth accumulation.

In short, if you want to get the best returns possible from P2P investing done on your own, then you should spend some hours first doing an analysis of the relevant loan history before you invest in a single Note. This is how to become serious about P2P lending. Only historical research on past loan performance will teach you how to pick the best P2P Notes.

According to the P2P companies, most investors on aggregate earn less than 10% on their Note investments, so to veer toward the double-digit returns you need to find some consistent strategy that balances the possible rewards with the risks.

No one can invest in, say, 15% Notes and expect to earn 15% on their investments. There will always be defaults that lower your expect rate of return. The net default rate on your loans will depend on a number of factors such as the type of loans, their creditworthiness and the health of the economy. Once again, picking the right loans to fund is key to higher returns.

Only through analysis will you find strategies that will maximize your ROI and possibly produce double-digit returns. The beauty is that analyzing past loan performance looking for winning criteria is likely to produce more stable returns with less volatility than if you tried to predict stock returns through some special type of mathematical analysis.

For the do-it-yourself investor, several websites provide some excellent analysis tools that allow you to delve into the P2P loan histories and discover some valuable investment criteria. For Lending Club investors you can do research on various loan strategies using the NickelSteamroller.com, InterestRadar.com or Lendstats.com websites while Prosper-Stats.com would be useful for investors in Prosper Notes.

How Do You Get Started?

P2P lending, offering net before tax returns typically between 6% and 12% annually, is surely a source of high yields for those seeking more income. Most investors are earning less than 10% per year, but at today's level of interest rates investing in P2P Notes can usually produce better returns than CDs or bonds if you manage the risks well. Smart investors even apportion a part of their IRA to this type of investment to avoid taxes, which is a strategy we particularly like if you choose to get into P2P lending. Putting P2P lending returns in an IRA account will definitely help you avoid taxes.

You can definitely earn higher returns by bypassing the banks and investing in P2P Notes, but you must remember to always invest in such a way as to prevent the possibility of catastrophic loss from too many defaults.

So how do you get started?

Don't make the mistake of going to a P2P exchange, opening an account, plunking down some cash and then immediately start investing blindly in Notes. You must first do some analysis and resist any temptation for instant fun and excitement. P2P investment profits do not happen automatically, and you certainly reduce your chances of making profits if you follow the road of hastiness. The best course of action, even if you elect the option of automated investing by some third party, is to initially do some analysis of P2P loan histories so that you can get a feel for the returns that this type of investment offers. You must certainly *educate yourself first* before entering into any investment or market but here is a formula for very profitable P2P investing.

If you are interested in P2P lending for the extra returns it can offer, first go to the Lending Club and Prosper sites and study them. You might also consider subscribing to Peter Renton's excellent publication, Lending Academy (Lendingacademy.com), to get a better feel for this field before risking any of your money. Other websites that stay abreast of P2P lending include LendingMemo.com, LendAcademy.com, PeerCube.com, and websites such as the Random Thoughts blog (andirog.blogspot.com) as well as the Lending Club and Prosper blogs. There is also the annual LendIt conference that is entirely devoted to the online lending space.

For deeper insights about this asset class, we should also remind you once again that it is useful to compare P2P Notes to credit card debt since the majority of loans are used for this purpose. Banks and credit card companies make plenty of money on this debt, and you can, too, if you learn how to invest wisely in the appropriate notes.

Whether we are going through rough recessions or rosy economic environments, for decades the consumer credit industry has been profitable for banks and credit card companies who provide credit at high rates on credit card balances. Even though default rates have fluctuated with the rise and fall of unemployment and general economic conditions, consumer term loans have also proven to generate positive returns over very long periods because their default rates have predictably fluctuated in a fairly narrow acceptable range.

P2P lending now gives you a way to participate in this arena, without having to be a credit card company or bank, so that you can make net profitable investments while suffering the inevitable loan defaults and missed payments that will occur. You simply have to learn how to invest in P2P Notes like a business. To do this you must employ lending criteria that have been discovered from backtesting their historical performance.

In getting started, if you want to earn a safe level of returns with the fewest defaults you might concentrate on investing in the lowest risk loans, such as those at Prosper. If you want higher returns then you will have to start investing in higher risk loans, such as the B or C Notes at Lending Club, but you will still need a judicious selection process to minimize the higher risks of defaults.

Always remember that if you want a particular level of returns that you must invest in loans being charged an even higher interest rate in order to achieve your target rate after defaults.

The careful judicious selection of Notes is one of the keys to profitable P2P investments. You can have Lending Club or Prosper select loans for you automatically, you can do it yourself, or use a third party firm like LendingRobot or others to automate the process. I always prefer the automated process myself if it has been scientifically backtested. With the current speed of funding loans that is now being experienced on these platforms, that is the way I would personally choose to invest.

Nevertheless, before deciding which of these options fits you best, you should visit sites like Nickelsteamroller.com, LendStats.com, Prosper-Stats.com, InterestRadar.com, PeerCube.com, and personally backtest different combinations of credit criteria to get a feel for what has historically worked well. After some preliminary analysis, you can then decide what to do to move forward.

There is no way around this truth: you should spend some time at this analysis before investing a single dime in P2P Notes. If you don't select the automatic investment options available to you then you should definitely use some of the historical research tools publicly available to determine how you can best select future loans and build a highly profitable Note portfolio.

Remember that even though you perform a historical analysis of loan performance, the past performance for any set of loan criteria is no guarantee that those same criteria will perform equally as well into the future. However, if you are going to risk money at all then this is the best way to select loans.

Much of future loan performance will definitely depend on the state of the economy because in aggregate this will affect the borrowers' abilities to repay their loans. If you want to invest in P2P Notes, you should recognize that the trend of the economy (such as the unemployment rate or the health of the housing market) will affect your investment results. If the unemployment rates are rising or economy is worsening, the performance of the 3-year and 5-year loans should worsen and visa versa. In short, the performance of P2P investing will have a lot to do with the economy and credit cycle.

A well-diversified portfolio is the key for getting safer, higher returns with P2P investing. As Lending Club has Noted on their website, studies historically show that owning 100+ Notes reduces the risk in your returns, and "investors with more diversified accounts have generally experienced less volatility and more solid returns than investors with more concentrated holdings. Diversification increases when you purchase additional Notes related to different borrower loans. ... Accounts with more than 100 Notes and with no Note representing more than 1% of the total account value are the most likely to have positive returns. Accounts with fewer than 100 Notes and with some Notes possibly representing more than 1% of the total account value are the most likely to have negative returns."

With this in mind, you should stick to the $25 Note size when getting started with P2P investing. This simple strategy will maximize your level of diversification and chances for a profitable outcome. To further minimize your potential losses, you should not consider P2P investing unless you can invest in at least 146 Notes, which was the number statistically computed by Emmanuel Marot of LendingRobot as necessary to help insure a profitable investment outcome. This translates into a minimum of $3,650 for an investment account composed of $25 Notes.

If we make this an even 150 Notes, we are actually talking about investing a minimum of $3,750 (or $4,000 if we choose a higher round number) to give yourself the best chances at earning great returns. Peter Renton of Lend Academy has statistically computed that a 500 Note portfolio at Prosper, which comes to $12,500 using the $25 minimum, is what you would need to be sufficiently diversified to insure that you will not lose money at all.

The gist of it is this: the more Notes you judiciously buy, the higher your chances for success.

If you want to invest a lot more money and want to employ larger Note sizes, you should still make sure that no loan is more than 1% of your total P2P investing portfolio. You should never dedicate a very large portion of your capital to a single loan and in terms of your entire net worth, you should follow the government's regulatory guidance and refrain from putting more than 10% into this asset class. Furthermore, regardless of the stable returns it usually produces when you do it well, you should not put all your eggs into this one investment basket.

If you are the type of shrewd investor who wants to pick loans on your own, including those with riskier credit ratings, we would suggest that you first develop a carefully researched investment strategy *before* opening a P2P account. Otherwise you may feel some pressure to get started right away after an account opening, and this might cause you to make certain costly mistakes.

You should never put yourself in a situation where you feel there is pressure to invest *before* you are qualified to make the best decisions, otherwise the resulting impatience is likely to cause investment mistakes. In other words, don't feel overly excited when getting started with P2P lending. When first starting out there is no need to invest your entire portfolio all at once. Start slowly and invest your money gradually over time rather than all at once. Also, try not to let cash build up in your loan account, but continue investing over time as your loans get repaid.

You should certainly analyze the relevant loan histories for various loan criteria, otherwise you won't even be able to decide whether you should select the automatic investing options offered by Prosper, Lending Club or third-party firms like LendingRobot. The ability to analyze the historical performance of various loan criteria provides investors with the ability to "create an alpha of extra returns" when they select loans based on the best performing criteria they discover.

If you have enough money and want the most diversification, there is also good reason to open separate accounts at both Lending Club and Prosper. You should consider spreading your investment across multiple platforms so that you don't overexpose yourself to one particular style of underwriting. If you had to start with just one P2P platform, Lending Club offers more loan choices whereas there currently seems to be less competition for loans at Prosper.

Summary

Overall, P2P lending is an exciting new asset class that offers great returns if you avoid the fundamental errors most people make. If you want to jump in to reap these high returns, it is essential that you invest in multiple Notes. You should diversify in multiple loan grades as well. Consider staying in the 3-year debt to avoid liquidity risks.

Success at P2P lending is really a mathematical game of diversifying to manage your risks. You should be investing in multiple notes and multiple grades because the name of the game is diversification!

Because this investment class is new, try to understand all the risks before you take the plunge into P2P lending. Do some research on the past performance of various loan criteria because understanding loan history can help you increase your returns. If you don't come up with any winning criteria yourself, consider trusting your portfolio to tested strategies that are managed through automation. That's probably the best advice for getting the maximum benefits from peer-to-peer lending.

CHAPTER 6:
OIL AND GAS ROYALTY TRUSTS

World oil prices are incredibly low right now, and that spells opportunity for buying any oil assets that are depressed in price. If you want to buy an oil well, the best time to do so is when prices are low.

Some analysts are arguing that crude oil prices are so low because Saudi Arabia has been overproducing in order to crush the higher cost U.S. shale oil producers and put these potential competitors out of business. OPEC's refusal to cut oil production certainly makes it seem like the oil price drop is an oil price war between Saudi Arabia and the US.

Some (such as the President of Venezuela) say it is because the US government wants to harm Russia, so the government is cooperating with Saudi Arabia and repeating an old move from its geopolitical playbook, used near the end of the Cold War. It is suppressing oil prices in order to destabilize and possibly bankrupt Russia. In other words, the price of oil is being suppressed for foreign policy objectives. The basic idea is that there is a battle going on over the long-term control of oil and gas prices in the Middle East, and this battle also involves the weakening of Russia (as well as Syria and Iran) by flooding the market with cheap oil.

Some say the low prices exist because despite all the central bank money printing, we are in a worldwide recession with reduced oil demand. With reduced oil demand because of lower economic demand, oil prices should naturally fall! The reasoning is that the low prices are all because of supply and demand.

Some say the low oil prices are due to a broken Petro-dollar system.

It doesn't matter why oil prices are currently so low for the fact is that prices *are* low. One of the rules to getting rich is to remember that the time to buy an asset is exactly when there is a pregnant opportunity of low prices.

You want to be buying valuable assets when they are underpriced, and *especially when the price is catastrophically low because blood is running in the streets.*

No one can ever forecast when currently low oil prices mark the *exact* bottom in oil prices, which would be the perfect time to buy. You can never say that this is the *exact* moment for certain that you should be buying oil and gas properties as long-term assets either. You will have to decide that timing on your own. However at this moment in time when oil prices are historically low, in order to increase your wealth over the long run you should be thinking about whether you should buy oil and gas wells as direct investments. You should be figuring out how you can take advantage of a temporary low price situation and invest in oil!

At some moment in the future oil will reach a rock bottom price, and that is the time when you might want to buy this hard asset *if you think prices are destined to rise thereafter.* Maybe you will decide that oil prices have bottomed from watching some long-term MACD chart using weekly or monthly prices. Maybe from looking at some long-term cycles chart of oil prices that also suggest higher prices in the future. No one can predict when that time is. However …

It is 100% certain that *now* is the time you should be *educating yourself* about oil and gas assets and how to analyze them – when currently there is no pressure to act - so that you can act in the future when you finally think prices have bottomed.

Real assets such as gold, silver or farmland, are in vogue right now. There is a worldwide scramble for accumulating real assets in people's portfolios. Individuals everywhere have woken up to realize that there is a potential disaster looming in their portfolios if they just hold fiat currencies and paper assets that represent nothing in terms of real wealth.

An oil or gas well, on the other hand, is a *real asset.* It represents *real wealth* because it is an actual income producing well that produces oil and gas that, like food, is a needed commodity that can be readily sold on the market at any point in time.

Owning an oil or gas well certainly means you own an income-producing asset, but if you just want to own the well to claim the income without having to operate it, how can you do this?

Simple. You can buy a share in an U.S. Oil and Gas Royalty Trust.

A typical U.S. Oil and Gas Royalty Trust often owns hundreds of oil and gas wells along with the revenue stream from those wells. An Oil and Gas Royalty Trust therefore represents a convenient way for an investor to own a share of a diversified number of oil and gas producing properties that are currently throwing off royalty income.

Other than drilling a well yourself (or buying into an oil company that owns wells), owning part of an energy trust is probably the only way available to you to directly own an oil or gas well.

There are approximately two-dozen Oil and Gas Royalty Trusts that are publicly traded on the exchanges just like stocks. A few of the largest trusts are as follows:

BP Prudhoe Bay Royalty Trust (BPT)
Chesapeake Granite Wash Trust (CHKR)
Cross Timbers Royalty Trust (CRT)
Hugoton Royalty Trust (HGT)
MV Oil Trust (MVO)
Sandridge Mississipian Trust I (SDT)
Sandridge Mississipian Trust II (SDR)
San Juan Basin Royalty Trust (SJT)
Pacific Coast Oil Trust (ROYT)
Permian Basin Royalty Trust (PBT)
Sabine Royalty Trust (SBR)
VOC Energy Trust (VOC)

Using these tickers you can follow prices on most free charting services, such as bigcharts.marketwatch.com, where you can readily see that prices for the trusts have fallen off dramatically and are screaming new lows. The result is that the yield on many of these trusts is over 10% at present because of the recent decline in oil prices.

This is a time to be analyzing these instruments! You can buy any of the trusts through your brokerage account just as easily as you can buy shares of Walmart, Citibank or IBM.

While the Oil and Gas Royalty Trusts own oil and natural gas producing properties, they don't actually operate the wells on those properties themselves. They just own the land and the royalty rights that encompass the oil and gas fields.

The trusts typically have no physical operations of their own and have no management or employees. They are merely financing vehicles that are usually managed by a bank officer. Their only annual expenses usually come down to just a few auditors and board members (who oversee the trust) as well as the administrative costs of collecting the royalties from the productive properties and distributing them to shareholders.

Since the trusts are not operating companies they make no business judgments about what to produce or where to drill. The way that they are typically set up is that other companies perform all the actual operations of extracting the oil or gas (or mineral) resources, and then pay royalties on those resources to the trust. The field operator is typically a well-established oil production firm that might be someone like BP (British Petroleum), Chesapeake Energy, Sandridge Energy, Conocophillips, Chevron or Exxonmobil.

The Oil and Gas Royalty Trust itself is therefore just a passive participant in the entire oil and gas pumping process. It simply collects its share of whatever the operating company earns from the appropriate oil or gas well/field.

When you invest in an Oil and Gas Royalty Trust, it is therefore a way to establish a direct ownership stake in a large collection of oil or gas wells. The trust lets you buy a share of the wells and in turn this entitles you to a share of the profits that they generate. A share in any oil or gas trust entitles the owner to a proportionate share of the cash flow generated by the wells, and any trust will continue to distribute most of the cash earned by its wells until those natural resources are depleted.

T. Boone Pickens created the first Texas Oil & Gas Royalty Trust in 1979 involving Mesa Petroleum. Since then other oil and gas producers have set up these trusts so that they could sell their slow-declining but long-lived productive assets to individuals who valued them more than the companies themselves. By selling off their wells via trusts, the oil companies could offload properties to individuals who were seeking long-term yields. In return, the companies could then use the cash they received to pay off debts or reinvest in newer discoveries.

The special interest in U.S. Oil and Gas Royalty Trusts comes from the fact that they are not only a way to directly own a *real wealth producing asset* (oil or gas), but the returns are often *double digit yields* on your investment when oil and gas prices are high.

Because the returns of the trusts are based on actual commodity prices, when oil and gas prices fall then the revenues from the trusts will be lower as well, and the value of the trusts will also decline. That's the risky nature of buying an oil or gas well … if oil or gas prices go up then you look smart but if prices decline you look dumb. That's the nature of risk. The best time to buy a well, therefore, is when you think prices have bottomed and are on their way up. That is why you must educate yourself about these energy trusts ahead of any potential bottoms.

In any case, the beauty of the Oil and Gas Royalty Trusts is that they are set up to generate real income from the production of oil and gas, so it is natural that the cash flows are subject to how much is produced along with the swing of commodity prices. The questions for you to consider are *if and when you should buy*.

If you get the timing right by buying oil and gas wells when there is a long-term low in oil and gas prices, you will look like a genius. If you buy and prices keep falling then you will probably see major losses in your investment. On the other hand, if you want to own a real hard asset, that is the beauty or advantage of these investments. It is all a matter of pricing and pricing is a matter of timing.

Like MLPs and REITs, Oil and Gas Royalty Trusts also have some special tax advantages that sometimes make them of special interest.

The trusts are pass-through entities, like Master Limited Partnerships (MLPs), which means they are exempt from corporate taxes. They distribute the lion's share of the profits from their wells (over 90%) to their investors, but those distributions are considered a return of capital that reduce an owner's cost basis in the trust. An investor in the trust is a part owner of the wells, and therefore can also depreciate the assets to lower his cost basis, too.

Now here is the bad side to owning an oil well - it is destined to have a finite life. You should think of it as being like a bond that pays interest, but which has a shelf life after which it will pay you no more. In other words, after all the oil or gas is extracted, naturally a well will be worthless as a source of revenue.

When an ordinary corporation owns oil or natural gas wells, the corporation can add to its properties over time by acquisition or expansion. That will keep the entity alive and going. However, an energy trust becomes fixed when it is initially set up, and thereafter it cannot buy new wells or expand its operations. You cannot know the amount of money you will be able to extract from the well, but can only know that the amount is fixed because it won't go on forever.

Hence, by nature a trust is doomed to have a finite lifetime due to eventual depletion of its resources. Because it cannot expand its fields, the trust's fixed quantity of reserve assets will decline gradually as the resources are extracted and sold. Depending on how the trust is set up, higher oil and gas prices might entice the producer who manages the wells to enhance oil recovery from the fields, but in general the value of the trust will decline over time as the reserves are extracted (since less resources are left remaining over time) until it become worthless.

Still interested? You should be if you want to own a *real asset*. Basically, there are various benefits as well as many drawbacks to owning this type of asset that can be summarized as follows:

Benefits:

- Commodity Play – Since the value of any Oil and Gas Royalty Trust is directly tied to its production output and the underlying price of oil or gas, the trusts are pure plays on the price of oil and gas. They enable you to participate in these markets through a vehicle that avoids dabbling in the dangerous futures market. If you believe the price of gas/oil will go up, you should consider buying an Oil and Gas Royalty Trust.

- Possible High Yield – The energy trusts typically pay out the majority (90+%) of their cash flow as distributions. When oil/gas prices are rising this typically produces very high yielding investments that can pay more than bank accounts or government bonds.

- Tax Advantages – The trusts are pass-through vehicles, so their cash distributions are not double-taxed like dividends. Furthermore, there are various non-cash depletion or depreciation expenses available from owning trusts that can lower your tax liabilities. As an owner, the cash flow returns can be used to reduce your income tax cost basis (the trust pays out a share of its assets rather than actual income), so you are taxed at the lower capital gains rate when the trust is sold.

Drawbacks:

- Volatile Yield and Unstable Royalty Checks – Fluctuations in oil and gas prices will affect a trust's income, distributions and thus share prices. Because yields fluctuate, there is a risk when buying a trust that you will not get all of your principal back. Trusts typically pay out distributions on a monthly or quarterly basis but the distributions are neither guaranteed nor fixed. Furthermore, it is impossible to know what oil or gas prices will be like in five or ten years time so the price of a trust could fall dramatically if commodity prices declined severely. Because of these risks, many trusts hedge their oil and gas exposure price in order to smooth out royalty payments because of their inherent unpredictable volatility.

- Depletion – Oil and Gas Trusts are not allowed to acquire new assets or expand themselves by buying more wells. Since they are not allowed to acquire additional properties, their resources are fixed and must eventually decline. That is their destiny - the royalties of a trust will fall and eventually reach zero. Trusts therefore have an ultimate termination value of zero. In short, they are depleting assets with a finite production life. Since a trust will reduce the amount it disburses to investors as the wells mature, you should look for a reserve life of at least ten years or more for a good investment. The best way to estimate the remaining shelf life of a trust is to divide the current reserves by the annual production to see how many productive years are left.

- Predetermined Termination Dates - Many trusts are set up with a predetermined termination date, at which point the assets will be liquidated and the proceeds distributed to investors. Or, they are sometimes set up with a production termination clause that specifies when the trust should be liquidated based on the inability to produce a minimum amount of revenue for two consecutive years. In other words, once a trust's oil or gas field fails to produce output then that trust might cease to exist and therefore the trust will be liquidated.

- Tax Complexity – Owning an oil or gas trust entails some complexity at tax time. Owners of oil and gas trusts must often pay income taxes in the states in which the trust operates. They must also report the pro rata portion of the trust's income and expenses on their tax returns, which requires that owners file Schedule E and B on their tax forms. If you want to own one of these vehicles, it is recommended that you employ a CPA to prepare your taxes.

How to Select an Oil & Gas Trust

Once you have decided that it is a good time to buy oil or gas wells for the revenues they will throw off into the future, you must be selective as to which Oil and Gas Trust you will buy. There are only about two-dozen choices available, but you must evaluate your choices carefully.

Naturally your concerns should be the price of oil and gas going into the future. You must also factor in how many years that the trust will probably remain active, meaning for how long the wells you buy will continue to actively produce oil or gas (which entails the rate at which those resources will decline).

The general rule is that you want a remaining shelf life of at least 10 years for any oil and gas royalty trust you might invest in. But how can you get this figure? You can gain an idea of this number and the value of a trust by examining its PV-10 report, which is included in the 10-K filed be each trust during March of every year.

The PV-10 is the present value of the estimated future net oil and gas revenues from the well's proven reserves, net of estimated direct expenses, discounted at 10% per annum. The discounting reflects the timing of future cash flows for a trust and is calculated without deducting income taxes on future net revenues. The PV-10 estimate is *not* intended to represent an estimate of the fair market value of a royalty trust. The PV-10 estimate is just a consistent means of measuring the value of a trust's remaining oil and gas reserves that helps you make comparisons between various trusts. You can use it to help compare the relative size and value of the proved reserves held by trusts without regard to the specific tax characteristics of such entities.

There is a caveat, however: the PV-10 calculation uses constant price level assumptions for the life of the proven reserves. Therefore, because the PV-10 uses a static oil and gas price level to value reserves, to find the estimated value of a trust you need a valuation model that reflects other factors that may impact the trust's unit value.

Now, the Oil and Gas Trusts are not a surefire way to collect growing dividends because many trusts can fail to meet expectations. You have to do your homework in order to select the right trust that will keep performing for years. Nonetheless, the trusts are unique investments with unique tax benefits. If you buy them when prices are at a bottom and about to rise, you can be a big winner.

Right now, like P2P lending, some of these trusts are paying the equivalent of a 10% yield or more. Who knows how long it will last, or whether oil prices will fall even further.

You should not try to predict petroleum prices, stock prices or any type of prices. You should be looking for cash cornerstones for your portfolio, methods to generate cash that will keep operating for a long time. And to be perfectly honest, you should really look for cash being thrown off by hard assets, such as genuine oil or gas wells, rather than businesses that can shut down during a recession or depression. It is true that in a severe recession that the demand for oil will drop and prices can go even lower, but then you still own the oil in the reservoirs when you buy an oil or gas trust. You will still own a hard asset, a physical commodity that people will need.

Right now the world is waking up to the idea that people should diversify into real assets. These are real assets but they suffer when oil prices are low. Nonetheless you can start to do research on your own so that you are an informed, educated investor who knows what trust to buy when the price is exactly right.

CHAPTER 7

MASTER LIMITED PARTNERSHIPS (MLPs)

There are several different types of investments available on stock exchanges which people can buy when they are seeking high yields. The MLP, or Master Limited Partnership, is one of these high yield investment alternatives.

An MLP is simply a *limited partnership* (rather than a corporation) that is traded on a securities exchange just like a common stock. It has one or more general partners who run the business and thousands of limited partners who receive quarterly cash distributions from its operations. The limited partners receive most of the returns because they provide the MLP with capital, but the general partner typically holds a 2% stake in the firm and receives his percentage of the profits before the limited partners get their cut.

MLPs are very popular with income investors because their cash distributions usually translate into very high yields and appear in a regular, consistent cash flow stream. Those cash flows are composed of returns from both income and growth, and are designed to defer taxes.

MLPs are usually businesses with very resilient profit models that usually represent an excellent diversification to your portfolio. Typically these businesses are continually striving to grow because the general partner is given an incentive to maximize distributions by pursuing various acquisitions and growth projects. This tends to increase distributions to unit holders over time. Furthermore, MLPs typically protect against inflation and they have the tax benefits of being a partnership rather than a corporation.

The terminology for MLP investing is different than for corporations. When you buy into a MLP you are called a "unit holder" rather than "shareholder." Being a "unit holder" means you are a part owner of a partnership business whereas a "shareholder" is part owner of a corporation. MLPs throw off cash to you every year, but the payments are also called "distributions" rather than "dividends."

The major difference between an MLP and traditional corporation is how they treat taxes. Because MLPs are partnerships they "pass through" income to you the investor; the MLP pays no tax itself. The reason that MLPs are so attractive to yield investors is precisely because of this fact that they escape federal income taxes by passing the tax burden onto you. In this way you avoid double taxation.

Most stocks are structured as C-corporations, which means that the companies pay corporate taxes on their profits at both state and federal levels. MLPs, however, avoid corporate taxes. As partnerships they pass all the tax obligations though to their unit holders (owners). Since one level of taxation is removed, MLPs therefore allow investors to receive a larger annual cash distribution than if the business was set up as a typical corporation.

The pass-through tax structure of an MLP also means a lower cost of capital for the underlying business, which is very important in capital-intensive industries. It allows companies to build and operate low-return assets that cost a lot of money - such as long pipeline networks - but still provide a sufficient rate of return to attract investors to the projects.

Traditional corporations can choose to pay or not pay a dividend to shareholders, but by law MLPs *must* distribute most of their income to unit holders in order to keep their special status. MLPs are not legally bound to a specific level of distributions, but in practice MLPs usually pay their investors through quarterly distributions, the amount being stated in the contract between the limited partners (the investors) and the general partner.

As a general rule MLPs distribute 100% of their cash flow to the limited partners (unit holders), less a reserve determined by the general partner. Because they are apportioned a share of the MLP's depreciation, the unit holders also typically receive a tax shield on 80-90% of their annual cash distribution until their unit (share) is sold. Thus, MLPs can let you pocket very high yields for years and years until you sell your units.

By law MLPs must generate at least 90% of their income from certain types of "qualifying" activities. Here are a few examples:

Enterprise Products Partners (EPD) provides a wide range of services to producer and consumers of natural gas and crude oil, owning onshore and offshore pipelines.

Plains All American Pipeline (PAA) owns crude oil and refined products pipelines and associated facilities. It is also involved in the marketing and storage of liquefied petroleum gas.

Kinder Morgan Energy Partners (KMP) owns and operates natural gas, gasoline, and other petroleum product pipelines as well as crude oil terminals and gas processing facilities. It also operates coal and other dry-bulk materials terminals and provides CO_2 for enhanced oil recovery projects.

Energy Transfer Partners (ETP) is a leading natural gas pipeline operator and owns associated facilities. ETP also markets propane to retail customers in 40 states.

Historically speaking, the very first MLPs were set up primarily for tax purposes and appeared in the oil and gas field. Their special structure was developed to encourage investment into U.S. energy infrastructure, so the majority of MLPs today are still related to the natural resource activities, especially the energy industries of oil, natural gas and coal. Oil and gas producers typically transfer their pipeline assets to an MLP and then the producer usually becomes the general partner of the operations.

After they came into being MLPs began to appear in other industries, too. Eventually Congress passed legislation limiting MLP tax treatment to entities earning more than 90% of their income from special sources. That is the general rule that now applies across all the MLP industries.

Most of the energy MLPs usually include pipelines, crude and refined product storage tanks, terminals, and processing plants for natural gas, gasoline or oil that move energy from producer to user. However, MLPs can be involved in other areas such as timber, coal, sand mining, etc. as long as the business operations qualify as "natural resource" activities under MLP regulations.

By far the vast majority of MLPs are pipeline businesses, which earn very stable incomes from transporting oil, gasoline or natural gas. The typical asset is a very long natural gas pipeline stretching for thousands of miles. These pipelines are expensive to build and leased out under long-term contracts to various utilities or energy producers to transport their products.

The pipeline MLPs usually make their money via a toll-road business model that charges a fee for the products that flow through them. When you invest in these MLPs you are making a play on the growing demand for energy and aiming to receive tax-advantaged income that profits from that growing sector.

While the majority of MLPs engage in the transportation and storage of oil and natural gas, these MLPs do not take title to the commodities transported through them. They are free of any commodity credit risks. They are just paid a fixed fee for moving a product over a certain distance through their pipelines, and sometimes paid fees that are indexed to inflation.   This is the basic toll-road business model.

Since pipelines and storage facilities entail substantial construction costs and serve specific geographical areas, typically they experience very little competition. Basically, they usually hold a near monopoly within their locale. Since they are constructed to last a very long time, they are also expected to have very long lives of functional usefulness. Thus they can be expected to generate long-term revenue flows that will enable them to continue making their distributions for a long time, namely as long as product keeps flowing through them.

Investment Benefits

There are a lot of benefits to buying MLPs, as mentioned, but the primary benefit to income investors is their yield, which can average 5-10%. To track the performance of various MLPs or just get an idea of the possible yields you should keep your eye on the Alerian Index, which is a composite of the top 50 MLPs capturing about 75% of available market capitalization.

The most recent figures of 2015 show MLP yields varying from 1.5-18%, with an average of 6.5%. This is a much better return than what you are getting on CDs, bonds and bank accounts. Typically the median yield spread between MLPs and the 10-year Treasury Bond has been about 331 bps (basis points), but it has been as low as 27 bps and as high as 1205 bps over time.

Besides the actual yield of an MLP, unit holders can usually count on the growth of the distribution over time which will vary according to the MLP, economic environment and conditions. For instance, the per share distributions of the Alerian Index components grew at a compounded rate of 9-11% during 2005-2008. These numbers are not typical of what you can expect because a more conservative long-term CAGR for the cash distributions is a growth of 3%-5%. If you take a 6.5% yield and add a distribution growth of 3%-5%, this results in a 9%-11% total return.

Alerian also reports that the sector has seen a CAGR (compound annual growth rate) of 25% in market capitalization since 1995. In 1995, there were 16 MLPs with a total market cap of $7 billion. In recent years, due to various legal changes and IRS rulings, many non-traditional businesses have monetized their assets into the MLP structure, including frac sand, frac water disposal, fertilizer, and refining companies.

Over the past 10 years, MLPs have generated 249% on a total return basis, as compared to 122% for the S&P 500, 117% for REITs, 118% for Utility stocks, and 59% for Bonds. On an annual basis, this translates to a CAGR of 13.3% for MLPs, 8.1% for REITs, 8.3% for the S&P 500, 8.1% for Utilities, and 4.7% for Bonds.

Investment Risks

There are many benefits to investing in MLPs, and there are risks as well. Let's review some of the risks that investors should know about.

Cash Distribution Sustainability Risk - The primary reason you buy a MLP is for the income it provides, so a key concern is whether it will be able to continue generating cash for its unit holders after you buy it. You should prefer an MLP that will generate sustainable distributions that will grow year after year.

This ability to continually throw off cash will depend on the business structure of the MLP and its management. For instance, pipeline operators usually try to build, expand, or acquire new pipelines so that MLP revenues can grow. They also try to pay out to investors any cash that isn't needed for current operations or the maintenance of equipment as long as it is prudent.

The best general partners have a track record of keeping their capital costs under control, generating cash to finance consistent distributions and also successfully investing in new assets. Large market cap MLPs are usually more skilled at this than smaller players, which are inherently riskier than larger firms.

Economy Risk - Most MLPs have a lower volatility than the stock market because they operate in the energy sector and usually don't own the underlying commodities (oil, gas, etc.). The price of the commodity being transported may rise or fall, but many MLPs have a fixed-fee arrangement. If the volume of product transported through a pipeline remains steady, the revenue it generates will therefore not fluctuate.

On the other hand, if the US economy turns down and the demand for energy products decreases, many MLPs will transport less product and thus see reduced cash flows. However, while a slowing US economy might reduce the volume of products transported, it probably won't drop by much because of a steady level of minimum demand. Nonetheless, you need to know that the profitability of pipeline and remember that transportation MLPs are susceptible to recessions and other economic shocks.

In uncertain economic times, MLPs remain a solid source of income. In 2008-2009, 78% of all energy MLPs either maintained or increased their distributions. In comparison, 85% of real estate investment trusts (REITs) either cut or suspended dividend payments.

While most pipeline, storage or processing MLPs don't own the commodities that pass through them, some MLPs can be exposed to commodity risk (coal, propane, and oil exploration and production MLPs, among others).

Interest Rate Risk - Because MLPs typically take on debt in order to grow, when interest rates rise their cost of capital therefore rises. With higher borrowing costs the profits of an MLP will usually then take a hit. Interest rates can therefore affect the profitability of MLPs and therefore they suffer from interest rate risks.

The safest MLPs generate enough capital internally to finance their growth, and so they don't run the risk of having to borrow money and take out loans for their projects at unfavorable interest rates.

When interest rates rise, yields on bonds and other investments will often start to look more attractive than that of an MLP. When T-bond rates rise, one therefore has to look carefully at the risks between owning MLPs for their returns and investing in other interest rate instruments.

Liability Risk - One of the problems with an MLP is that creditors can seek the return of cash distributions made to unit holders if a liability to the creditor arose *before* the distributions were paid. Even if a unit holder sells their units, such a liability will still stay attached to the unit holder.

Legal Regulatory Risk - Since the fees that pipeline MLPs charge for the transportation of oil and gas products are regulated by the government, any regulatory changes affecting these matters could affect the MLP's revenue stream.

The current tax law is that partnerships usually enjoy "pass through" taxation of their income to partners, which is why MLPs enjoy high cash distributions. Even though unlikely, if the government were to change the tax laws regulating the MLP structure, unit holders might not be able to enjoy the high yields in the sector.

How to Buy MLPs

There are currently around 130 MLPs trading on major exchanges. If you don't want to invest in single MLPs, there are also closed-end MLP mutual funds, open-end MLP mutual funds, MLP exchange traded notes (ETNs) and MLP exchange traded funds (ETFs) that will help you balance your risks by investing in a variety of successful MLPs.

Each different MLP vehicle has its own advantages and disadvantages, and their tax characteristics differ greatly. Because the tax situation can be complicated, let's discuss just the pure MLP investments that you can buy on the stock market exchanges. However, remember to check with your tax professional on whether holding MLPs directly is a good idea for a retirement fund because other alternatives, such as MLP funds, are available.

You can easily locate these MLPs through various online screeners such as the ones sponsored by Alerian MLP, MLP Data or Capital Link:

www.alerian.com/mlp-screener/
www.mlpdata.com/mlps
mlp.capitallink.com/tools/mlp_screener.html

The friendly FINIZ screener (www.finiz.com/screener/ashx) is also very popular.

As a yield investor, other than the protection of capital there are two primary factors you should look for in selecting investments: (1) dividend yield and (2) growing earnings if that growth means increasing distributions into the future. You can easily zero in on these factors using the FINIZ screener.

There are many different types of MLP you can consider, but a beginner might find it easiest to get started with natural gas pipeline, crude oil, refined petroleum product or propane distribution operators since they typically pay high yields and are the easiest to understand.

On the FINIZ screener you can select the "Oil & Gas Pipelines" industry for review, select a minimum dividend yield (because you are looking for high-dividend candidates), and then can select MLPs by their "return on equity," which is a measure of their profitability. Since you are looking for growing distributions, you can also select "Over 5%" for "EPS Growth Next Five Years" to see whether analysts are expecting at least a 5% annual long-term earnings growth. You can also screen for large cap operators to weed out the riskier, smaller players. Since institutional ownership is usually interpreted as "smart money," you can add this as one of your filters to come up with a short list of current investment candidates.

The Taxes

MLPs can be very profitable high yield investments, but the big complication with owning them comes at tax time. While MLPs give you income sheltered tax benefits, with those benefits come some paperwork headaches. That complexity is the price you pay for the high yields.

If you use a CPA for your taxes then handling MLP distributions will be no big tax time hurdle because you can simply give the filing problems over to your accountant. However, if you do your own taxes then you should expect to spend some extra time dealing with K-1s. At tax time you will be mailed a K-1, which details your previous year's portion of the MLP's income, gain, losses, deductions and credits.

As a unit holder you must enter these items on your tax return to compute the tax you owe at your own tax rate. It is simple to handle stock dividends and bond interest taxes, but MLP accounting gets a little more complex because of these calculations.

Here's the reason for the complexity, which also explains why MLPs are so attractive. An MLP makes its cash distributions to investors based on the MLP's "distributable cash flow" rather than its income. The MLP distributions do not include depreciation or amortization expenses. Hence, the cash distribution you receive from an MLP is *not* the same as your share of the MLP's income. It is possible that the distributions you receive will *exceed* your portion of the MLP's net income for the year.

When that is the case, any excess distributions are considered a "return *of* capital." These returns are considered a payback of what you originally paid for the company and therefore reduce the cost basis of your original investment accordingly. You are not taxed on these excess distributions until you sell your shares in the partnership at which time your reduced cost basis is taken into consideration when computing the net profit or loss of your investment.

On average, roughly 75% to 90% of an MLP's distribution is classified as this tax-free "return *of* capital." The remaining balance of the distribution, typically in the 10% to 25% range of the total, is considered a "return *on* capital." Whereas a "return of capital" is not taxable until you sell your MLP holdings, a "return on capital" is just ordinary income, and is therefore taxed in the year it is received.

Let's restate it another way. With MLP investing, only 10-25% of the MLP distribution is usually taxable income for the year. As to the other 75-90% of your annual distribution, you receive a tax shield on this money until your unit is sold. When you finally sell your units, you have to compute whether you made a gain or loss on the investment. Upon selling, the cost basis for your investment is not what you originally paid. It is lower than your original cost by adjustments that take into account your yearly distributions minus your net partnership income.

Many tax professionals feel that most people should not hold MLP units in an IRA, 401(K) or other tax deferred account. The tax law is such that any unrelated business taxable income (UBTI) of over $1,000 in a tax-deferred account is subject to federal income taxes, and substantial MLP cash distributions may put you over this limit. Since most MLPs increase their cash distributions over time, this becomes more likely the more units you have and the longer you hold your units.

MLPs fall into the category of high yield passive income investments. They offer a regular, consistent stream of tax-deferred income that can actually grow over time, and which currently beats the yields of Treasury Bonds. You can easily see the high yields that many are offering by using some of the stock screeners we have already cited. The only big drawback to MLPs is a little bit of complexity at tax time.

The final bit of advice is to talk to a tax professional, or MLP expert, before you get involved in MLP investing. You do not want to inherit an unwanted tax situation because of ignorance. You should not really fret the taxes, but just need to be sure you understand the obligations.

Because of the tax treatment, investors who are looking into a MLP investments should probably look to holding for the long-term, and thus should concentrate on those which can increase their distributions over time. The combination of high-yielding distributions and preferential tax treatment make MLPs a good investment for income investors and anyone looking for yield.

CHAPTER 8:
REAL ESTATE INVESTMENT TRUSTS (REITs)

A close cousin of the MLP is the real estate investment trust, or REIT, which gives small investors the chance to participate in owning large income-producing real estate investments. REITs are not only a way to diversify into real estate properties but are usually high yield investments as well.

The typical road of real estate investment is to directly own property, but as a small investor it is impossible to create an extremely well-diversified real estate portfolio since your capital is limited. After all, real estate investing is capital intensive and you need a large sum of money to be involved in many properties. It also requires active labor-intensive management, which often involves an extraordinary amount of work and headaches.

Large investors, such as insurance companies, pension funds and other financial institutions have no problems providing the amount of capital needed for well-managed properties and can therefore easily invest in large real estate projects. This gives them access to the property diversification that they want for their portfolios.

REITs were created by Congress in 1960 in order to give all investors the opportunity to invest in large-scale, diversified portfolios of real estate. The law enabled shareholders in a REIT to invest in large-scale properties the same way you can become a partial owner of other industries, which is through the purchase of stock shares.

A REIT usually generates its income through the renting, leasing and selling of property. The stockholders earn a share of that income without actually having to go out and buy, manage or finance any property themselves. Thus REITs allow small investors to invest in larger pools of real estate, and this provides you with the same advantages that institutions have when they invest in large real estate development funds. REITs enable you to play the same game with far less capital.

Many countries have REITs, but we will restrict our discussion to those in the United States. To qualify as a REIT under U.S. tax rules the company must be structured as a corporation, trust or association and must invest only in real estate, mortgages or other real estate collateralized investments. The REIT cannot be a financial institution or insurance company. Nevertheless it is a company that buys, develops, manages and sells real estate assets.

An REIT must be managed by trustees or a board of directors that conducts investment management decisions on its behalf. All REITs must have a minimum of at least one hundred shareholders, and no five can together hold more than 50% of shares between them. In other words, any group of five or fewer members can hold no more than 50% of its shares.

As another requirement, at least 75% of a REIT's total assets must be invested in real estate, cash or U.S. Treasuries and 75% of its gross income must be derived from real estate (such as from property rents, mortgage interest or from sales of real estate). No more than 25% of its assets can be invested in taxable REIT subsidiaries.

An REIT will pay little or no U.S. federal income tax if it pays out at least 90% of its taxable income in the form of shareholder dividends each year. Therefore REITs typically pay out nearly all of their taxable income as dividends to shareholders who, in turn, pay the income taxes on those dividends. This is why REITs are of interest to most investors. It's because they are dividend plays, and high yield dividend plays at that.

There are several types of REITs you can invest in - Health Care, Industrial/Office, Lodging/Resorts, Self Storage, Timber, Infrastructure, Retail (shopping centers, regional malls, free standing), Residential (apartments, manufactured homes), Diversified, etc. - but two are the most important. Those are equity REITs and mortgage REITs.

Equity REITs

Equity REITs account for the vast majority of REITs. They own physical properties such as shopping centers, malls, hotels, office buildings or apartment complexes and their revenues come principally from leasing space in properties (such as office buildings) to tenants, or from the sales of the properties they own. Naturally, they distribute the rents they receive or any capital appreciation (gain) from property sales as dividends to their shareholders.

Equity REITs may invest in any type of real estate, but most specialize in a particular type of property such as office buildings and commercial property or residential real estate. While some are diversified in their holdings, and some are very specialized such as a REIT that owns golf courses.

An investment in an equity REIT is usually an investment in a large real estate portfolio that is professionally managed and tends to be somewhat diversified.

Mortgage REITs

Mortgage REITs do not own real estate properties, but instead invest in property mortgages or mortgage securities for their income. They basically loan money for mortgages to real estate owners, or they purchase existing mortgages or mortgage-backed securities. In other words, just like a bank they make their money by providing the financing for real estate projects. Mortgage REITs either originate or purchase mortgages and originate mortgage-backed securities to earn income.

The earnings of a mortgage REIT come primarily from the spread between the interest they earn on mortgage loans and the cost of funding these loans. Since they are making their money on an interest rate spread, this makes them sensitive to interest rate increases. Mortgage REITs usually have a higher ratio of equity to debt than commercial mortgage lenders.

Why Invest?

In short, people invest in REITs when seeking high yields because dividends tend to be the key attraction of this industry. Investors typically invest in REITs for their high levels of continuing current income and to participate in any real estate opportunities for long-term capital appreciation. The long-term total returns of REIT stocks are usually less than the returns of high-growth stocks but more than the returns of bonds.

REITs also provide a very liquid but non capital intensive way to invest in real estate. Thus they can provide your stock portfolio with exposure/diversification into real estate, which is a natural inflation hedge. If you were to try to mimic a REIT on your own you would need substantial capital and management skills in order to buy and maintain a large number of investment properties that themselves might not be very liquid. REITs on the other hand basically let you enjoy the ownership benefits of real estate without actually becoming landlords.

Remember that REITs must distribute nearly 90% of their yearly taxable income, created by income producing real estate, to their shareholders. By distributing all or almost all of its profits (90%) and skipping the taxation, REITs are strong income vehicles for yield investors who only have to pay one level of taxation for the distributions paid and can also benefit from the appreciation of the underlying assets.

The attraction to yield investors is that many have dividend yields in excess of 10% and their returns are also largely uncorrelated with stocks and bonds.

How to Invest

Individuals can invest in REITs either by purchasing their shares on a major stock exchange or by investing in REIT ETFs. Some REITs are public but not listed on an exchange and others are private. For those listed on the stock market, before investing you need to perform an analysis of the company to determine if it is a worthwhile candidate for your portfolio. Because of their liquidity, public REITs are of primary interest to most investors.

Generally the equity REITs are considered safer than the mortgage REITs — become one holds and manages property while the other holds paper and simply finances deals that could go bad — but you'll have to individually analyze each company to determine whether or not it is a good investment. Because of their accounting rules, REITS are analyzed using the "funds from operations" figure that gives a better idea of the company's earnings than just the net earnings figure. A variety of free web sources can teach you how to analyze the income statements from these real estate plays.

You can follow how the REIT industry is performing overall by tracking the FTSE NAREIT All REITs Index, FTSE NAREIT All Equity REITs Index, and FTSE NAREIT Mortgage REITs Index. Reit.com also keeps stats on the industry and is usually a one-stop portal for stock information, returns, and yield comparisons. In 2015 it reported that there are over 223 REITs in the FTSE NAREIT All REITs Index for a total market capitalization of nearly $1 trillion and nearly $2 trillion in real estate assets.

Basically, REITs are total return investments that can offer you very high yields at over 6% per annum, which is much better than a bank account or long-term bonds. Since REITs are required by law to distribute at least 90% of their taxable income to shareholders each year, this means that you usually get both high dividends – which is important for the high yield investor – and the potential for long-term capital appreciation.

By holding an REIT you are also diversifying yourself away from companies by exposing yourself to real estate, which is an asset protection strategy you might consider.

CHAPTER 9:
YIELD COS

Yield investors are always looking for investment vehicles that might pay more than CDs and bank accounts. This is why they commonly turn to MLPs, REITs, P2P Lending and Energy Trusts as high yield cash flow investments. There is yet another yield vehicle that has started to become popular over the years, and that is the "Yield Co." This is a publicly traded company – usually in the renewable energy field - designed specifically to produce cash flow for investors. Like an MLP or REIT, this cash flow is distributed to investors as dividends.

Yield Cos serve the same function as MLPs and REITs in that they are established to own low-risk operating assets producing a predictable cash flow stream that is passed on to investors. Like MLPs and REITs they are also structured to avoid the double-taxation of income. People invest in the Yield Cos because they like the current yield and also because they expect that the low-risk returns (yields) will increase over time.

The Yield Co is sometimes referred to as a "synthetic MLP" because of various similarities with the basic MLP structure. Basically, it is structured to simulate the avoided double-taxation benefit of MLPs and REITs but achieves this in a different way. It does so by matching positive cash flows from assets with losses due to the asset's depreciation and expenses that exceed taxable income. The net operating losses thereby reduce the Yield Co's taxable income so that it is taxed on much lower annual earnings, or the math may work out such that it may not even owe any taxes at all.

Since net operating losses can carry forward for future taxable events, this often enables Yield Cos to avoid paying significant income tax for many years into the future. Furthermore, the dividends paid by a Yield Co may also receive favorable tax treatment at the investor level if they are treated as the return *of* the original investment as opposed to a return *on* investment.

As with most energy-related MLPs, a Yield Co is typically created by placing alternative energy operating assets in a public company while keeping development assets in a parent or affiliate company, and by setting up various arrangements between the two.

Now there are a few important differences between Yield Cos and MLPs. First, laws limit the kinds of assets that are eligible for MLPs while the renewables of a Yield Co usually cannot be included within them unless certain conditions are met. Second, while MLPs rely on a partnership structure to lower the taxes on their assets (partnerships are not taxed at the corporate level but only on the investor/partner level), Yield Cos do not have this benefit. As explained, Yield Cos typically rely on depreciation or tax loss carryforwards to mitigate corporate tax expenses.

Many Yield Cos have been created in the renewable energy field to enable investors to participate in renewable energy projects while avoiding most of the risks associated with the industry. Renewable energy companies are often perceived as risky businesses because the technology utilized in these projects is often unproven. Think operating solar, wind, and geothermal projects. Also, the future cash flow projections of many renewable energy projects are often based largely on estimates, which makes them risky. There are various regulatory risks as well.

Yield Cos are designed to have significantly lower risk profiles than their larger parent companies. They are typically designed to contain only stable energy producing assets with predictable cash flows (so that they can be easily sold to the public) and are not usually involved in the riskier aspects of bringing new projects online.

As with MLP pipeline companies, to create a Yield Co a parent company (ex. SunEdison) might bundle renewable and/or conventional long-term contracted operating assets into the Yield Co in order to generate a stream of predictable cash flow. The creation of the Yield Co therefore allows investors to buy a single vehicle that contains operating projects with stable, reliable cash flows.

For instance, a large energy company may have completed several energy projects such as a group of solar energy farms. While it may still be developing other projects, the selected solar farms might already be selling power and generating revenue because of energy purchase agreements with an electric utility. Now if the larger parent company chooses to maintain the ownership of these solar energy farms, they will regularly return cash for years. However, it will also take years for the parent firm to completely recover the initial investment involved in their creation. Instead of having to wait years to be paid back by the earnings of the project(s), the parent company can bundle these projects together into a Yield Co separate company and list it on the public markets. Investors can then buy shares of the predictable future income of these solar farm projects, which have been bundled together into a Yield Co, and the money raised will give the parent company some needed capital that it can reinvest in other projects.

That's how it works.

As a general rule, investors are usually willing to pay more for assets that have a proven history of cash generation than for assets that are volatile or still under development. A proven track record means something is more of a low-risk opportunity, and that makes all the difference to investors. This is why they snap these up.

By separating the more volatile activities of development and construction from the more stable and less volatile cash flows of operating assets (putting operating assets in a publicly traded vehicle while the development activities are in a separate entity) a parent company can raise capital to pay off expensive debt or finance new projects at rates lower than those available through tax equity finance.

In other words, a Yield Co is usually formed by a larger company to take operating assets that have been de-risked to produce a predictable cash flow stream of interest to investors seeking high yields. It then uses the Yield Co to raise capital from retail investors interested in a stream of cash flow. Many utilities are using them to recoup investment capital from various already-developed projects. Thereby they raise money and free up some capital that they can use for reinvestment and to develop even more energy projects.

Investors, of course, are using them to invest in stable renewables and to get a higher yield than bank accounts and CDs.

How much do the Yield Cos pay?

Right now the yields are rather decent compared to what you can now get from "risk-free" 10-year Treasury bills. For instance, Yield Cos are currently paying annual dividends of 5-6%. That's a lot!

If you are interested in investing in Yield Cos, rather than do the research yourself there is also a Yield Co ETF that was set up by Global X whose ticker symbol is YLCO. This ETF seeks investment results that correspond to the price and yield performance of the Indxx Global YieldCo Index (TR), which is an adjusted market cap weighted index designed to provide access to globally listed Yield Co securities.

That would be the first place to start in terms of investment research to select a Yield Co for your portfolio.

CHAPTER 10:
DIM SUM BONDS

If you want to invest in foreign bonds that pay a higher interest rate than U.S. Treasuries then you have to worry about the currency risk. You also have to worry about sovereign country risks if you are buying foreign government debt as well as normal credit risks – namely the health of the company issuing the bonds - if you are investing in foreign corporate debt.

The Holy Grail of foreign debt is a *safe foreign bond* that pays a *higher interest rate* than U.S. bonds and which is denominated in *an appreciating currency* so that you get a currency boost to boot. As stated, you want the underlying issuer to be financially sound so that you don't have to worry about not receiving your interest payments or the return of your principal.

With this in mind, why not consider buying Chinese bonds?

"Huh?"

Yes, most people are flabbergasted when they hear of that suggestion. Few have ever even considered this. What most investors don't know is that various forms of Chinese bonds are now highly sought after debt instruments across the world and the trend is growing. Investors are buying and few are selling.

Previously, investing in Chinese renminbi debt meant that you had to take the difficult steps of opening up a bank account inside China. There were capital controls that affected the transaction, and you had to really question as to whether you really trusted the debt in the first place. The most difficult issue was the fact that anyone who put their money into China to invest in any sort of renminbi debt had to have a plan for how to get their money out. Now everything has changed.

The demand for renminbi currency is soaring because of China's growth in international trade, but when people hold renminbi they want to park it in either short-term or long-term debt instruments denominated in renminbi. While previously you had to go inside China to buy renminbi debt, now you can buy reminbi-denominated bonds *issued offshore and held offshore* that pay hefty interest rates and may even rise in value as China's currency goes international.

The Chinese government is working very hard to internationalize its tightly controlled currency in order to make it fully convertible worldwide. Therefore a rising proportion of China's international trade is being directly settled in renminbi rather than U.S. dollars, and China is encouraging this trend in every way possible.

China is already the world's second largest economy and largest exporter, so there is a very large and growing demand for its currency in order to conduct trade with the nation. To facilitate trade, the People's Bank of China has taken steps to establish bilateral currency swap arrangements (that bypass the dollar) with over thirty other central banks including those within Australia, South Korea, Malaysia, Indonesia, Argentina, Iceland, Singapore, New Zealand, Thailand, Pakistan, UAE, Turkey, Brazil, United Kingdom, and Switzerland.

The renminbi is now the second-most used currency in global trade finance after the dollar. While for trade financing it is number two, by the end of 2014 it entered the top five of world payment currencies behind the dollar, Euro, pound and yen. It is likely to further increase in usage (and value) as demand further increases, so buying renminbi bonds might be a smart move as a currency play, especially if the yield is better than that of U.S. Treasury bonds and especially if the currency is expected to appreciate in value.

Some analysts also say that China wants to make the renminbi the predominant currency of the near future, and thereby amplify China's influence on the world stage. China, they speculate, first wants to position the renminbi alongside the dollar as both a transactional currency *and* part of the IMF's reserve currency basket, and then gradually replace the dollar as the most dependable reserve currency of the bunch.

Whether China wants the renminbi to become the major reserve currency of the world is just speculation, but what is definite is that China does indeed want to make its currency more popular and more easily convertible than how things stand at present. It also wants to reduce the influence of the dollar in international trade.

Beijing also wants—for various financial and strategic reasons—to slow the growth of its enormous dollar reserves. Therefore it wants more countries to start using the renminbi instead of the dollar for international trade settlements, and the RMB swap facilities are helping to accomplish this so that it stops accumulating dollars. Another benefit desired by China is that any increase in renminbi internationalization will help insulate it against the possibility that the U.S. will be able to cut it off from the dollar-denominated international financial system, which the U.S. has shown (through its actions toward Russia) that it is willing to do to countries that don't follow it will.

Now no currency can become freely convertible, as China wishes the RMB to become, unless nations have a way to park that currency in interest paying bonds while the money is waiting to be used. If you buy renminbi while you are waiting to use it for foreign exchange you want your funds to gain interest. The only way to do so is if you hold that renminbi in interest paying renminbi accounts, bonds or notes. For large sums banks prefer short-term bonds and notes. For safety reasons most RMB investors would want those renminbi bonds held outside of China. Hence, if China wants the renminbi to become fully convertible as well as a reserve currency then the Chinese government must start issuing more international-grade bonds that foreigners feel are safe for investment purposes.

So what is happening in the world to make this possible?

Dim Sum Bonds

One of the first steps in this direction is that China encouraged the creation of "dim sum" bonds. These are bonds *issued outside of China* but denominated in Chinese renminbi rather than the local currency of their issuing location. The name "dim sum" comes from a popular style of cuisine in Hong Kong, which is where the bonds were issued for the very first time. Dim sum are very delicious plates of bite-sized Hong Kong delicacies.

A "dim sum" bond is therefore a bond that is denominated in the Chinese national currency, the renminbi/yuan (RMB), but it is issued offshore rather than by China. Denominated in Chinese RMB and but issued elsewhere, dim sum bonds represent a growing portion of China's total local-currency debt and their issuance has given a huge boost to the international popularity of the renminbi currency.

If you want to put some of your money in Chinese renminbi, but not within the Chinese banking system, then you might consider buying dim sum bonds.

The first Hong Kong dim sum bond was issued in July 2007 by the Chinese Development Bank, one of the three major policy banks of China. It was the first offshore renminbi bond in the world and entities flocked to the issue to access China's closed debt markets.

In September 2009, a second step was taken in this direction. At that time, China's Ministry of Finance issued the first Chinese government dim sum bond in Hong Kong for the offshore market. In July 2010, the People's Bank of China and the Hong Kong Monetary Authority then worked out an agreement to help establish an offshore renminbi bond market in Hong Kong. The purpose was to now encourage non-bank issuers to offer renminbi-denominated bonds. McDonald's then became the first nonfinancial company to issue a dim sum bond.

McDonald's decision to issue a dim sum bond was a no-brainer if there is such a thing. The company needed renminbi in order to finance its expansion plans for China. By issuing a three-year dim sum bond, it raised the RMB 200 million loan it needed at a cheaper bond coupon rate than the interest rates it would have been charged by local Chinese banks for a loan. McDonalds only had to pay a 3% interest rate to subscribers compared to the 7% rate that Chinese banks would have charged.

After McDonalds, the international firms Volkswagen AG and Caterpillar also floated dim sum issues to finance their operations within China. Caterpillar's dim sum bond issuance totaled one billion RMB! Dim sum bonds had mainstream acceptance. Since that time, many other companies doing business in mainland China have also floated dim sum issues. Most of these offshore dim sum bond issues have generally been of short duration.

In November 2010, China's Ministry of Finance next sold 8 billion renminbi ($1.3 billion) of bonds of varying maturities in Hong Kong in order to help form an offshore renminbi yield curve that would help others to price their issues. Thus, step-by-step through its creation of a bond market China has gradually been making positive moves to help the renminbi become more liquid and convertible.

In January 2012, the China Development Bank also started selling a 15-year bond in the effort to establish longer offshore renminbi maturities, and from that point on renminbi bonds started to be issued everywhere.

In April 2012, for instance, another offshore renminbi bond was issued in

London and then listed on the London Stock exchange. In February 2013, Taiwan issued its first offshore renminbi bond. Singapore saw its first renminbi-denominated bond issued in May 2013 and then in 2014 Germany's KfW Development Bank issued a 1 billion renminbi bond, which is now listed on the Frankfurt stock Exchange.

By July of 2014, offshore renminbi-denominated bond issues had totaled over 350 billion renminbi!

Each local market now uses a different nickname for these offshore renminbi bonds. While Hong Kong calls them "dim sum" bonds, Singapore calls them "Lion City" bonds, and Frankfurt traders in Germany call them "Goethe bonds" in a nod to the city's famous poet. Luxembourg-listed renminbi bonds are called "Schengen bonds." Basically, locations other than Hong Kong have become more active in the issuance market.

The Luxembourg Stock Exchange was the first European stock exchange to issue a dim sum bond in May 2011. Approximately 80% of Eurobonds are issued in Luxembourg and today the Luxembourg Stock Exchange also issues approximately 20% of the global market of dim sum bonds. This ranks Luxembourg as third in the world after Hong Kong and Singapore. Currently in 2015, over 45 dim sum bonds from nearly 30 international issuers with a volume of 34.7 billion RMB are listed on the Luxembourg Stock Exchange. Financial institutions account for 65% of these issues while corporations and international organizations stand for 28% and 7% of issues respectively.

If you were a company, why would you want to issue bonds denominated in renminbi? As the case of McDonalds illustrated, companies with business in China can use the renminbi currency they receive from their offering to help fund expansion of their operations. They can often obtain cheaper funding from foreigners than they can from the domestic China market, so issuing dim sum bonds to foreign investors is a smart move.

Had McDonalds (a non-Chinese issuer) sold a renminbi-denominated bond inside China it would have then been called a "Panda bond." This is another alternative, but McDonalds would also have had to pay a higher interest rate on a Panda bond than from issuing a dim sum bond.

Panda bonds are only sold to Chinese investors. For instance, German luxury carmaker Daimler AG needed money to overhaul its factories in China. For various reasons, it decided to sell a 500 million renminbi ($81.5 million) bond to Chinese investors. That made it the first foreign non-financial bond issue in China's domestic market. If you are a company with Chinese operations, previously you could only fund operations through bank loans but now you have both the Panda bond and dim sum bond options. As foreign investors, it's the dim sum bonds we are interested in.

Foreign banks also are not interested in Panda bonds, but in the dim sum issues since those bonds are held outside of China and avoid all the Chinese internal regulatory red tape. There can at times still be various restrictions on domestic renminbi funds, making it difficult to move RMB around or exchange it freely, so wise foreigners prefer the offshore dim sum option. Most dim sum issues have been highly oversubscribed and when I once interviewed a Bank of China fund manager in Hong Kong he said that everyone wants to buy them and no one wants to sell them!

To date over 95% of all dim sum bond issuances have been for fixed-rate coupons and the average coupon rate has been approximately 4.1% for the bonds issued between 2011 and 2014. About 90% of dim sum bonds carry durations of one to three years, which is the duration preferred by investors who expect the renminbi to one day appreciate against the U.S. dollar. Between 2007 and 2012 more than 50% of dim sum investors were private banks or commercial banks.

Just as the size of specific dim sum issues is insignificant compared to typical government-bond issues, the overall size of the dim sum market in aggregate is still very small compared to the total $1.5 trillion local renminbi bond market. According to Fitch, it is less than 5% of the size of China's domestic renminbi bond market, yet is destined to grow because of growing interest in offshore RMB debt and China's strategic aspirations that will cause it to support the growth of this market.

While China may one day very well overtake the U.S. as the world's biggest corporate debt issuer, right now China seems to just be more concerned with developing the RMB bond market. The dim sum bonds are a way of seeding the global banking system with RMB bonds so that the renminbi becomes more popular, and they represent a diversification away from U.S. Treasury issues.

Renminbi Hubs

Basically, renminbi-denominated bonds are being issued to help internationalize the wider popularity and acceptance of renminbi bonds. They don't just enable foreign firms to find lower cost funding for Chinese operations than from within China, but the dim sum bonds also enable the Chinese government to prepare the way for the RMB currency to become freely convertible on the international stage.

Dim sum bonds are seeding the way for this to happen. They are kick-starting the liquidity needed for Chinese debt instruments and are thus helping to pave the way for the renminbi to become a more openly traded currency. China is also doing this by establishing renminbi "clearing centers" in many countries.

A renminbi clearing center is a place where you can directly exchange the local currency for renminbi and vice versa. For instance, at the Frankfurt clearing center in Germany you can exchange euros for the renminbi without having to first turn the euros into dollars. With renminbi in hand, you can then buy dim sum bonds or the local Goethe bonds issued in Frankfurt.

With a RMB hub in a country any trade transactions with China become more efficient because you replace a two-step clearing process with a one-step process. You no longer need any intermediate conversions to the U.S. dollar and thus an extra additional layer of currency transaction costs is avoided along with banking fees. Because of the reduced costs a currency hub in a country gives its companies a bidding advantage for commodity products such as agricultural goods or metals.

Renminbi clearing centers have already been established in Hong Kong, Macau, Taiwan, Singapore, Australia, South Korea, Japan, Germany, France, UK, Luxembourg, Qatar, Canada, Malaysia, Thailand, and more are coming. Each time the Bank of China established a clearing centers in one of these markets, in most cases the move was quickly followed by the issuance of renminbi bonds by Chinese banks selling into those markets.

As mentioned, Germany signed agreements with Chinese financial authorities in March 2014 that permitted the sale of dim sum bonds at the Frankfurt Stock Exchange. Then in April 2014, Germany's KfW development bank issued the first renminbi bond in the country. It was a two-year bond with the volume of 1 billion renminbi at the Frankfurt Stock Exchange. KfW said it was targeting institutional investors and was issuing its dim sum bond because of growing demand for the currency as a global asset.

Since renminbi clearing banks are now in Europe, European investors have been inspired to increase their renminbi holdings. The RMB currency is definitely becoming more convertible, its usage is dramatically growing in world trade, and now renminbi bonds are being issued in many places. If you ever expect the RMB to increase in value versus the dollar, renminbi bonds are your most likely bet.

While Hong Kong will most probably remain the primary offshore renminbi market, Deutsche Bank feels that Europe is likely to be the second most important market. Hong Kong is the clear present winner because it has the most established offshore renminbi infrastructure, its funding costs are cheaper than elsewhere, and at the end of September 2014 it had the largest offshore renminbi pool with RMB 1.1 trillion in deposits.

How have the returns been with dim sum bond? A study by Fitch showed that offshore renminbi bonds typically offered investors higher yields than comparatively rated U.S. dollar-denominated bonds. They offer higher stable yields, too. Furthermore, renminbi bonds are not as vulnerable to U.S. financial shenanigans, such as QE or QE tapering, as the foreign bonds of other emerging economies. These bonds have typically been yielding between 4-6% over the past two years.

The market for renminbi bonds will definitely continue to grow. It offers investors a stable, high yielding alternative to government bonds issued by the United States, Europe, and Japan. The likely net result of the growing popularity of these bonds will be higher relative yields in these western markets because those bonds will have to raise their yields to compete.

In terms of the big picture, international investors are increasingly realizing that the renminbi is a major international currency for which they need some substantial exposure. They don't want to open up any type of financial account in China so they are cautiously adding dim sum bonds to their portfolios. Until familiarity grows, they would rather have an offshore renminbi bond as an investment rather than be positioned in anything issued within China.

In the future we might even see foreign nations issuing other types of domestic bonds denominated in the renminbi just as Japan does with uridashi bonds, which are Japanese bonds denominated in high-yielding currencies such as the Aussie dollar and New Zealand dollar. Russia's largest bank (Sberbank) has just issued renminbi-denominated letters of credit, in concert with the Chinese Export-Import bank, which highlights the coming trends in this direction. Russia's Deputy Finance Minister Sergei Storchak also announced that it is considering issuing debt in Chinese renminbi in the coming years in order to facilitate Russian corporate borrowers' access to the Chinese market. The basic trend in all this is that you might see an explosion of foreign bonds denominated in renminbi where they are not Chinese in origin.

China has been trying to get the renminbi accepted in the IMF's basket of currencies. If that happens, countries will accelerate their purchasing of Chinese bonds of various types, including dim sum issues. All countries will recognize that the RMB is not a legitimate currency, so they will add more RMB bonds to their banking reserves. If they add the renminbi, they have to remove something and the currency that will lose market share will undoubtedly be the U.S. dollar.

China is very eager to join the IMF's SDR basket (which contains the dollar, euro, pound and yen) so it really wants to seed the entire global banking system with renminbi bonds in preparation. As banks around the world endorse the RMB and include Chinese bonds in their banking industry, they will start to discharge U.S. Treasury bonds and drop the dollar. Perhaps they will redeem the T-bonds, cash them out, or simply let them mature. In any case, many countries will see others discharging the T-bonds so in order to prevent getting the worse price in the dumping, many will sell the T-bonds and dollars and convert it into gold. This is a trend that the U.S. fears but China absolutely wants more acceptance of its currency.

If you expect the long-term price appreciation of the renminbi due to these or other reasons, this means that accumulating renminbi reserves is a wise strategic decision. America is being increasingly viewed in the world as a hegemon in relative decline, while China is being looked at as the preeminent rising power, so dim sum bonds or renminbi bonds represent an investment in the rising power. With dim sum bonds you are diversifying investments into the rising power of Asia.

As an investor, you can now gain direct exposure to China's currency via the dim sum market through three exchange-traded funds. They include:

Guggenheim Yuan Bond ETF (Ticker: RMB)
PowerShares Chinese Dim Sum Bond Portfolio (Ticker: DSUM)
Van Eck's Market Vectors Renminbi Bond ETF (Ticker: CHLC)

All three are traded in the U.S. and have $5 million to $6 million in assets. In addition, fund powerhouse BlackRock (NYSE: BLK) launched its first mutual fund of dim sum bonds in November 2011, targeting qualified investors mainly in Asia. These are all possibilities for tapping into the dim sum issues.

In the future the demand for RMB bonds will grow for a variety of reasons, including the fact that any endorsement by the IMF will be an open door for China, and nations around the world will therefore want to add the renminbi to their banking reserves. If they add RMB to their savings account then they will have to remove something, which will undoubtedly be the U.S. dollar. If you trade with China, which is now the "world's manufacturer," you will need RMB currency for direct exchange in the future and with that growing demand for renminbi you are sure to see an increasing desire for dim sum bonds, namely renminbi denominated debt instruments paying interest in RMB.

CHAPTER 11:
FARMLAND INVESTMENTS

If you want to grow your wealth over the long-term through investments but want a vehicle that preserves its value through inflation or during other adverse economic conditions, there is one type of asset class you have probably overlooked. This hard asset class has the strong potential of increasing in value over time because they are not making any more of it, and it can produce a current yield as well. This asset class is income-producing farmland.

Most investors today focus solely on investing in paper assets such as CDs, stocks and bonds. However, due to growing global financial risks there is a definite trend in the world to switch out of paper assets into "hard assets."

Hard assets are also called "real assets" because they represent real, tangible goods rather than just paper promises. Therefore, when most people hear of "hard assets" they typically think of the precious metals like gold and silver. However, hard or tangible assets also include oil and gas wells, timber (a great investment in itself), mining property, collectibles and income-producing farmland. The question is, what is so special about this last asset class of farmland?

Right now there are about 7 billion mouths to be fed in the world. That number will rise to approximately 9.5 billion in about 35 years (by 2050). By that time, the available acreage of farmland in the world will have been cut in half. In other words, the demand for farmland will rise over the next few decades to feed more hungry mouths while its supply will decrease, and that supply-demand imbalance spells a great set-up for farmland as a long-term investment.

Let's examine just the supply part of this imbalance. Right now there are approximately 3.5 billion acres of arable land worldwide. This amount of total global arable land is expected to marginally increase by less than 5% by 2050. The Oakland Institute notes, "over the last 50 years, the amount of global arable land per capita shrank by roughly 45 percent, and it is expected to continue declining, albeit more moderately, going toward 2050." From another angle it is estimated that there is only a limited potential to increase arable land (capable of growing crops) by only 20% over the next 20 years, so the possible supply of farmland is estimated to be limited over the long run while hungry mouths are going to increase.

As to the hungry mouth or demand side of this imbalance, we should note the following trends. All over the world, especially in China, India and many Third World countries, new middle classes have been emerging. The behavioral trends show that as these individuals make more money they then want to spend some of that money on a better diet.

A better diet usually translates into more meat consumption, which will propel the demand for meat upwards for many decades. Meat production requires more livestock, and this in turn requires that more grain will need to be grown to feed the animals. Thus, an increasing world population translates into a growing demand for agricultural grains and livestock, which in turn requires more farmland and farm production. Those are the basics behind the supply-demand imbalance.

Even if we didn't have burgeoning middle classes growing all over the globe, the world's population is still slated to increase regardless, which will in turn lead to an increased demand for food and then farmland. The demand for greater quantities of meat and protein will therefore rise over time just from basic arithmetic, and since their production relies primarily on grains (as animal feed) grown by the world's grain farmers, this will require sufficient farmland and water supplies – both of which are being imperiled. In short, the supply-demand imbalance of farmland suggests that it is positioned for price increases over the long run, and this is a sure trend that astute hedge funds have noticed.

Farmland will play a big role in satisfying these growth trends, and is also a recognized inflation hedge with a big benefit. Unlike hard assets such as gold and silver, farmland can produce a stable income stream. It can pay a yield while it appreciates in value, and that is something precious metals cannot do.

If we evaluate farm ownership using the traditional measures for investments we'll find that farm ownership has historically offered strong financial returns, is not highly correlated to other assets, and indeed serves as a good hedge to protect against inflation. Those are all positive reasons to consider it in a large investment portfolio.

Because they were burned badly by mortgage backed assets and other paper instruments, hedge funds, pension funds and wealthy investors have been recently pouring money into this asset class and farmland prices have been rising fast, so let's go beyond the basics and perform a "deep dive" analysis to better understand why farmland investments have been attracting all this special interest.

First, let us turn to the NCREIF Farmland Index, which records a quarterly time series composite return measure of investment performance for a large pool of individual agricultural properties acquired in the private market for investment purposes. The NCREIF Farmland Index only reflects the returns on American farmland investments. All properties in the Farmland Index have been acquired, at least in part, on behalf of tax-exempt institutional investors with the great majority being pension funds. As such, all properties are held in a fiduciary environment.

The historical track record of this index shows that farmland investments have returned approximately 12.4% per year since 1992. So the total annual returns over the last two decades have averaged 12.4% with low volatility. This is due to a combination of land value appreciation and current income from rental contracts. While this index only tracks American farmland the fact is that *European, Australian and South American farmland have all seen similar trends in long-term price appreciation.*

This is looking back over just the last twenty years so let's go back further. In the inflationary 1970s the price of farmland boomed, as did the price of agricultural commodities. When that inflation was conquered in the early 1980s, the farmland price boom collapsed hurting those who had purchased expensive farmland at its peak. Even so, farmland has done well since then.

Basically, due to current income and capital appreciation it turns out that farmland has been one of the top performing investments over the last century. Over the last one hundred years, based on income and capital appreciation, farmland has consistently delivered positive returns with only three brief periods of negative returns (1930s, 1980s, and 2008). This explains the long-term trends, but why have current prices been skyrocketing just recently? The current rise in local land prices has been fueled largely by three trends:

- A worldwide agricultural commodities boom that has driven food prices up by more than 100% since 2003, according to the Food and Agriculture Organization of the United Nations (FAO), and with the rise in food prices has come a rise in farmland prices.

- Individuals who are worried about potential inflation (or the possible destruction of the dollar) and who have therefore put their money into farmland investments since they can generate income that matches inflation.

- A mass movement from paper assets into hard assets (by well-off investors) which has increased the desire for farmland investments.

Let's put aside the financial concerns of these reasons and only concentrate on the factors of supply and demand. Can we expect the supply-demand imbalance between farmland and food supplies to continue? Here is where farmland investors get excited.

Growing Global Food Demand

As stated, globally we can expect an increase in the demand for farmland over time. This is because the global demand for food will rise as the global population rises and as nations, such as the emerging markets, also become more prosperous. Since food demand is actually growing faster than population growth this calls for either more efficient farms or more farmland to supply that food.

The United Nations' Food and Agriculture Organization (FAO) estimates that the world population will reach 9.2 billion by 2050, requiring 70% more food production over 2010 levels. Over the last ten years, agricultural output has grown by 2.4% annually and to feed those future hungry mouths the output will have to increase by 3.4% per year.

Reaching this goal will be difficult, especially since good farmland is becoming scarce and some agricultural crops (such as corn) have been diverted to producing biofuels rather than edibles. Our farmland output must increase to feed a growing world population, and since even oceanic food sources are now being adversely affected by the radiation spilling into the ocean from the Fukushima power plant, this will put even more pressure on increasing the world's agricultural output.

Agricultural food has to come from farmland and yet farmland is limited in supply. In most places farming acreage is even decreasing as more and more land is diverted into property development. Fossil water supplies to water crops are also declining or becoming polluted by fracking, which is making farming just that much more difficult since it needs to draw on these underground water supplies to irrigate crops. Desertification, soil depletion, water shortages, urbanization, and fracking are just some of the trends that are slowly destroying available farmland.

Furthermore, whether or not one believes in the premise of climate change and the prospect of warmer temperatures, the fact is that many crops, including GMO varieties, show less tolerance for extreme heat. This may imperil food production in the future if high temperatures (and lower water supplies) continue. Farmland that was once productive may no longer be so if weather patterns become permanently unfavorable for crops.

Some countries, such as China, understand these factors and foresee the forthcoming demand for agricultural land skyrocketing just from population demands alone, so are strategically buying up farmland all over the world in Africa, Asia, South America and even Russia. Many sovereign wealth funds, seeking food security, have also purchased vast quantities of farmland in countries such as Brazil, Tanzania, Argentina, Australia and the United States.

For instance, 1% of Australia's landmass, which is prime for growing cattle, has passed to Indonesian interests. Long-term buyers from Asia, especially Chinese, are said to be hunting for grain-growing land wherever they can find it. There is basically a growing demand for farmland and shrinking supply available in the world. As a perfect example, Chinese entrepreneurs now own alfalfa farms in seven predominantly western American states, and a significant portion of this alfalfa crop is being exported to China to feed its animals. It is being converted to hay and sent to China to feed livestock.

It might seem strange to Americans, but eventually you may see a price effect from increasing numbers of farmland crops being entirely sold to Asia or other international locations. In the case of alfalfa, this is being done to meet owner desires rather than because the farms want to accumulate foreign currency such as the renminbi.

In Third World countries, farmers specifically export their crops - rather than just sell them on the local market - to gain foreign currency since their own domestic currency is usually weak (and sometimes worthless). Exporting crops in order to earn foreign income helps to keep a currency stable, so this is a common strategy used by Third World nations when their currencies are experiencing devaluation.

Venezuela is a prime example of this trend; countries experiencing currency devaluation will export goods in exchange for more stable currencies with the result that food scarcity will be experienced domestically since fewer goods stay within national borders. In other words, as farmers export their best crops for foreign exchange, this often leads to domestic food shortages and higher domestic prices, which is yet another reason that long-term planners consider farming investments as a way to protect the value of their money.

If investors are worried about the potential collapse of the dollar one day because of the incessant money printing being orchestrated by QE that might possibly lead to currency debasement, large farmland investments that produce exportable crops offer some possibility of protection. In the case of the dollar being destroyed, they can produce exportable crops that will earn non-dollar income. This is a positive means of dealing with inflation if the dollar ever collapses on the world stage. Should the U.S. dollar ever suffer the fate of a severe decline, which would normally produce severe domestic inflation, income-producing farmland would be seen as a protective investment.

Jimmy Rogers Gives His Opinion

Sophisticated investors, such as Jimmy Rogers (who launched the international Quantum Fund with George Soros in the early 1970s), don't even look at *these* factors but believe that farmland investments will pay off big this decade simply because of the supply-demand imbalance and especially due to the demand-boosting trends. Rogers has continually advised today's younger generation to get into farming as a career rather than to get an MBA. He predicts that farming incomes will rise dramatically in the next few decades, and expects the farming income growth rate to be greater than in most other industries — including Wall Street. Farming, he feels, is the place to be if you want to make money in the future. That's where he sees some of the brightest investment prospects.

The essence of Rogers' argument is this: We don't need more bankers. What we need are more farmers. "The world has got a serious food problem," says Rogers. "The only real way to solve it is to draw more people back to agriculture." In an interview with *Barron's*, Rogers recently stated:

> I think agriculture is going to be one of the best investments over the next few decades. The world has consumed more than it has produced for much of the last decade, so inventories are near historic lows. The average farmer is 58 in the U.S. and Australia, 66 in Japan. Old farmers are dying or retiring, and young people aren't going into agriculture. Young Americans go into PR, not agriculture. Prices have to go much higher to attract labor, management, capital or we're not going to have enough food in the long run.

> I could buy farmland and become a farmer—although I would be hopeless at it—or buy farmland and lease it out. Buy shares in farms, farm equipment, fertilizer and seed companies that trade on exchanges around the world. Stock markets in agriculture-producing countries should do better than those in agriculture-importing ones. Retailers, restaurants, banks in agricultural areas will do well. Buy a vacation home on a lake in Iowa, not Massachusetts. And there are listed indexes like the RJA [Elements Rogers Agriculture Total Return exchange-traded note], or the RGRA [RBS Rogers Enhanced Agriculture ETN].

An interesting point that Rogers brought up is that while the demand for food and farmland will rise over time, farmers themselves have a particularly troublesome demographics problem that will lead to its own supply and demand issues. In the U.S., the average farmer is around 58 years old with a life expectancy of less than 15 years more to live. Farmers will therefore be disappearing because of both retirement and mortality rates. As trends stand, most children of farmers are not going to become farmers. Hence, we have the situation where fewer people are getting into the farming business in the future, including a farmer's next generation since it is usually not interested in farming.

Farmland is usually held for very long periods of time and rarely comes on the market until an owner passes away. Since the next generation usually isn't interested in becoming farmers, these facts open up a window of opportunity to invest in farmland, and that opportunity is now. It is estimated that over the next twenty years nearly half of U.S. farmland—about 400 million acres—will be up for sale as our aging base of farmers moves into retirement or passes away. This is an opportunity for those who want to get into farmland investing.

At least that is the conclusion of many wealthy international investors, hedge funds and corporations who for various reasons are buying up much of America's usable land at astronomical prices per acre, turning the farmers into their tenants or repurposing the land altogether. Acreage is being purchased at a crazy clip by farmers and investors, and many of them are from overseas.

A recent report by the Oakland Institute documents the little known trend that even corporations are starting to buy up U.S. farmland. The strange thing is this. The biggest land-grabbing companies aren't the giant Monsanto and Cargill agribusinesses. The big buyers are actually financial firms such as banks, pension funds, hedge funds, insurance companies and the like. The Oakland Institute notes that Wall Street is viewing farmland as a sound tangible commodity that has the potential for "solid, if not excellent, returns" and has adopted this view after being burned by credit-default swaps and securities backed by trashy mortgages.

Buying a Local Farm

Now for the small investor, any interest in owning and operating a small scale farm is usually the matter of a lifestyle choice rather than an investment decision. It usually isn't a decision made because of inflationary expectations, United Nations estimates of future food scarcity, or recognition of a world commodities boom. Many people just like the farming life-style as well as the idea of food self-sufficiency. Farmland investments are especially interesting to the self-sufficient who love the land. They even appeal to "preppers" since they can produce consumables during a crisis when food sources might be scarce. The problem, however, is affording a farm (even if you already know how to run one, which is yet another issue) because farmland has become quite expensive.

Not many people have the income or the accumulated funds that enables them to buy a farm, nor the wisdom to even know what type of farm to buy and how to run it. As a business, a farm has to make money to stay afloat and so you need to know how to profitably manage it. For those interested in organic, holistic, or sustainable farming there are publishers like Acres U.S.A. that will introduce you to successful small scale farms and successful farming models, such as the Polyface Farm in Virginia and Singing Frogs Farm in California. Furthermore, information is readily available on the internet to introduce you to other successful small scale farms as well.

As an investor, are you sophisticated enough to buy a farm and manage it? Most people don't have the skills to do so, which is why tangible asset investors typically confine their real asset investments to other purchases. Other hard assets such as precious metals are more liquid, portable and easier to handle but they don't pay a yield and cannot feed you during a crisis.

Farming indeed has complications. The major consideration is that you want any farming investment to be an income-producing asset. If you buy farmland and it sits idle without yielding any output then you still have expenses such as maintenance and property taxes. However, operating a farm takes skill, expertise, special knowledge and commitment. You want to grow crops that can be sold competitively, which in turn requires land that has the best prospects for appreciation returns.

If you cannot outright purchase a farm, another option is to simply invest in a farm. Private farmland investors can create companies and pool their money to buy farmland, which they often have to because average-sized farms (420 acres) now cost $1 million or more to buy. Managers can even be hired to oversee the day-to-day operations of very large farms. The returns from such investments have to be looked at through a long-term horizon of typically 10 to 15 years.

The problem with farmland investments is finding a suitable investment vehicle because locating a suitable farm is not as easy as one might think. Surprisingly few opportunities are appropriate because of the size of the land or types of crops being grown (usually you want crops that can be exported). Furthermore, because of their large size most farms can usually be purchased only by wealthy investors, pooled money or investment funds. This brings up another option for investing in farmland, which is to buy shares in U.S. farmland funds which specialize in income-producing farmland property.

Before dealing with that topic, let's first ask what can you earn from farmland. To answer that, let's put aside the annual appreciation value of farmland and assume that crop production is normally financed by the owner/investor. As a performing asset, you can expect a farm to generate modest cash returns before taxes and depreciation (but net of all overhead and management fees) of about 4% - 6% per year depending on its location and crop. Specialty or permanent crops, such as almonds or grapes, can produce annual returns of 6% - 10%.

Farmland investments, when rented out, can produce a steady income in the form of rents paid by farmers who are growing crops or trees that they sell to paper and furniture companies. According to a USDA report, nearly 40% of U.S. farmland acres are rented, and in the Ag-heavy farm states (such as Iowa, Illinois, and California) the number tops 50%. Since 1967, farmland cash rents have yielded between 4% - 8% and approximately 5.7% on average. In addition to the direct cash rents, the ancillary sources of farmland income include timber sales, oil & gas royalties, hunting leases, billboard rents, and even windmill leases. These are great returns, especially since they represent a steady income stream while the farmland itself has appreciation potential.

How to Invest in Farmland

Since we are interested in farmland, let's stay focused on evaluating farming investments themselves rather than alternative ways to invest in agriculture. But before we focus on direct farmland investments, let's review some of the related alternatives. Since our topic is income-producing farmland we can dispense with other agricultural investments such as banks in agricultural areas or shares in farm equipment, fertilizer or seed companies. We can also avoid the topic of ETF agricultural funds such as the PowerShares DB Commodity Index (DBC), which tracks an entire basket of agricultural commodities grown on farms such as soybeans, wheat, corn, coffee and so on.

Similarly, the Market Vectors Agribusiness Fund (MOO) seeks to replicate the performance of the DAXglobal Agribusiness Index, and consists of global companies engaged in the agriculture business. Many of these companies have large farmland holdings but the MOO share prices are driven more by commodity prices than by land prices. We can also stay away from evaluating agriculture-related stocks such as John Deere (DE), which sells farming equipment. There are also fertilizer companies, phosphate and potash companies (PotashCorp and Mosaic) or other companies that deal in direct or indirect farming inputs.

Since not many vehicles offer pure farmland exposure, one indirect way to play farmland values is to invest in a large U.S.-traded agribusiness company. Overall there are 50-100 agricultural stocks, most of which own or lease large chunks of land in conjunction with their other operations. These corporations include Bunge (BG), Archer Daniels Midland (ADM), Monsanto (MON), Cresud Sociedad (CRESY), and Cosan (CZZ). Since these are not direct farmland investments, we will ignore these as well.

There are also REITs (real estate investment trusts) such as Gladstone Land Corp. (LAND) or Farmland Partners Inc. (FPI) that invest in farmland. Gladstone Land owns over $100 million worth of farmland in the U.S., which it rents to farmers and corporations to produce an investment yield. Farmland Partners buys farming related companies such as grain storage facilities, feedlots, grain elevators, processing plants and distribution centers, as well as livestock farms or ranches. Next there are also land management companies, such as Limoneira Co. (LMNR) and Alico Inc. (LCO). Alico operates 130,000 acres of U.S. farmland in Central where it grows citrus and sugarcane, and provides land to cattle ranchers whereas Limoneira owns farmland that produces lemons and avocados.

With all these options put aside, what you have left is the option of farmland investment vehicles if your wallet is big enough. Many of these farmland investment vehicles offer international exposure, and a short list of popular candidates includes the following:

- Adecoagro S.S. (AGRO), which is 20% owned by George Soros buys, operates and develops farms/farmland. The Luxembourg-based company owns significant farmland holdings that it operates in South America and farms 217,000 hectares spread across multiple farms in Argentina, Brazil, and Uruguay.

- Jimmy Rogers is said to be launching a farmland fund in New South Wales.

- The Agcapita Farmland Investment Partnership of Canada is a farmland private equity fund with significant holdings in western Canadian farmland (Saskatchewan, Alberta and Manitoba). It allows investors to effectively allocate a portion of their portfolios to farmland without the need to take on the complex ownership responsibilities themselves.

- Ceres Partners in Indiana invests in farmland and has produced astonishing 16% annual returns since its launch in 2008. Ceres Partners manages $346 million for 259 investors in its farmland fund, which is open to qualified investors but requires a minimum investment of $250,000. The fund charges a fee of up to 2% of assets each year and 20% of profits as a commission.

- Pharos Miro Agricultural Fund, a joint venture between Dubai-based Pharos Financial Group and London-based Miro Holdings International, is looking to invest $350 million in farmland across Africa, Eastern Europe and Eurasia.

- UBS AgriVest, a unit of the Swiss banking giant UBS, specializes in farmland real estate investments. Its strategy: "Rather than gambling its profits on commodity prices that could rise or fall, AgriVest prefers the predictable income that comes from renting to tenants, usually through lease agreements that last one to five years." Clients with a minimum of $1 million can invest in a commingled fund (which is technically a REIT) in which money from numerous investors is pooled together to collectively purchase farmland properties. Clients with $50 million can buy an exclusively owned farmland equity portfolio tailored by AgriVest to the risk-return appetites of the client.

- Hancock Agricultural Investment Group (HAIG), a division of Canadian insurance giant Manulife, operates solely through individually managed accounts but enables individuals with a minimum of $50 million to buy a farmland portfolio that they own exclusively. Clients include pension plans and private equity firms.

- US-based South American Soy LLC, run by Phil Corzine, owns thousands of acres of farmland and agribusiness in Brazil.

- UK-based DGC Business Consulting Limited develops investment opportunities in Argentinian farmland.

International farmland holdings come with their own risks, which include possible weather changes (due to global warming trends), unfavorable operating fundamentals and even political risks. Nonetheless farmland investments are a natural hedge against inflation (it has a high correlation to inflation of 90% to 95%), so as inflation soars a good farmland investment can offset some inflation pains. Its value should also benefit from the increasing global demand for food that keeps pace with the growth in global population. No one can deny that the global food demand is rising due to population trends, especially in the emerging markets, and the demand for agricultural commodities is consequentially outpacing supply.

For many nations with growing populations, food security concerns will definitely require more farmland in the future, but arable land is becoming increasingly scarce. The continued demand for ethanol and biofuels as well as the diversion of productive crop farmland to these ends or property development should also impact farmland availability. From these trends alone we should expect that farmland is positioned for long-term appreciation and one should expect to see farmland investments rise in value over time.

We also did not mention the fact that farmland is a special asset class whose returns are not directly correlated to stocks and bonds, and that makes this an attractive investment vehicle, too. Historically speaking, farmland returns have been negatively correlated with bonds and equities and have shown only a modest positive correlation with commercial real estate. Therefore farmland can help to diversify a large investment portfolio concentrated in paper assets.

Since its returns are uncorrelated with these other asset classes that typically reflect the state of the economy, farmland profits turn out to be somewhat insulated from the economic shocks that usually affect stocks and bonds. Farmland even offers a degree of protection during certain types of crises based largely on the fact that everyone has to eat to stay alive. When the economy goes sour people still need food to survive. An investment in self-sufficient farmland is not just an investment in profits but in food supplies.

Overall, the basic investment fundamentals to remember are that farmland offers portfolio diversification, stable returns, and a means of long-term wealth preservation. Farmland investments can also diversify and balance a portfolio to offset financial and commercial real estate market volatility. The worldwide supply of farmland is shrinking for various reasons while demand is increasing, so the demand-supply imbalance should position farmland for long-term price appreciation. Furthermore, when commodity prices rise then farmland usually increases in value, too, so it is a natural hedge against inflation.

An investment in farmland over the long-term can thus provide a steady stream of income *and* capital gains. It all depends upon a judicious selection of the property you purchase and crops you produce. In a world that is diversifying away from paper instruments and turning to hard assets, it is an asset worth considering if and when you can afford it.

Former Morgan Stanley analyst Barton Biggs once said, "Farmland is a theoretically safe, income-producing, inflation-protected hedge," which summarizes the situation entirely. This is why farmland investments might one day attract some of your attention, especially if you have a large enough portfolio or simply enjoy the lifestyle because you want to operate one yourself.

CHAPTER 12:
REAL ESTATE CROWDFUNDING

You have probably heard of crowdfunding sites like Kickstarter, IndieGoGo, Booster and GoFundMe. They help entrepreneurs raise capital for their new business ventures. They typically work as follows. Entrepreneurs list their particular project on a website and people who are interested in helping out a listed project can contribute money to the venture through the website.

As an investor you are most probably interested in owning property as an asset for your portfolio, but did you know that crowdfunding is also available for the real estate market? Sites such as Patch of Land, RealtyShares, Realty Mogul, iFunding, CrowdStreet, Collaperty, Groundbreaker, CrowdBaron, Prodigy Network, FundRise and Money360 list real estate projects that investors can fund for a share of the action. Developers use these websites as a mechanism to raise money for their projects.

There are over 75 real estate crowdfunding platforms in the United States alone and perhaps over 150 in the world at this moment in time. Most of the crowdfunding opportunities are for commercial projects such as hotels, retail centers (shopping malls) and multifamily residences. However, some of the crowdfunding platforms raise money for singe-family homes that developers want to buy for "fix and flip" projects. These are quick projects where they can buy, rehabilitate or rebuild, and then resell the properties.

Normally your participation in a real estate project would require substantial capital, perhaps $50,000 or $100,000 or more. However, crowdfunding enables multiple investors to pool their money into a single investment, and the existence of multiple funders greatly lowers the price of entry.

For instance, a single apartment complex might cost a few million dollars to build or finance, but with crowdfunding the investors might be able to participate in the project with a smaller sum such as $5,000 each. This lower-cost entry enables investors to diversify their risks over dozens or hundreds of investments, something they might be able to achieve only by directly doing the projects themselves or by investing in multiple REITs.

Crowdfunding allows an investor to allocate the same money that they would otherwise put into a single property (or REIT stock) across multiple properties in different geographies, thereby achieving greater diversification. An investor can participate in attractive real estate projects and still avoid all the headaches of property management.

To be eligible to invest at any of the real estate crowdfunding websites, the SEC stipulates that you must be an "accredited investor," meaning you must have a net worth of $1 million (not including the value of your home) or an annual income of at least $200K in each of the two most recent years, or joint income with a spouse exceeding $300,000 for those years and a reasonable expectation of the same income in the current year. This requirement was set up because investors can get hurt in real estate crowdfunding if there is fraud, if the property drops in value or the project defaults. These real estate investments are not insured by the FDIC and therefore without government guarantees, so the accredited investor requirement helps to make sure that only investors who can should the risks and know what they are doing can participate.

Let's summarize real estate crowdfunding in this way ...

The Pros:

- Investors need not rely on their traditional "country-club" model to find attractive real estate projects.
- Investors can now access the real estate market with very small amounts of money instead of the substantial sums usually required for large projects. They can invest a sum like $100K in many smaller projects.
- Traditional real estate investing is inherently fragmented and inefficient. Investors have access to myriad projects across the nation and of all types, both debt and equity, so choice and options aren't a problem.
- Investors can even work with real estate developers directly, because of the crowdfunding platforms to have a voice in the process.
- Investors now have another new way of adding real estate assets to their portfolio.

The Cons:

- As with all real estate investors, crowdfunding investors assume the risk that the real estate market goes south, which will cause them to lose money. In other words, you are investing in real estate and therefore must bear the real estate market risks.
- A major danger is that the risk of investment default (from real estate developers) for crowdfunding is higher compared to peer-to-peer and direct real estate investment funding. This is something you must remember when selecting both projects and platforms to use.
- There is also a lack of liquidity for your investment, once made, due to the absence of a secondary market.

To understand this new vehicle for accumulating real estate assets, let's look at RealityShares, which is one of the more popular real estate crowdfunding platforms. The RealityShares online investment platform, RealityShares.com allows accredited investors access to nationwide real estate investment opportunities in pre-screened and professionally managed residential, commercial, retail, and mixed-use projects. The projects can be sorted by asset type (i.e. single family home or apartment building) or geography. Investors can purchase shares in these opportunities for as little as $5,000 each.

RealityShares raised $300 million for over 200 projects across 59 cities in 2015. Depending on the type of project funded, the average return on investment varied between 8% and 29%. Looking forward, RealityShares is looking at five specific markets with attractive tech and real estate sectors where it hopes to find more investment opportunities in the future - the Seattle, Dallas, Austin, Miami and Chicago areas.

If you qualify as an investor, you have two options as a RealityShares investor: (1) debt investment and (2) equity investment. As a *debt investor* your contribution funds a loan for the company that is responsible for the real estate project, and depending on your investment level, your portion of the money earned from monthly interest charges will be deposited into your account. An *equity investor* is paid a monthly percentage of the project's cash flow from rent, or is paid a share of the profits if the project is sold.

Information on every project is available on the project's Investment Overview page, which includes information such as the project's "hold period" that can last anywhere from less than six months to more than five years. This is the expected amount of time that will pass before investors recoup their money. Typically you recoup your money after a project has been either paid off or sold. Investors also have access to an investor dashboard where they can monitor their investments, returns and tax documents.

RealityShares is just one of the many crowdfunding companies out there and not all of them are created equal. The important thing is to work with a reputable firm whose senior management has previous business experience and with a platform that will survive because it is well capitalized. You want to use a platform that not only delivers great customer service during the fundraising process, but continues that excellent service after the real estate deal is fully funded and closed.

If you are interested in this form of real estate investing, some of the larger crowdfunding companies you therefore might want to check into include:

Fundrise, operated by brothers Dan and Ben Miller, specializes in commercial projects in urban areas under $30 million. Projects are normally $2 million to $5 million per deal. So far they have raised over $60 million for real estate projects. The fee is 0-3%.

Realty Mogul, founded by Jilliene Helman, lets you invest in real estate loans and cash-flowing equity investments with as little as $5,000. Fees depend on the type of investment and the nature of the transaction. It has financed over 265 properties valued at over $600 million.

RealityShares allows investors to invest in various real estate classes:

residential, commercial, retail and mixed usage. Investors pay no fees because the platform makes money from listings and other related fees.

CrowdStreet lists professionally managed real estate investments including both equity and debt investment opportunities.

Patch of Land requires a $5,000 minimum for its real state crowdfunding, which is called online syndication. It offers the chance to purchase loans for residential fix and flip investments as well as equity positions in commercial property. It has raised over $29 million in debt finance to date.

iFunding founded by William Skelley, Jules Kwan, Sohin Shah and S. Alice Chen, lets you invest in both debt and equity for projects You will benefit from low minimums starting at $5,000.

Prodigy Network, founded by Columbian entrepreneur Rodrigo Nino, has raised over $106 million for Manhattan real estate and is one of the largest crowdfunding platforms in the world. The minimum is $20,000 an investment.

Money360, founded in 2010, invests in projects under $10 million across the United States. It has since completed over $30 in funded projects.

AssetAvenue, which launched in 2013, is a LA based crowdfunding operation that has raised over $24 million for real estate projects.

There are plenty of other platforms, but you understand their nature from this small list. Basically, crowdfunding for real estate offers you (the investor) various pros and cons versus your other options of buying real estate stocks, REITs, or directly investing in large real estate projects as a substantial investor. It is definitely going to grow in the future because it solves a host of problems, so now is a good time to get acquainted.

Consider this. Less than a decade ago you could not search for a home via the internet, yet millions of online searches per year are now made using Zillow.com. When you look at Facebook, Twitter, or Wordpress you will find that they started relatively small and then became larger and more institutional over time. This will also happen for real estate crowdfunding.

Crowdfunding is sure to grow in the same organic way as these giants because it solves a major problem for both developers and real estate investors. It creates efficiency for private commercial real estate transactions.

Institutional investors, for instance, will rarely invest in any real estate project for less than $10 million simply because they manage multibillion dollar funds and they cannot manage small investments. Those projects, over time, will more and more turn to crowdfunding as their method of financing. Crowdfunding therefore allows small time developers to mid-sized operators (with $20 million deals) to get financed, and lets investors participate in those deals that they otherwise would never hear of and get access to.

If you are interested in becoming a hard asset real estate investor without undergoing all the hassles of managing a project yourself, crowdfunding is a new real estate investment opportunity giver you should look into. It can help you add real estate – a recognized hard asset – to your portfolio as either debt or equity, and is very easy to manage.

CHAPTER 13:
PHYSICAL GOLD AND SILVER

"Buy gold and silver!"

Most of us have heard this from time to time and wonder whether it is sound advice. After all, the press usually does everything in its power to belittle precious metals investors by calling them "gold nuts," "gold bugs," or other derogatory names.

Gold and silver are near multi-year lows, and whenever that happens in any market then a bearish consensus begins to dominate all the participants in that marketplace. Everyone who thinks differently tends to be ridiculed and belittled so buyers tend to leave the market. Few people want to touch the precious metals sector when the market is ruled by a bearish mentality.

Therefore should you consider holding precious metals in your portfolio, especially when their prices have been falling for the past several years, they pay no interest and the establishment seems to treat them with disdain? Here is something to think about on this large topic.

Do you remember the American Express commercial that went, "When it absolutely, positively has to be there overnight"? In terms of the safety of your financial assets, there are absolutely, positively and perfectly good reasons for you to have some physical gold and silver bullion coins and/or bars in your wealth portfolio. Rather than holding 100% of your wealth in paper assets, a portion of your wealth should definitely reside in precious metals. There are simple reasons why you should consider holding some gold and silver in your hands using the best means to do so. The proposal for consideration involves generally sound principles that have historically held throughout time and should apply regardless of the economic and financial environment.

Gold is a Means to Store Wealth

The very first principle to recognize when considering gold and silver investments is that you should look at precious metals investments as *a form of savings and insurance rather than as a speculative play*. In other words, you should not buy gold and silver to trade them. They are meant to help you preserve your assets and you should consider them as a form of wealth insurance or wealth protection rather than just a trade.

Historically speaking, precious metal investments are a mechanism of savings that has been used for thousands of years, outlasting every world currency. You must therefore think of gold and silver as a means for protecting your wealth in the long term regardless of the fate of paper currencies. There have been many difficult periods in history when protecting your wealth became more important than trying to earn a higher return on that wealth. Our present era of zero interest rates due to QE (quantitative easing) money printing policies is one of those times when you should be more concerned with the risks overshadowing the safety of your assets rather than the possible yield on those assets.

Mark Twain once jokingly stated, "I am more concerned about the return of my money than the return on my money," and that short quip summarizes the dangers of today's financial environment. We are living in a financial world similar to a Ponzi scheme because central banks (governments) are so indebted that they are printing money to cover their own financing of interest rate debt. They must also keep low interests low to lower their own financial burdens, and to top it off they even have to buy their own debt since no one else will! They are doing so in order to save their financial systems and *that need to save their systems means that your own assets are someway at risk.*

This is something you must deeply consider, especially in light of the fact that many analysts believe we have entered an "endgame" time for fiat paper currencies, the supremacy of the U.S. dollar in global trade, and unchecked central bank money-printing policies. All these possibilities suggest potential future chaos in the financial markets for which we should buy some type of insurance for protection. Because central banks are currently printing unlimited quantities of money and keeping interest rates low in order to fund giant liabilities and prevent massive debt defaults, present financial times are now matching various historical situations where similar policies led to financial destruction.

During previous periods of unlimited government spending and money printing to satisfy those government debts, one of the ways people preserved their wealth was by investing in safer stores of value other than paper assets, and the safest alternatives were always the precious metals.

Why are the precious metals a way to store your wealth? The answer is because they are internationally traded assets with no counterparty risks. When you own precious metals they are yours entirely. Their prices will also never go to zero so they can serve as a stable global medium of exchange. Their prices even tend to increase during financial crises because they represent a form of financial value storage and insurance. They also embody a variety of other beneficial characteristics.

All debt that you buy carries a risk that the counterparty issuing it won't pay back what is owed to you. This is counterparty risk. Even government currency has a risk that the paper may not retain its value over time. The Zimbabwean dollar, for instance, has suffered such massive hyperinflation that the currency has become virtually worthless paper. Inflation or hyperinflation are just two of the risks that might destroy the value of a currency so that it is worth little and can buy practically nothing at all.

Whenever a company or country goes bankrupt then any debt it owes decreases in value. Most paper assets, such as stocks and bonds, carry this risk of lower prices in some way. While tangible real assets that produce income (such as farmland, oil wells, timber, etc.) also carry these risks to some extent, the fact that they can independently throw off income even during bad financial times tends to make them valuable during severe financial times that become survival emergencies.

The point is that when you want to preserve wealth in a fragile financial system or during fragile financial times then you need to invest some money in assets that will retain their values better than everything else. They should have no counterparty claims on them so that they cannot drop in value. Precious metals fit this bill nicely and are one of the safest ways to store your wealth for all sorts of financial conditions.

To understand the reasons why everyone should hold some precious metals at the moment we need to understand the risks to our current global financial system, and to do that we first need to understand some paper currency basics.

The U.S. Dollar is a Fiat Currency

To get started, we must first understand that the U.S. dollar is presently the world's "reserve currency." It is also a "fiat currency." A *fiat currency* is a paper currency that a government has declared to be its legal tender, but which is not backed by any tangible physical commodity such as petroleum, timber, gold or silver. The currency might be backed by tax dollars or government promises, but it is not backed by the ownership of any tangible assets whatsoever.

The U.S. dollar used to be a hard currency because at one time you could readily convert it into gold upon demand, but it became a fiat currency in 1971 when President Richard Nixon cancelled this convertibility. Prior to that time the world followed the Bretton Woods system where the value of the U.S. dollar was tied to a fixed interchangeability ratio of USD $35 to one ounce of gold. Because of Nixon's decoupling, the value of the U.S. dollar became independent of gold and totally dependent on its prudent management by the Federal Reserve.

The abandonment of the Bretton Woods agreement in 1971 by the USA is just one more illustration of an important lesson from history that *all fiat currencies eventually fail.* They have all failed previously due to some from of destruction, and from the principles of sound thinking you can come to realize that one hundred percent of fiat currencies are destined to fail in the future. Fiat currencies never succeed in holding their value over long periods of time but always eventually fail due to some reason such as too much government debt, currency devaluation, hyperinflation, war, monetary reforms and many other reasons. As I wrote in *Super Investing,*

A study of 775 fiat currencies by DollarDaze.org reported that 21% were destroyed by war, 20% failed through hyperinflation, 12% were destroyed through independence, 24% had to be monetarily reformed, and 23% were still in circulation awaiting one of these outcomes. Researcher Vince Cate researched the fate of 599 dead paper currencies and though he came up with different figures, every single one of the 599 paper money systems he analyzed disappeared. Cate found that 28% were destroyed by war, 27% were destroyed by hyperinflation, 15% ended through acts of national independence (the new states renamed or reissued new currency), and 30% ended through monetary unions or reforms (such as the creation of the Euro).

It is one of my advisory principles that every generation can expect to live through a war, banking crisis, economic depression, hyperinflation, fiat currency collapse, period of massive unemployment, loss of freedoms, or some type of political takeover that throws out the established status quo. During your lifetime you will certainly live through some sort of major disaster like this which will threaten all your previous efforts at wealth accumulation.

It is therefore just a matter of time before U.S. dollar ultimately fails one day because as strong as it is and as well accepted as it is no currency has ever been granted the boon of perpetuity. Paper currencies have always failed eventually and always will whereas gold and silver have been with us throughout thousands of years and will always retain value. Historically they have done this because they served as an independent store of value without any counterparty risk.

The U.S. Dollar is the World's Reserve Currency

While being a fiat currency, the reason that the U.S. dollar is so popular in the world today is because it is presently the world's "reserve currency" and used for oil payments, which is essence makes it backed by oil. The world's *reserve currency* is the most popular currency in the world used for international trade. Central banks hold large quantities of the global reserve currency in order to help their countries conduct world trade. It is basically the primary currency used to settle transactions in world trade, and thus all other currencies (and commodities) usually have values quoted in terms of their exchange rate to that currency.

This is one reason why the dollar is used to price many world commodities, especially the energy commodities related to oil. Unfortunately, the role of the dollar in quoting petroleum prices in the Middle East is fast disappearing and this will threaten the dollar's usage as the world's primary reserve currency. The Petrodollar (the necessity to use dollars to buy oil) will disappear eventually and the economic supremacy of U.S. will disappear as it does.

If you are the one who issues the world's reserve currency, wealth travels into your country as you export your currency because you are exchanging paper you can just print up for *real goods and services*. A fantastic exchange of paper for real wealth becomes possible in this way. In being the issuer of reserve currency, your country can become fantastically richer if it spends its money wisely to build itself rather than just engage in conspicuous consumption. Unfortunately we did not do this.

American dollars being exported as the world's reserve currency can bring more wealth into America whenever the dollars travel outside of the country. When those dollars are not needed in the future for world trade then the dollars will be sold (traded) for other currencies instead. That selling will drive the U.S. dollar down in price, thus producing great inflation within the United States. This is happening now.

Since most global trade transactions are denominated in dollars, especially oil, there has always been a great demand for dollars worldwide in order to conduct country-to-country trade. Countries have needed to hold large quantities of dollars on hand for ready usage since they are the in-between currency required for global trade. Accordingly they park those dollar holdings in U.S. T-bonds and T-bills when they aren't needed for transactions. In other words, countries need to hold U.S. dollars to conduct world trade since that is the common transactional currency used to conduct trade, and while waiting to be used they commonly hold those dollars in T-bonds and T-bills in order to collect interest.

The volume of money in T-bonds and T-bills would certainly be in jeopardy if countries found out that they didn't need to hold dollars anymore. They would dump the dollars for other currencies en masse and foreign banks would not be buying U.S. Treasury-bonds anymore. This dollar dumping, or de-dollarization, would be catastrophic for the dollar and for the U.S. financial system and economy if it ever happened. It would totally turn the U.S. economy and financial system on its head.

The great benefit to the U.S. from everyone buying its T-bonds and T-bills (its debt) is that it can essentially borrow money from everyone else in its own currency. As a reserve currency that everyone needs and accepts, the ability to print dollars is like holding a credit card with unlimited spending privileges. The U.S. can buy things from overseas to power its economy just by printing more dollars ex nihilo and foreigners will happily accept them. Then those dollars come back to the U.S. to buy T-bonds, T-bills and other dollar-denominated assets all because the U.S. was able to create paper out of the air.

Imagine what it would mean if instead of printing off dollars and having foreign countries accept them other countries didn't want the dollar. This capability for acceptance of its policies – due to the dollar being the world's reserve currency - allows the U.S. to do many things that other countries simply cannot do, such as fund expensive foreign wars just by printing paper!

You need to understand this point deeply because it is one of the key reasons that some nations are objecting to the dollar's dominant reserve status and also a reason as to why the dollar has not yet been replaced as the world's reserve currency. Another unspoken truth is that the U.S. will use military actions to defend the dollar's role as the world's reserve currency so that it doesn't lose that status. It would be an economic, financial, political, social and military catastrophe to America if the USD lost its role as the major reserve currency of the world. Therefore the U.S. military defends the dollar's role in world trade, which in turn also preserves the military's ability to rage war.

The U.S. military can station troops across the world in part because it can print up money to fund those foreign ventures without limit, and the rest of the world will readily accept those notes for local expenses with no complaints or questions asked. As long as other countries accept its money the U.S. has virtually unlimited spending power to maintain its global dominance, which in turn the U.S. uses to keep protecting the dollar's status. It never wants to see this status diminished or it will lose its ability to do many things in the world at will.

Remember that if dollars weren't needed for conducting world trade then U.S. dollars would be sold for other foreign currencies. This in turn would drive the dollar down in price. This would certainly lead to inflation in the United States. In fact, inflation would skyrocket in the U.S. causing untold economic and social chaos. Its dominance in many fields would decline if that ever happened.

In short, the benefits of being able to print up money that the world will blindly accept without question, objection or complaint is so great that the U.S. has, does, and will use all its military might to protect the dollar's status as the world's reserve currency. The purpose behind many of the most recent American wars has been to protect the U.S. dollar, especially the dollar's role in global oil trade (the Petrodollar).

Other countries know of the privileges afforded the U.S. by the dollar's reserve status and have accepted it for a long time. However, recently they have started objecting to this state of affairs because they believe that the U.S. has gone too far in some respects and has been increasingly abusive in over-using some of its dollar-given privileges.

Since the U.S. never wants to see any country stop using the dollar for trade, it will fight tooth and nail to make sure that any possible trend to replace the dollar is stopped dead in its tracks. For instance, small countries that have tried to remove the dollar from their trade equation in the past, or even hinted that they would do so, have quickly met with military invasions that in hindsight were never really justified.

Consider that Iraq was invaded just months after Saddam Hussein announced plans to drop the dollar for its oil trade and use the Euro instead. Libya's Muammar Gaddafi was also toppled after trying to rally African nations around a new dollar-free African gold-backed dinar for conducting trade. He too was toppled just months after proposing to abandon the dollar. When Iran began considering selling oil in Euros, it was immediately identified as a nation planning for nuclear war and sanctions were raised against it to try to bring about its downfall. Only a series of greatly fortunate events has prevented its invasion. Over the past 14 years the U.S. has launched military aggression against numerous countries, and many of these cases can be linked with threats to the dollar's status.

Basically, the U.S. does not want any currency to be competing with the dollar so as to threaten its reserve currency status and dominance in world trade, especially the Petrodollar status of the dollar (which means that the world's oil trade is conducted in dollars). It also doesn't want other central banks in the world to be independent of its power and influence because that would threaten the dollar and its other hegemonic policies too.

For instance, prior to 9-11 seven countries had independent central banks that were not easily controlled by Washington or the network of western powers in general: Afghanistan, Iraq, Sudan, Libya, Cuba, North Korea and Iran. After the military invasions of western powers, the independence of central banks in those countries was immediately curtailed.

Let's take a look at Libya as just one example. The rebels in Libya, which had a 100% state-owned central bank, even declared a new central bank and national oil company while still fighting with Muammar Gadaffi! As Michael Snyder wrote:

The rebels in Libya are in the middle of a life or death civil war and Moammar Gadhafi is still in power and yet somehow the Libyan rebels have had enough time to establish a new Central Bank of Libya and form a new national oil company. Perhaps when this conflict is over those rebels can become time management consultants. They sure do get a lot done. What a skilled bunch of rebels – they can fight a war during the day and draw up a new central bank and a new national oil company at night without any outside help whatsoever. If only the rest of us were so versatile! But isn't forming a central bank something that could be done after the civil war is over? According to Bloomberg, the Transitional National Council has "designated the Central Bank of Benghazi as a monetary authority competent in monetary policies in Libya and the appointment of a governor to the Central Bank of Libya, with a temporary headquarters in Benghazi." Apparently someone felt that it was very important to get pesky matters such as control of the banks and control of the money supply out of the way even before a new government is formed.

It is 100% certain that the U.S. does not want to see other countries stop using the dollar in world trade. It therefore never wants to ever see a return to the gold standard since gold represents an independent competitor to the dollar. Gold's global recognition as a vehicle for conducting trade, in any form whatsoever, would immediately reduce the usage of the dollar and essentially handcuff America's ability to print money on demand.

Since other countries would stop investing in its debt should this ever happen you can now understand the screaming ridicule that often appears in America's press attacking any type of gold standard, gold-based or gold-backed currency system since these would destroy the dollar's predominance in world trade and its status as a reserve currency. This explains a lot of the negative sentiment you usually see against gold (and silver).

Once again, the military reasons for wanting to retain dollar dominance must also be understood. As a history lesson, prior to 1914 the world was using the gold standard for world trade. In 1914, the world abandoned the gold standard because if European governments had continued maintaining it they would not have been able to fund World War I. They could not afford to go to war if they were still bound by the financial restrictions imposed by adhering to a gold standard, and so they chucked it out of the window so that they could engage in unchecked money printing. The gold standard prevents war!

You can therefore now understand that a return to the gold standard would quickly squash the ability of the U.S., or any other country, to wage war in the world today. It would put financial limits on the process. That's why other nations actually want this restraint placed on the U.S. for it has definitely shown a tendency toward incessant invasions over the last few years. In short, pegging a currency to the price of gold, rather than having the free reign to simply print it at whim, would require fiscal, monetary and military discipline that governments have never shown an ability to keep without that constraint.

The World's Reserve Currency Always Changes

Yet another historical fact ties into the United States government's worries about keeping the dollar globally dominant. It is the undeniable fact that the major reserve currency of the world also *always changes over time.*

Nothing in existence can withstand the law of impermanence, so the U.S. is in a constant battle to fight the fact that the world's reserve currency has, can and will change over time. This fact foretells of an inevitable doom for dollar's status one day, but you simply don't know when. It could take years, decades or centuries but it is only a matter of time before the world's reserve currency once again changes due to overwhelming circumstances.

At any moment, however, the currency that serves the greatest importance to world trade is usually the one that serves as the reserve currency and that is the USD. It will certainly serve that function as long as it remains the most useful currency compared to its possible contenders. Nonetheless, please remember that what the reserve currency of today is not what it was 100, 200, or even 300 years ago. Prior to the U.S. dollar, the world's reserve currency was the British pound sterling, which served as the world's leading currency all the way back to the 19th century. The pound had in turn replaced the French franc that had served as the previous reserve currency, the franc had replaced the Dutch guilder, and so on it goes. The global reserve currency always has its day, but only lasts so long before it is eventually replaced by a stronger contender. That is the way of the world.

History clearly shows that all fiat currencies eventually collapse over time, and even reserve currencies come and go to be replaced by one another. This happens when countries en masse start moving away from using one currency in preference to another, and this is a worrying observation since there are enormous shifts away from the U.S. dollar going on at present.

Aside from these facts that (1) fiat currencies eventually go bust and that (2) reserve currencies change over time, you must also understand that (3) every few decades *the reigning monetary system in the world also fails* in some overall way and has to be rejiggered to restore confidence to the system so that it can all get going again. This, too, is not opinion but rather just a historical fact. Monetary scholar Edwin Vieira has pointed out that every 30-40 years the reigning monetary system usually fails in some way, and then has to be retooled to start again. Author Jim Rickards has identified three times within the last 100 years alone - namely in 1914, 1939, and 1971 – where the international monetary system has already collapsed and had to be changed. Every few decades it certainly has had to be reset.

A clear thinker would therefore never deny that another future collapse of the entire system is impossible. They will not maintain that things will always be okay and that we will never need substantial reforms in the future. That would just be a stupid, silly and incorrect bet. History proves from many examples that the world's financial system always evolves and is sometimes radically replaced rather than just adjusted.

Heaven has not granted the boon of perpetuity to any country or currency or financial system. The question of when, where and how things change is just a matter of timing and circumstances. Whenever a collapse has occurred in the past, however, it has never been the end of the world nor will it be so in the future whenever financial necessity happens again to cause a reset, as it inevitably will. *There will always be a new normal after the world resets,* and then the world will proceed forwards again. If it didn't get up again, brush off the dust and heal its bruises after a crisis then the world would freeze up and stop forever, and that just isn't going to happen.

Therefore the key is to be able to survive and thrive through such crisis periods without losing everything. The key is to preserve your assets during those difficult times. There is always an eventual end to the crisis *because people absolutely need some form of money as a unit of exchange* (other than just barter, which they often turn to during a crisis). There is always an end to any turmoil and then a new normal becomes established. This is inevitable because society cannot operate without some stable form of exchange, and so it must move to a new one. The question is how to preserve your wealth through the period of destruction, and possibly how to even increase it because a crisis always represents opportunities. Whenever you can buy assets at a discount whose prices will return to fair values after the crisis, this is the way to most safely accumulate wealth over the long run.

Whether a future set of inevitable financial troubles is accompanied by the chaos of war, debt, deflation, devaluation, hyperinflation, depression, unemployment, social unrest, exchange controls, capital destruction, surging interest rates, currency destruction, falling asset prices, or financial warfare, those living through the pain must remember that eventually there is always a new normal.

Once again the reason is simple. All countries need stable mediums of exchange in order to function and survive. They all need functional economic systems where trade and exchange can function. After a financial crisis or even total collapse happens, the major powers need trade and exchange to begin again so they simply sit down and reform the system so that this can once again happen.

The Times Press Ahead

Since Americans abandoned the gold standard in 1971, over forty years have gone by. Historically speaking, this is about the average time one has had to wait before a fiat currency usually goes bust. It is also longer than the usual time taken in this century before the world's monetary system has been periodically retooled. Right now, the world financial system is at its one of its most fragile times in history due to the buildup of excessive debts and money printing policies run amok by central banks. It is near one of those potential pivot points for a necessary reset. Excessive debts and money printing have brought us to an unstable extreme.

Many analysts are now openly worrying that systemic failure is a distinct possibility since the excessive government, corporate and private debt obligations have grown so large that they can never be repaid. They represent a domino chain of interlinked bankruptcies if any weak link in the chain ever fails. The problems have been several decades in the making so their size has become unmanageable. The attempts to paper them over by issuing more debt to solve a problem of too much debt have spread everywhere and now that "non-solution solution" itself threatens the entire system with collapse.

If any sort of financial crisis or collapse happens that is related to this, people will be scrambling for assets that have no counterparty risks and which can hold their value. Gold and silver are two such assets. Their further benefit is that they have been used as money, and *can be used as money*, in just such a perilous situation while other assets cannot be so used.

Events currently happening in the world definitely suggest that the tipping point for a new reset of the world's monetary system may be close at hand. Various countries, especially the BRICs nations (Brazil, Russia, India, China and South Africa) and other associate countries are silently making changes that will have a big impact on the current international monetary system and the current dominance of the dollar, which they wish to see reduced. Many countries are actively and openly seeking a dollar alternative, and their cooperation may even spell the end of the dollar's reign as the world's reserve currency. In early 2015, after a meeting between the foreign ministers of China, Russia and India the nations issued a press release containing the vision of a new world order: "Russia, India and China are determined to build a more just, fair and stable international political and economic order."

Previously under the gold standard, the money printing abilities of central bankers were constrained by the discipline of gold. When money was freed of the need to be backed by gold then that's when an era of unrestrained money creation by central bankers began.

Over the past several years the intensity of this money creation has increased exponentially. Central banks are now running expansive monetary policies that are even looser than those seen during the Great Depression, and government debts are ever mounting as this printing continues. Some governments are even printing new debt to cover their debt obligations of interest payments on the debt they previously created! When it comes to world debt, we are seeing the creation of a Ponzi scheme of gigantic proportions that is ultimately destined to collapse because there is no way to grow oneself out of it.

The government debt levels for many nations are now so high that they can only be maintained by artificially low interest rate policies (QE quantitative easing), otherwise the nations could never prevent systemic insolvencies or even pay the interest owed on their debts. All the while, the debt levels are building still larger due to all the excess money printing.

Take the case of Japan as an example. Currently the government debt levels for Japan are so large that they are mathematically impossible to be repaid. For instance, fund manager Kyle Bass has warned that Japanese debt levels are north of 20 times the government's tax revenues. *The country is therefore technically insolvent.* Bass flatly warns, "There's no chance at Japan repaying their debt." The most recent numbers show that nearly 43% of central government tax revenues are now used to pay the interest on Japan's national debt. If Japan's interest rates were raised the country would certainly face insolvency.

When we look at these extreme debt levels in various nations, and the inability of nations to reduce them, we have to remember one reliable conclusion from history, which is the banking principle that *debts that cannot be repaid will not be repaid*. That means financial crisis in the future for which you, as an investor, must be prepared.

Let us now look at the debt situation of the United States in brief because a comprehensive summary of its debt situation, instead of just sound bites, would require an entire book. The renowned economist, Boston University professor Laurence Kotlikoff just recently testified to the United States Senate about the state of the U.S. budget, explaining:

> I told them the real (2014) deficit was $5 trillion, not the $500 billion or $300 billion or whatever it was announced to be this year. Almost all the liabilities of the government are being kept off the books by bogus accounting. ... The government is 58% underfinanced. ... Social Security is 33% underfinanced. ... So, the entire government enterprise is in worse fiscal shape than Social Security is, but they are both in terrible shape. So, how much is America on the hook for in the future? ... If you take all the expenditures that the government is expected to make, as projected by the Congressional Budget Office (CBO), all the spending on defense, repairing the roads, paying for the Supreme Court Justices' salaries, Social Security, Medicare, Medicaid, welfare, everything and take all those expenditures into the future ... and compare that to all the taxes that are projected to come in, and the difference is $210 trillion. That's the fiscal gap. That's our true debt. ... It will collapse. It is just a matter of when. I can't say when, but all I can say it's going to be too late. ... It will collapse. It is just a matter of when. I can't say when, but all I can say it's going to be too late. ... We are seeing signs of this in the economy, but we are not picking it up that clearly. The macro economy is not doing all that well. ... I think our financial system is really built to fail because it combines two things which really haven't been addressed. ... It combines leverage, borrowing by the financial middlemen and then investing in things that they don't tell you they are investing in. So, there is opacity and leverage. These are the two major problems for the banking system. What we need to do is get rid of the leverage and get rid of the opacity. We need full disclosure of the investments of our financial institutions. ... I think [Treasury-bonds] are one of the riskiest securities in the world because interest rates are likely to go up. I think the Fed is going to have to keep printing money because Congress isn't paying our bills, and that's going to lead to inflation eventually. So, I think long term Treasuries are extremely risky, and they can drop 5%, 10% or 20% overnight. That could put my bank that was viewed as perfectly safe today out of business. So we could have inflation take off and interest rates go up. We could have banks fail, and that could lead to runs on other banks. That's the scenario.

Throughout the last several hundred years of history, most episodes of excessive debt creation have resulted in excessive fiat money creation that has in turn been followed by pronounced periods of debt defaults, extreme inflation or even extreme cases of hyperinflation. This usually resulted in political instabilities and has commonly culminated in wars, dictatorships, or political collapse.

What we also need to know, as students of history, is that the money printing used to avert debt defaults usually brings about tremendous asset price inflation prior to a collapse, but there is always an eventual collapse in the end. Excessive money printing can bring about a boom in asset prices for some time, but then the bubble must always pop and asset prices must deflate downwards. All booms have a shelf life that eventually sees an end, so this is something you should be wary of in today's ultra-propped up stock market.

Ludwig von Mises once said, "There is no means of avoiding the final collapse of a boom brought about by credit expansion (debt creation). The alternative is only whether the crisis should come sooner as the result of a voluntary abandonment of further credit expansion, or later as a final and total catastrophe of the currency system involved."

The case of Japan is just one instance which shows that global debt has reached such high levels that a global debt restructuring or even debt Jubilee will eventually be needed in the world and that you need to protect yourself should this happen.

Here's the kicker. Due to the tremendously large U.S. debts and other related financial conditions that reveal weakness rather than strength in America, many analysts conclude that the dollar may one day no longer be seen as a credible global reserve currency, and so a new global reserve system may eventually be needed to replace the current failing dollar system.

When nations grow debts that become too large, historically speaking they have typically handled them in one of two ways. The first way is to suffer massive debt defaults, whereby the country undergoes deflation due to the collapse in bonds and other assets. This will cause a subsequent contraction of the economy. The financial elites in a country, who hold the most money and have the most options because of that money, don't want to see this happen. The Federal Reserve has publicly stated that they want to avoid this at all costs, which is why they are using massive amounts of QE quantitative easing and other strategies to avoid deflation and to try to bring about inflation instead.

This has done nothing for the real U.S. economy, which is suffering from extremely high levels of unemployment hidden by doctored statistics. It has only artificially propped up the price of paper assets (stock and bonds) that will one day fall dramatically when the artificial prop of easy money printing is removed from the marketplace and the bubble collapses, as must happen. Then prices of debt and other paper assets will certainly decline in earnest.

The second avenue of remedy is that a nation can choose to print more and more currency while keeping domestic interest rates low in order to prevent debts from defaulting. A nation can only do this so long until inflation and then hyperinflation takes hold of the financial landscape. It can then use the large quantities of worthless money in the system to pay off the accumulated debts with worthless currency, but the whole system will still suffer systemic destruction.

A currency in this instance eventually becomes worthless and then the whole system still has to be restructured. Any country taking this route eventually suffers an inflationary collapse, and then it has to undergo some type of currency reform to establish a new normal after suffering tremendous wealth destruction.

Which of these two extremes is the likely fate of our current financial system? No one knows for sure although plenty of arguments abound. Many analysts think we are in the endgame for these matters, but arguments abound on both sides as to whether deflation, inflation or both is likely to reign supreme when the bubble finally bursts. I believe that we are probably veering toward experiencing both of these outcomes to some extent, namely the collapse of debt and high inflation.

We do not believe that the Federal Reserve, which is owned by the major banks, will ever allow its banking members to go bust so that they must write off their debts with a default and be reorganized. The Fed won't let any of its members lose power and influence. Nevertheless there will still be banking defaults and bankruptcies in the system. Since the U.S. itself probably won't default on its own government debts (T-bonds and T-bills) saying, "Sorry, but we can't afford to pay you," it will probably choose to just keep printing money to pay people off with devalued currency, too. It will just keep printing money until the dollar is eventually worthless.

Everyone knows that the U.S. government has recently been printing money without limit through its QE quantitative easing program. This policy has not made the common man on the street richer or saved the economy, but has served to enrich elites holding paper assets. For instance, it has rescued and greatly enriched the bankrupt Wall Street banks that were holding reams of toxic debt instruments they helped to create. Furthermore, QE has accelerated anti-dollar developments across the globe.

The QE policy of keeping interest rates artificially low has certainly suppressed U.S. government interest payment burdens for T-bonds and T-bills. QE has reduced interest obligations to a much lower and more manageable level for the government, so the Fed isn't in any hurry to raise interest rates.

The clear track record of the Federal Reserve over the last few years shows that it is willing to keep printing ever-larger sums of money to cover various losses, paper over financial crevices and prevent the financial bankruptcies caused by debt defaults. The long list of reasons for QE also includes keeping the U.S. interest burdens low, as paradoxically as that may seem since it requires that the U.S. print up more debt.

Unfortunately, it has been *confusing liquidity with solvency* as a solution to its debt problems. Liquidity may "feel good" but is no solution to debt insolvency. *You absolutely cannot print more debt to solve a problem of having too much debt.* When entities do that, people eventually lose confidence in the debt and it eventually becomes worthless. That is why we expect debt defaults to accompany inflation in the eventual endgame resolution to our own current era of financial excess.

Since the U.S. has consistently chosen a course of money printing to solve its problems, and since practically every other country in history has also consistently chosen this course of action, the best bet is that the U.S. will continue to do this into the future rather than bite the bullet and accept massive debt defaults, which are destined to happen anyway. The money printing will not enable it to save its current financial system in the shape or form that it currently stands, and thus the whole system, dependent upon the dollar, is likely to be reorganized and reformed.

This money printing will eventually cause inflation, which the Federal Reserve dearly wants, and a drop in the value of the USD currency. As the currency drops in value, import prices will rise in the U.S. that in turn will cause inflation to rise dramatically. In the 70s a *higher demand for goods* caused prices to go up, but this type of inflation will be caused by *currency debasement*.

If inflation rises sufficiently, the rule of human nature is that eventually people will start saying, "Hey, this piece of paper, this paper currency called the 'dollar' isn't worth much of anything. This money printing isn't making anyone richer. None of us is getting wealthier through money printing except the banks whose coffers are getting larger. All I'm seeing is inflation and lower purchasing power for my cash. My cash in the bank is also generating no return so I am going to sell this currency and get something else that's stronger such as another currency or gold and silver."

When this crisis of confidence finally hits the dollar, the world will start rejecting the dollar as toxic paper. There has always been a tipping point when investors in government debt from money printing nations began to doubt the ability of those nations to service the debt and refrain from cheapening it through massive paper money printing. Much past precedent exists – in France, Spain, Rome, and other countries and empires – showing that a crisis of confidence can then lead to hyperinflation, the collapse of a nation's economy and the total reorganization of a nation's currency.

The killer is the following. Since U.S. debt levels are so high while the Fed has clearly chosen the road of inflation, the dollar's status as the world's reserve currency will be threatened if the dollar suffers a loss of confidence and becomes worthless. People will look toward more stable currencies, which might at that time might even include the ruble and renminbi.

Once again, the status of the USD as the global reserve currency will be threatened if there is ever a crisis of confidence in the worth of the dollar. That being the case, *we better think ahead and be prepared with some type of financial insurance if we ever expect this to happen.* The chances are very high that this will occur. History and present conditions show this is likely.

For us, the key to remember is that the precious metals are fantastic assets to hold during such times because they can both hold their value during monetary crises and benefit from monetary inflation.

International Moves by China and Russia

China and Russia certainly believe that the U.S. may eventually lose its reserve currency status, or at the minimum think that the dollar will be imperiled because of all the excessive debt and money printing.

They are buying large quantities of gold in preparation of this possibility because if countries worldwide stopped buying T-bonds and T-bills because they no longer wanted dollars, then gold (the only major asset without any counterparty risked that has historically been used as the backbone of currencies and trade for thousands of years) might skyrocket while T-bonds, T-bills and the dollar might fall.

These countries hold plenty of dollars, which puts them severely at risk should the dollar ever fail dramatically or just simply weaken. However, whatever they might lose on their dollar holdings, should the dollar severely decline in value for any reason whatsoever, those losses would in part or whole (and even then some) be made back again by an opposite gain in their gold holdings.

Here is where the danger comes in to the U.S. through their recognition of the dollar's weakness. Both China and Russia are not just preparing for the U.S. dollar to decline or lose its reserve currency status due to financial mismanagement. Together they are *actively* working to weaken the dollar. For many reasons they, and other nations, wish to dethrone the United States from its position of world financial, commercial and military leadership that is strengthened in part by being the global reserve currency. It is only by putting restraints on the unlimited credit card provided by being the reserve currency that they can reign in the power of the United States.

Along with other nations, they feel that de-dollarizing world trade will somewhat protect them from U.S. excesses and abuses of self-interest including unchecked military interferences everywhere. China has its own reasons for wanting to reduce the world's dependence on the dollar, as does Russia, which dearly wants security because its history has been one of invasion.

In their eyes, dethroning the dollar will hamper the U.S. military's ability to project its power and influence across the world, which both countries dislike since this threatens their own preeminence and safety in their own spheres of influence. Both of these superpowers gain to benefit militarily, financially and economically if the dollar is in any way knocked down a few pegs, and especially if the United States loses a measure of its monopolistic financial dominance.

To reduce the need for the dollar, China has initiated direct currency swap arrangements for its bilateral trade with leading trade partners such as Australia, Brazil, Russia and so on. It is setting up renminbi (RMB or yuan) swap facilities across the world so that it no longer has to conduct trade settlement in dollars. It wants to reduce its dependence on dollars in any way, shape or form possible.

China also knows that if it establishes some relationship between its currency and gold, China will not just be protecting itself in case of a dollar collapse but will be giving its own currency an extra boost of the credibility it needs for more nations to hold it as part of their banking reserves basket. China has recently created various commodity exchanges, open to the world, that compete with western systems to trade the physical commodities of gold and oil via contracts denominated in Chinese renminbi rather than the dollar. Financially strong, the Chinese are diversifying away from the dollar and pricing more and more goods in renminbi instead. *All its various efforts mean that proportional-wise there will eventually be less and less need in the future for the dollar in world trade.*

Recently the Chinese openly publicized their objective to reduce their dependence on the dollar (as has Russia) so that everyone knows what they are doing and so that their plan could attract more international adherents. The Chinese state news agency even published articles openly calling for a new global currency to replace the dollar, which proves everything just stated.

China doesn't want to replace the dollar entirely. That doesn't help anyone, least of all China. It doesn't even want to hurt the U.S. either and neither does Russia. However, it does want the world to get away from its myopic dependence on the dollar, as does Russia and many other nations who have been hurt by America-centric policies taken to the extreme. China certainly wants to give its own currency, the renminbi, a greater level of credibility in cross border trade so that people choose to hold it and this is part of their set of reasons for de-dollarization.

The first step along this path is to popularize the renminbi's usage in trade settlement. The subsequent step is to encourage foreign banking systems to diversify out of the dollar into the renminbi, which benefits China in many ways. China is progressing along these lines because a few years ago China's renminbi was not even in the top ten traded currencies of the world, but now it is number five on the list. If nations choose to store some of their wealth in China's currency, those Chinese bonds would push out U.S. Treasuries.

Over the past three decades China has grown its manufacturing capabilities to become the manufacturing powerhouse of the world. It started off making cheap goods, following the example of Japan, and now produces higher quality and even technologically sophisticated goods. All the world wants to buy Chinese goods, and now they need the renminbi to do so.

Geopolitically speaking, Russia has extensive untapped natural resources that the West covets while China has the capability to turn them into finished products. Together the two nations want to create a trading bloc that gets away from the dollar and both are working towards that end, which is why both are politically demonized by the West. Now you know why. The Chinese and Russians are simply acting in their own best interests, which is what every nation does, and the West demonizes them because it does not want to see any power or influence deserting its shores. While the West currently dominates the banking system in the world, we can say that Asia is fast dominating the manufacturing or commercial sector of the world, which is worrying the West.

The two nations of Russia and China aren't attaching human rights or other conditional demands to their trade. Trade is just business. They just want to increase their trade to get richer, and each wants to develop their own market without competition or interference from the West. China sees its natural marketplace as the whole of Asia since it is close to home both geographically and culturally, and as much of Eastern Europe as they can grab a hold of. Russia has its own sphere of influence that it wants control of without interference from Western powers, and sees de-dollarization as one of the ways to protect itself.

The Chinese, as students of history, firmly believe that one day the U.S. is probably going to default on its debt through the road of money printed inflation and currency debasement. The Chinese believe this since (a) this is already the road that the U.S. has embarked upon with earnest and (b) the path which most nations historically take. They therefore suspect that U.S. T-bond and T-bill paper will eventually become worthless, and that their holdings of those debt instruments will collapse in value in the future. Like many other nations, in their minds they actually view U.S. Treasury debt as sub-prime!

The Chinese hold too much U.S. debt to get rid of it all entirely although they have various ways of quietly chipping away at the entire amount that don't attract much attention. The Chinese also know that if their central bank stocks up on gold, which will outlast the dollar and preserve its value, the renminbi may be one of the few currencies left after all the smoke of a possible default clears because that gold would rise in value and help protect the country's finances.

Holding gold and silver will position the Chinese to make a fortune if the dollar ever collapses. By holding precious metals that would retain their value when everything else becomes worthless, the Chinese would be able to buy up assets everywhere on the cheap and then claim uncontested wealth and world financial dominance. It would all happen because other people tried to deny reality and slept at the wheel.

Therefore the Chinese are actively accumulating incredibly large amounts of gold, which is a undisputed fact. No gold mined within China, for instance, ever leaves the country. China is also importing staggering quantities of bullion through Hong Kong. The amount is as much bullion as it possibly can. The Chinese government is *even encouraging its citizens to buy physical gold* so that more and more of it is pulled into the country.

Remember that the Chinese do not want to destroy the dollar since that would destroy the world financial system and their own ability to survive. That road of destruction benefits no one, least of all the Chinese and the assets they own in America. They are not in a rush to do anything and don't want any blame. Nevertheless, they just want to reduce the predominance of the USD so that they can benefit and get what they want.

Every country operates along these lines, along the principles of self-interest. If China tried to reduce dollar dominance through attempts to directly replace the dollar with a gold-based currency system, its moves would quickly be countered by the U.S. and its financial allies. However, it can actually accomplish this through an alternative gold-based route, which is by *installing a gold trade standard for global commercial transactions*. Because it is starting to dominate world trade, China can go after this objective through the route of trade, which is the route it has chosen.

If the dollar's role was weakened via the route of global trade then that would solve many international issues for many countries who have complaints. Having accumulated substantial quantities of gold itself, a gold trade standard that would mean posting trade notes backed by gold for world trade, would certainly strengthen the role of the renminbi in a system based on gold.

Both the Chinese and Russians see the predominance of the dollar as an underlying problem to many global issues, and believe that replacing the dollar is a grand solution to problems such as excessive national debt levels, baseless currency regimes, unsound trade payment systems, potential bank insolvencies, unchecked military invasions, and so on. They see that the system will probably break down and the only remedy to a collapse always involves gold.

If a fiat currency ever broke down then no paper currency replacement could be used as a solution to the problem. Paper currency cannot be used to replace other fiat paper currency! The great economist Von Mises talked about this problem saying that when it loses its soundness, a paper-based fiat currency cannot replace a broken debt-saturated paper-based currency system. There is absolutely no credibility to the replacement. New paper cannot replace bad old paper.

The only way out is with gold or silver, and this has been seen countless times in past history. When an old monetary system is destroyed, a new currency involving gold and silver can quickly bring stability to the markets and so this is the route that successful governments take. Most of the stable solutions to currency destruction that have worked in the past involved a return to asset-backed currencies, such as the gold standard, to stabilize the markets.

In 2012, billionaire Hugo Salinas or Mexico once wrote a letter to the Prime Minister of Greece, Alexis Tsipras, and the contents of the letter illustrate this principle. Salinas urged Tsipras to establish a new Greek silver coin, and said that this action would solve many of Greece's monetary problems. His ideas are so informative about the issues at stake and the reasons that the precious metals may rise in price that we should carefully read his letter. His ideas may one day catch hold in the world so learning of them may affect your decision on whether or not to be buying precious metals:

> Mr. Tsipras, the desperate situation of Greece offers you a unique opportunity to do something fundamentally great for Greece and to establish yourself as a great national leader. You are a young man and thanks to this, you have a brilliant opportunity to build a long career as a Statesman - not as a politician, but as a Statesman.
>
> In effect, the return of the Drachma would allow Greece to pull itself together once more. It would definitely not make matters worse, for the present situation is so bad that the Drachma will give Greece an immediate respite.
>
> Thus, the monetary heart of Greece would once again begin to beat and furnish the necessary liquidity to get the economy "moving" again.
>
> However, this measure will inevitably entail monetary inflation through the creation of increasing amounts of Drachma to cover the budget deficits of the Greek government for some time, and the inflation will bring about the constant devaluation of the Drachma.
>
> This will allow the renovation of Greek exports and a rebirth of Tourism to Greece, since Europeans will prefer to travel to Greece due to the advantages which the rate of exchange with the Drachma will offer.
>
> However, it is clear that a permanent inflation cannot be acceptable and cannot offer political stability for Greece.
>
> It is on this point, that I present to your government an alternative that no "accredited" economist has had the will, or the necessary understanding of human affairs to consider.
>
> All "accredited" economists in the world will say that the Government of Greece should "eliminate the fiscal deficit" to put a stop

to pernicious inflation. However, these economists are not in Government; they are not politicians or Statesmen and they ignore the huge problem of convincing a population accustomed to spending, to save money. The keynesians, who are the majority of economists today, detest the idea that the population should save; they attempt to solve all problems by increasing spending, until finally the whole economy collapses. The Greek economy has collapsed because the money to spend, which came from foreign loans in Euros, has finally dried up: there is no more money to spend.

Mr. Tsipras, the way to lead the Greek people to stability is through real money, and not through fictitious money such as the Euro, which has led to the present chaos. The present European disaster was guaranteed from the day of birth of the Euro as a fictitious - fiat - money, of a symbolic nature, and not real money.

It will be only by giving Greeks a silver coin in parallel with the Drachma, that you and your Party may gradually lead Greece to fiscal equilibrium. Your government will have to modify profoundly the mentality of the Greeks, before achieving this goal. Let us think of all the great leaders the world has seen, and we shall see that all of them governed by means of the ideas which they inspired in their nations.

With a silver coin in their power, Greeks will feel an enormous pride in Greece and there will be a renewed hope of a better future, a condition which is indispensable in order to achieve a recovery. Modern "economists" never mention "pride" and "hope" as important factors in economic matters. And, of course they are supremely important!

Thanks to a renewed pride and hope, Greeks will be better disposed to accept the measures which your government may wish to implement, and to tolerate the difficult transition to fiscal balance; a period during which your government will have to control gradually the level of expenditures and government investment, until a sustainable level is attained.

Not only this: the conservative sector of your population - for whom you will also have to govern - will watch the continual devaluation of the Drachma (necessary as a part of government planning) with disapproval, and will strive to remove you from your position, unless they see in you the Statesman that has given Greece a silver coin, which may be used by those who wish to protect their savings, and who will, in the main, be conservatives. Thus, the conservatives will want to see you remain in power, so that you may continue your policy of placing silver money in the hands of Greeks.

The silver coin in parallel with the Drachma is the formula for national unity and reconstruction. The reconstruction of Greece will require of savings and nothing furthers saving more efficiently that silver money.

How can a silver coin be put into circulation in Greece?

I outline the basic principles:

1. The silver coin will circulate in parallel with the Drachma. The Drachma will remain the monetary unit of Greece. The silver coin will have a monetary value expressed in Drachmas. (Note as of March 17, 2015: Alternatively, the silver coin might have a monetary value expressed in terms of the Euro or of the Dollar.)

2 . Greece will coin a small silver coin, using the Greek symbols: Athene on one side, with the Owl on the other, following a tradition of thousands of years.

3. This small coin - the "Owl" - will contain 1/10 of a Troy ounce of silver, alloyed with copper to .9166 to give it hardness.

4. This coin will be assigned a monetary value by the Monetary Authority, which shall be preferably, the Greek Treasury. This coin will bear no engraved value; otherwise, the coin will go out of circulation immediately as the price of silver rises, whether in Drachma, in Euros or in Dollars. (This phenomenon caused the disappearance of silver money from circulation in the world, in the course of the XXth Century).

5. The monetary value which is assigned to the coin shall be slightly higher than the value of the silver contained in the coin. This condition is necessary, to keep the coin in circulation and prevent its being melted down for a higher value in silver, than its value as Greek money.

6. Whenever the price of silver rises, the Monetary Authority will raise the monetary value of the coin, to a point always slightly higher than the value of the silver contained in the coin.

7. However, if the price of silver falls, the Monetary Authority will retain the last value assigned to the coin. All experience has shown, that a population does not fear falls in the value of silver contained in a silver coin.

8. The population will retain these coins as savings; these will not be susceptible to deposit in the banking system; there will be no "Silver Owl" bank accounts.

9. The banks may establish "Custody Accounts" for the public who wishes to store their "Owls" in a safe place. This will be a storage service, and the coins will remain the property of the owner of a Custody Account.

10. The public may carry out payments either in Drachmas or in "Owls" according to their monetary value. Most Greeks will retain "Owls" in savings, and spend their drachmas – "Gresham's Law".

There, in one page, you have the essentials of a formula to revive Greece and the Spirit of Greece.

I also can foresee that the Greek coin, the "Owl", of 1/10 of a Troy ounce of silver, will become much more desirable on the part of Greeks, than any foreign currency. Your government will have no further problems with "Capital Flight", because Greeks will prefer to own "Owls" rather than any other foreign currency. And banks will have no need to offer high interest rates to attract savings; the silver coin will be so desirable that people will save it simply for its superior quality and future rise in value.

Nor will the Greeks be the only ones to wish to own "Owls"; all of Europe, which uses no silver, will want them. Thus Greece will receive Capital from Europe, for the purchase of "Owls": the purchase of silver is subject to taxation, but the purchase of silver coins that are money is tax-free.

(Note as of March 17, 2015: The Greek Government may opt to receive silver objects from individuals, to be returned to them in the form of "Owls". Thus assisting the economic recovery.)

Mr. Tsipras: Can you imagine the power that this new joy and pride in being Greek and having such a superior money, will bring to your government?

As you can see, we are here not talking about "economics", we are talking about the fundamental levers that motivate human beings, levers that have always and everywhere produced great deeds in past ages, and that we, humans of this age, have forgotten while absorbed in electronic fantasies.

I have here outlined the bases to introduce a silver coin that may circulate in parallel with the Drachma.

I have attempted to convince you that this is a plan that you can follow, on your road to greatness as a Statesman who re-established prosperity and joy in his country.

Because the Chinese anticipate future problems with the dollar, this letter illustrates why the Chinese government is buying as much gold bullion as it possibly can. Gold may one day serve as the solution to the problem of needing a new financial system (gold-backed currency or trade) that replaces a decaying dollar. Even if it doesn't, gold is still inclined to go up in price! Gold investments by the Chinese are a win-win from any way you look at them.

The Chinese are actually sponsoring a move, along with the other BRICS nations, to create a new financial system with a gold underpinning to prevent the excesses of central bank fiat money printing. One of its de-dollarization moves has been the objective of establishing the AIIB Asian Infrastructure Investment Bank that competes with the IMF, which is dominated by the United States. China will be the lead manager for financing infrastructure projects primarily for the Asia-Pacific region that covers over half of the world's population. China holds 50% of the AIIB voting power, exactly like the U.S. with respect to the IMF. No one can afford to stay out of it, so there are currently over two dozen founding members.

Despite pressures by the U.S. discouraging nations from joining this IMF competitor, even Britain, France, Germany, Italy, Australia and other western nations have finally asked to join the bank, much to the disapproval of the United States. Remember that the World Bank and IMF are institutions upon which the dollar derives some of its power, and the AIIB will replace them. This spurning of the U.S.

by joining the AIIB is therefore a stinging rebuke to Washington from some of its closest allies. It shows the waning power of America. It shows a break away from the domination of the U.S. in the global financial system and illustrates the extent to which U.S. influence is dying.

The AIIB will logically replace the World Bank and IMF in its own Asian sphere of influence, and those institutions will see their influence diminished in precisely the nations most needing capital. The funny thing is that China and Russia, by having western nations put their money into the AIIB, have made a wonderfully brilliant strategic move in effectively defusing nations normally considered their enemies. Basically, on the world stage all roads are leading away from the U.S. and many are heading to China. There is decline ahead for the dollar.

Other BRIC countries, Brazil and India, are beginning to wean themselves off the dollar too. They have been taking baby steps to abandon dollars as the in-between currency by which they settle their foreign trade. The BRIC nations are even setting up their own development bank (known as the New Development Bank) as an alternative to the World Bank and IMF and are at work on creating other alternative financial supranational institutions for emerging economies. In addition to the AIIB, China is heading up this new alternative development bank, which is part of the BRICS system, that is being run out of Shanghai. It is also designed to end the dominance of the Western controlled World Bank and IMF.

Furthermore, various BRIC nations also want to create their own interbank currency transaction system to replace the Western-controlled SWIFT (Society of Worldwide Interbank Financial Telecommunications) international payments system that controls global bank transactions in over 200 countries and has been used for decades.

While Russia has already completed its own SWIFT alternative, China has announced that it will soon complete its own alternative, called CIPS (China International Payment System), which will become a competitor to SWIFT as well. As with the Russia alternative, CIPS will provide a way for banks to transfer funds to one another without having to use the U.S. banking system or the U.S. dollar.

In short, there are various moves underway on all fronts to cut out the U.S. dollar from its position of worldwide hegemony, which is a potential disaster for the U.S. and the dollar. Political and economic power is draining away from the U.S. because of its flawed policies of big debt, big government, broken promises and unchecked military invasions.

All of these countries are after one thing: to decrease their dependence on the dollar and to limit the ability of the U.S. to impose its will unilaterally upon other nations. Using the dollar less in world transactions will decrease the demand for dollars overall, which in turn will decrease its value. Whenever the dollar loses its value in foreign exchange markets, import prices in America must rise. This inflation, if it ever became severe, would put tremendous pressure on the American population and you would doubtless see social unrest if this happened due to a move away from the dollar on a grand scale.

Who Might Launch a Gold-Backed Currency?

If the world monetary system either (a) reduces its dependence on the dollar in world trade or (b) abandons it entirely as a reserve currency due to a lack of confidence or due to some other depreciating event such as hyperinflation, there are two means available to replace it:

- You either start issuing IMF Special Drawing Rights (a form of money issued by the International Monetary Fund based on a basket of dollars, Euros, British pounds and the Yen) to replace the dollar in world trade, or

- You can return to some sort of gold standard, namely gold-facilitated world trade. International trade based on gold can be conducted through either gold-backed currencies or gold-backed trade notes, instead of the dollar, since these would carry no counterparty risk.

If the market followed the first solution and was flooded with SDRs (Special Drawing Rights), this action would be highly inflationary, which would subsequently drive gold and silver prices higher. The big problem with the "SDR solution," which bodes failure for this route from the start, is that no paper currency can be used as a solution to the breakdown of a fiat paper currency. As stated, most all the solutions that have worked in the past to end the collapse of currencies and financial systems involved some measure of gold or silver (or other hard assets) to stabilize the markets.

If countries went back to some form of gold standard in order to quell the problems raised by a disintegrating dollar reserve currency, the majority of nations would have to agree on a gold price high enough to settle the marketplace. In other words, the price of gold would have to move upwards and become high enough to remonetize various banking systems. Gold (and silver) prices would subsequently skyrocket, which would be good for precious metals investors.

Both solutions therefore come down to just one expectation, which is that gold and silver prices will eventually increase in the future in the face of any potential financial disasters involving the dollar.

If the dollar ever decreases in importance in the reserve currency system or entire system of global trade, then gold may indeed have to return as part of a new monetary system to help replace it as a monetary anchor. Remember that the world's reserve currency has periodically changed over time, so one day the dollar will certainly be replaced and we just don't know when. We are simply running through all the scenarios to understand possible future landscapes should this ever happen. No one knows for sure if any of this will occur, but events right now are showing that the dollar is losing its importance.

The logical conclusion is that if gold and silver played any role in remonetizing the world's banking system, rejiggering the world's monetary system or replacing the dollar-dependent trading system, the demand for gold and silver would soar and we would certainly see new price highs. If gold ever becomes re-monetized for world trade, you would also expect that several countries would eventually go back to the gold standard themselves for their currencies.

Furthermore, if countries even expected the possibility of future dollar problems because the U.S. could not repay its debts or will repay them with greatly devalued dollars, they also would start to quietly reduce their financial risks of holding too many dollars in T-bonds and T-bills. To do so would be a matter of survival. They would quietly start to accumulate alternative international assets including the precious metals, which is what we are seeing happen on the world stage.

All countries clearly recognize that if the dollar loses value for any reason whatsoever then the value of their T-bonds and T-bills would also plummet while gold and silver would rise in price. Governments are already critical of the American QE policies because the Fed's money printing is ultimately cheapening the value of the dollar while the ever-increasing U.S. debt levels put it at risk, thus undermining their entire national savings and bank reserves. As a matter of diversification, any gold they might hold would therefore help offset any T-bond and T-bill losses if they ever occurred.

China alone holds over $3.5 trillion in dollar reserves, and therefore would lose over $350 billion for every 10% devaluation of the dollar. It holds nearly 23% of foreign held U.S. government debt. You can therefore see its concern with dollar hegemony purely as a matter of financial risks rather than geopolitical dominance. To protect themselves, the Chinese are shedding dollars as quickly as possible by purchasing resources across the world, and in particular they are buying gold because they want to park more money in things other than dollars that will hold their value in case of a dollar collapse.

If the majority of central bankers all over the world started acting like China and wanted to start using gold in the financial system, supplies would quickly become so tight that gold would be hard to find, and that marketplace scarcity would only disappear if prices rose high enough to clear supply and demand. As previously explained, this would be good for gold and silver investors.

Even if we never go back to a gold standard or in some way include gold in the world trade or financial system once again, there are extremely good reasons for countries to be accumulating precious metals for their reserves, and good reason for you to be owning gold and silver.

If fiat currencies ever failed while a country's own currency was backed by gold (or some other tradable asset such as oil), that country would be one of the last men standing in the world economy after all the smoke cleared due to financial ruin. It would have positioned itself with the strongest pair of legs available for the eventual reset and subsequent climb upwards that would happen after any carnage. Holding gold and silver would even enable to it retain enough purchasing power to buy up all sorts of valuable assets across the world at rock bottom prices. Many nations know this, which is why several are quietly accumulating gold and silver.

If the world ever starts returning to the gold standard, our thinking is that you might expect the following currencies to be the first ones in line to transform into gold-backed currencies: the Chinese Yuan, Russian Ruble, Panama Balboa, Gulf Dinar, Nordic Euro, and Norwegian Krone.

In this list, Russia and China have been extensively covered already. Both have been accumulating staggering amounts of gold, which for strategic reasons they underreport to the marketplace.

Panama has the capability of launching a gold-backed Panama Balboa supported by gold and possibly crude oil. Groups of resource-rich African nations, rich with energy resources and minerals, could also launch a few gold-backed or resource-backed currencies, too. The Saudis and other Arab nations are also rumored to have plans to launch a gold-backed dinar currency. Four Gulf states (Saudi Arabia, Bahrain, Qatar, and Kuwait) have already announced that they will create a new common currency pegged to the dollar, but can just as easily switch that backing to gold once created.

The Germans and fellow Europeans (Austria, Netherlands, Finland, etc.) could also easily launch a gold-backed Nordic Euro. Germany, for instance, is reported to have several thousand tons of gold as a national reserve while China and Russia are rumored to have several times that amount in storage. Italy, France and Switzerland also have tremendous gold holdings. Oil-rich Norway could also easily launch a gold-backed Norwegian Krone.

The Gold Vaults are Empty

While the demand side for gold is quietly bullish due to the recognition of such various risky possibilities, you also need to know that the supply side situation for the precious metals prices also bodes well for higher prices in the future, too.

This is because various sources of physical bullion are disappearing from the marketplace. Deep storage gold, which means gold that is still in the ground, is no longer reaching the marketplace. Mines are shutting down due to low metal prices that make mining uneconomical, and this is removing large quantities of physical supply from the marketplace. Ready supply is dwindling. The present scarcity is so bad, and potential future scarcity so likely, you may even see some companies start to buy gold and silver mines to insure their own precious metals supplies, which Rajesh Exports (India's largest jewelry-maker) has announced it is trying to do at the present with various mining projects.

Basically, gold and silver supply is decreasing as mines shut down production. The price of bullion has declined so much recently that for many mines it is near the incremental cost of production. Many high cost mines have therefore shut down their low grade gold and silver production facilities and those supplies no longer reach the marketplace. In other words, right now the supply of gold is dwindling worldwide.

A cardinal rule in asset investing is to buy an asset below its replacement value, and for the demand-side we are near that situation in the precious metals markets. At the same time, Asians are buying vast quantities of the precious metals and removing them from the marketplace too. Even the inventories of precious metals in the bullion banks are being severely depleted to satisfy this demand. Whenever there is not enough supply to meet demand for any commodity then prices will rise. That is a basic law of economics, and right now supply and demand are unbalanced. Demand is far above supply, but prices are being artificially suppressed so that you don't know this.

Various analysts have written that the Comex vaults are nearly empty of gold bullion, the LBME vaults in London are empty, and bullion banks are mostly depleted of inventory. They cannot supply this demand either. As stated, most of the physical gold has already been shipped to the East where it has found a new home in the coffers of various Asian nations, especially China. The actual physical quantity that has been shipped eastwards is so large that the ability for the West to meet purchases with supply has decreased dramatically. Economist and ex-Treasury official Paul Craig Roberts has said, "The Chinese and the Russians are not running out of dollars in which to buy gold. The Fed is running out of gold in which to make these deliveries."

If the warehouses of the Comex and LBME paper futures markets ever go empty, then those futures markets will have to convert to cash markets. By necessity a futures market without a warehouse packed with inventory will not function. It will lose its ability to trade volume so it must revert to a cash settlement market.

The gist of it all is this. On the demand and supply front, the long-term buy and hold prospects for gold and silver are very promising.

In terms of the international scene we have the following considerations. Because the dollar has been the world reserve currency since the end of WWII, countries all over earth have huge stocks of dollars. They have been parking those dollars in U.S. T-bonds and T-bills to get interest.

If the dollar is abandoned as the reserve currency or if its importance in world trade is reduced for any reason whatsoever, countries will no longer need to hold the same quantities of dollars and U.S. Treasury bonds for foreign trade. What will they then do? They will then move to convert them into other foreign currencies - or gold bullion since it is the anti-thesis of the dollar - just as they are presently doing. This will be a multi-year story, but hundreds of billions or even trillions of unemployed dollars will try to get back to America as other countries dump them.

Additionally, because they see the role of the dollar potentially shrinking in world trade, or recognize the fragility of a dollar based system overburdened with massive amounts of debt, these countries will make contingency plans on financial and economic systems that will bypass the dollar. They will start to build financial systems and platforms that no longer depend on the dollar at all. This in turn will put further pressure on the dollar's exchange value in the long run.

In the past, the way that any pressure on the dollar manifested itself was through the rising price of gold, which is why central banks have been actively suppressing the price over the past several years. The suppression prevents people from recognizing that the dollar is weakening and being abandoned across the world stage. To keep up the appearance of a strong, dollar, the U.S. government (via the Fed, U.S. Treasury department and the ESF) have tried to artificially suppress gold and silver prices just as various other financial markets have been rigged.

Countries that have privately suspected that a possible dollar collapse might occur are presently delighted at the low gold and silver prices, and are accumulating the low-priced bullion as insurance against this event. It is a potential hard asset backing for their currencies to shore up their values in case of a crisis.

How High Will Gold and Silver Rise?

No one knows how high gold and silver prices can ultimately go if there is ever any global financial crisis, so we cannot bank on any forecasts to guide our investment decisions in the metals. We should do is what we always recommend, which is refer back to an understanding of history to help guide our decisions.

Nonetheless, because it is of such great interest we would like to share some price possibilities put forth by top analysts we highly respect who have studied the matter deeply and - using various forms of historical analysis and calculations - come to some conclusions.

Super gold analyst Jim Willie, who is connected to high level insiders in the gold market, says it will probably hit $7,000 per ounce and may go to $15,000 per ounce or more. Jim Rickards, author of *Currency Wars* and *The Death of Money*, thinks that the price of gold may go to $7,000 or $9,000 per ounce because he believes that the dollar may be devalued by 80% or 90% for reasons we have already discussed. Famous gold trader, James Sinclair, believes that gold may go to $50,000 per ounce, in gradual steps, because of the collapse of the US dollar and the fiat currency system. Cycles expert Charles Nenner has said in interviews that long-term gold cycles suggest it will continue a bullish run upwards for several years.

No one knows for sure what gold's ultimate price trajectory will be if we indeed encounter a worldwide crisis due to excessive money printing and a loss of confidence in fiat currencies. I follow Warren Buffett's principle of never trusting in forecasts and predictions, which I emphasized in my book *Super Investing*, but always try to rely on historical analysis, basic investment principles and a deep-dive analysis of processes, procedures and likely events.

Even so, the bottom line is that we believe that all investors should hold some gold and silver in their portfolios as insurance against the demise of the dollar and restructuring of the financial system. The advantages for holding gold and silver will not change going into the future and are only getting stronger. The little price you pay for buying financial insurance, by investing in the precious metals, may one day seem just a fraction of the money you save through such action.

One day soon the suppression of gold (to eliminate dollar competition) will no longer be possible because its physical price will be emancipated from the manipulated price of the paper futures markets. Central banks or their agents currently enter the paper futures market during the thinnest trading periods of the day and then dump (sell) great quantities of gold contracts (equivalent to several years worth of gold production) on the paper market simply to drive prices down. If prices are kept down, people are less likely to consider gold as an alternative to the dollar.

This manipulation is unmistakable, yet is permitted to continue because it is used as a tool to help protect the value of the dollar. Soon, however, it will be gone. The ability to paper short the market will be curtailed because new exchanges are arising that will trade the actual physical metals on a 24-hour basis and those exchanges will bring discipline to the paper marketplaces in such a way that will curtail naked shorting. The physical exchanges require actual inventories of gold and silver that cannot just be printed into existence out of thin air.

The Chinese and many others have been accumulating gold at rock bottom prices when the prices are manipulated downwards anyway, profiting from this stupidity by central bankers, and central banks have been emptying their vaults to satisfy the demand for deliveries at low prices. Their own inventories have almost been emptied.

The demand for physical gold has been very high even though prices have reached multi-year lows. There is actually a very real shortage in the marketplace for actual physical gold. All the gold is going from the West to the East, from weak hands to stronger hands just as financial power is draining away from the USA and Europe. Previously any banks buying gold usually kept it in the London pool, but now China is buying it and asking for physical delivery, thus draining it from the Western system. The physical market is becoming strained, but the paper market is 100X larger, which is why the financial institutions are using it to manipulate gold prices and push them down. When the market eventually sees no gold to deliver against the paper longs then the bullion banks won't be able to deliver on the paper, cash settlement will happen, and the paper manipulation will cease.

This is not what central banks or bullion banks want, but the more they push down prices the higher the physical demand becomes for the precious metals. Because of artificially suppressed prices while inflation gains in the world and financial instabilities rise, the demand for physical gold bullion has become insatiable because wise individuals and countries see gold accumulation as a measure of prudence.

A day will come when the LBME and Comex exchanges will not be able to deliver any more gold and silver to meet the demand for physical deliveries. At that time the exchanges will have to make contract changes to avoid default, and then settle the paper futures contracts in cash. At that time the physical market will finally be emancipated from the futures markets. When that happens, you will suddenly see jumps of $100 or $200 per day in the prices of the precious metals. At that time, any physical forms of gold and silver will become hard to find, and that future scarcity is another reason to buy ahead of time and store them away for your wealth portfolio.

What has moved the market significantly along this road to higher prices is a recent but little known development in the gold pricing system. The gold market initiated a new price fixing arrangement, which is another big milestone since it will eventually remove the dominance of the twice-per-day London gold fix and reduce the ability for various bullion banks to manipulate gold prices. Because buyers and sellers are anonymous during the auction process, the new pricing platform ensures equal opportunity among buyers and sellers. All market participants will have direct access to the fixing process thus eliminating the undue influence, privileges and advantages previously enjoyed solely by the fixing banks.

We anticipate that market domination of the pricing mechanism for gold will fall away from the privileged fixing members and move in favor of the deepest pockets, which will probably be large Chinese banks since they already have firm control of the largest physical market in Asia, the Shanghai Gold Exchange (SGE). In other words, gold pricing power will move away from London to Shanghai. Once again China seems to be a key cog in these changes. Over time, more and more this will promote China's interests and provide it with growing influence over world gold prices.

Analyst Alasdair Macleod has wisely stated, "At some stage China with her SCO partner, Russia, will force the price of gold higher as part of their currency strategy. You can argue this from an economic point of view on the basis that possession of properly priced gold will give her a financial dominance over global trade at a time when we are trashing our fiat currencies, or more simply that there is no point in owning an asset and suppressing its value forever.

Therefore the failure of the London bullion market to see strategically beyond its short-term interests has opened the door to China's powerful state-owned banking monopoly to control the gold bullion market. This is probably the final link in China's long-standing gold strategy, and through it a planned domination of the global economy in partnership with Russia and the other SCO nations."

The Precious Metals Portfolio Allocation

Even with these changes making the markets more fair, you should not focus on becoming a gold and silver trader. Yes, you can trade those markets but the emphasis is on holding the precious metals as a long-term investment. Gold expert Jim Sinclair warns that in trying to trade gold you're up against some of the smartest minds in the world who have incredibly deep pockets. He says that gold trading on the Comex and LBME exchanges is an insider's game of a manipulated market, and you're not an insider. Since you therefore cannot compete, your best option is simply to buy physical gold and silver and hold it rather than trade it. Holding physical gold and silver is your insurance policy whereas trading gold and silver is not your key to wealth.

If you are going to buy gold and silver, the best advice is never to use margin to buy. Furthermore, you should buy physical bullion, bars and/or coins and always take delivery of the metals. It is imperative that you never store your holdings at a bank but always safely store them outside of the banking system simply because banks (and the government) cannot be trusted during financial crises.

How much do experts recommend you buy? Once again the answer is not cut and dry, but a general rule of thumb that analysts bandy about is between 10% and 30% of your portfolio. Dr. Marc Faber recently suggested a 25% allocation to precious metals.

Back when I worked for Wall Street in the 80s, I ran dozens of computer studies to determine the best composition of a buy-and-hold wealth portfolio consisting of stocks, bonds, gold, foreign currencies and commodities. At that time I found that allocating 10-20% of one's assets to precious metals was the optimal amount to help protect and grow such a fund over the long run. Recently I heard an interview with another analyst who, running more current studies entirely different from my own, also found that devoting 20% of one's portfolio to precious metals produced the best reward/risk performance in the long run. You should therefore think of possible allocations in terms of units such as 5%, 10%, 15%, 20% or 25%.

How much one invests in gold and silver, and in what form, depends upon how concerned you are about the current economic, financial and political situation and how much you can spare from income producing investments. In any case, an investor seeking diversification should have some gold and silver in hand.

Your Best Precious Metals Investment Options

All in all, everyone should probably buy some physical gold and silver (without margin) for their portfolio. The precious metals are a form of financial insurance and protection against wealth destruction. Individuals should also hold them *in some private way* that is outside of the pitfalls and manipulations of the banking system.

It is difficult to determine the best forms of gold and/or silver to buy because everyone's situation is different. Some forms will be more liquid or popular in different areas of the world. Some will be less risky, better suited for international diversification, or will outperform others if there is a sharp price run-up in metals prices. Some are easier or cheaper to buy or easier to sell, less likely to be targeted in a confiscation, or easier to store. Some will offer greater purchasing power protection than others. Even with all these possibilities, your best choices basically come down to bullion, bars and coins.

If you want to buy gold and silver coins, we suggest you should consider buying bullion coins rather than numismatic coins. You should stay away from exotic coins or rarities and collecting numismatic coins should primarily be for fun, not profit. They always cost you both a numismatic premium and a dealer's spread above the cost of the underlying metal. Furthermore, if you buy and then immediately try to sell a numismatic coin you are likely to lose between 30-50% of your investment, which is also something to consider. For investments you should rely on highly liquid, easily traded bullion coins or bars that are portable and easy to store.

For gold bullion coins, the most popular coin varies widely among world regions. The most popular gold coin in the U.S. is the Gold Eagle while the most popular in Canada is the Gold Maple Leaf. The most popular gold coin in Europe is the Gold Austrian Philharmonic. China issues the Gold Chinese Panda, South Africa issues the Krugerrand, and Australia issues the Gold Australian Kangaroo. These are the major gold coins to consider.

As regards silver bullion coins your most popular options are American Silver Eagles, Canadian Silver Maple Leafs, the Silver Austrian Philharmonic, the Silver Mexican Libertad or various Australian solver coins issued by the Perth Mint.

For gold and silver bars and rounds the options are even wider in scope. To buy bullion coins or bars there are a number of highly reputable dealers that you can easily find on the internet such as SD Bullion, Silver.com, Metals.com, and others. Always search around for whomever will provide bullion bars or coins at the lowest premium over the spot price of gold and silver.

If you want to diversify your bullion holdings and also buy precious metals stocks, there are two types to consider. First, there are stocks that represent trusts holding actual physical bullion, like the Sprott PHYS and PSLV funds or the CES Central Fund of Canada that holds mixed quantities of gold and silver bullion.

If you want to be holding physical bullion through stocks then PHYS, PSLV and CES fit the bill. Hard asset experts consistently give these three funds top marks because they are well managed and audits always show that the physical gold or silver is actually there. That is not the case with 90% of the "paper gold" products out there in the marketplace. Warnings are constantly issued along these lines about GLD and SLV because while they are good for trading, at the end of the day they are still just paper promises for owning precious metals. Paper promises are no replacement for holding the real thing. You want to be holding the actual metals themselves rather than pieces of paper that say some entity is holding metals for you yet which might not actually be doing so.

There are also gold and silver mining company shares you can invest in that are basically leveraged plays on the price of gold and silver. This is not our preferred form of investing over actual bullion holdings. Picking what you believe will be the best performing gold and silver mining stocks requires a lot of analysis, and an entire book could be devoted to this one objective because of many tangled issues. For instance, one of the potential dangers in mining shares is that those firms and their properties might be one day coveted by governments, or even become subject to massive windfall taxes if the price of gold and silver should ever skyrocket. If those properties are in foreign jurisdictions, there is little you can do about this.

This once again suggests that your "safety," "insurance" or "wealth protection" holdings of precious metals should primarily consist of readily tradable bullion bars and coins that you actually physically hold.

If you are going to buy bullion yourself, such as silver and gold coins and bullion bars, you'll need to store them. You can do that at home or by using a storage facility. Quite a few hard asset advocates stress that you should avoid the precious metals storage vaults located in the Western banking system, especially those located in New York, London and Switzerland.

For instance, gold experts Jim Willie and Egon von Greyerz have reported that wealthy families have stored their gold in allocated Swiss accounts for years, but many who recently asked for delivery have found that certain Swiss banks could not and would not supply the gold they were supposed to be holding. Fishy things are going on in Switzerland in regards to "allocated" gold accounts, but any lawsuits related to these matters are quietly kept out of the press because of the potential damage to the banking system.

London and the U.S. banks also do not have spotless reputations in managing allocated or "segregated" bullion accounts either. In many cases, in these locations it is also possible that your allocated bullion has been loaned out to other parties and also is not sitting in the vaults that you are paying storage for each month.

From my own analysis, I personally side with the opinions of many other analysts who believe that some financial institutions (especially in London and Switzerland) have likely been telling clients that they were holding bullion for them in allocated/segregated accounts but were leasing it out on the market. In other words, clients have been told their gold is sitting in the bank's vaults and they have been charged storage fees, but their gold isn't actually there. It was "loaned out" to another party, who doubtless sold it in the market, but who paid an interest fee to the bank for the "loan." If that has happened to your account in the banking system and you ask for your gold back, you may never see it. To protect yourself you should try to transfer it out and take possession of it *now*.

You should always try to store your gold outside the banking system. History has shown countless instances where the government, or large banking entities, will suddenly change their rules in such a way that the changes could harm you and your money. In the future such events might even include the confiscation of whatever precious metals you have in the financial system if larger entities feel they can get their hands on it.

Always, always remember that in addition to buying from reputable dealers, you should store any precious metals where no government can get its hands on them because of the simple rule that "what governments cannot find they cannot confiscate." This is why many people choose to store their gold and silver investments in offshore private vaults that are outside of domestic banking systems.

If you want to select a bullion storage provider, here are the due diligence concerns you should consider:

- Make sure that your bullion storage provider and sourcing provider both have adequate insurance cover
- Make sure that your bullion is being sourced from recognized refiners known for their integrity such as those within the LBMA chain (so that when you buy bullion you can be 100% sure it is actually physical bullion)
- Never choose paper, pooled or digital bullion, and only choose fully allocated bullion accounts that also offer segregated storage of your precious metals
- Make sure that your provider conducts regular audits, using internationally recognized auditors, and that owner directed audits are available on demand while standard audits are done according to a regular schedule
- Make sure that you can take delivery of your bullion, including the ability to have it shipped to you
- Make sure that you can keep track of your bullion holdings online, including being able to review the weight, quantity, fineness, purchase costs and dates and other characteristics of your holdings
- Make sure that you can visit your provider and actually view your bullion holdings (whether physical coins or bars)
- Make sure that the true ownership of your bullion always remains with you rather than that the provider or any other party holds it in your name (while you store it with someone else you must still own it and have real control over it)

- Make sure that your provider can facilitate the sale of your bullion, when you want, in a timely, efficient and expedited manner so that you can turn it into cash whenever you desire

Remember that some gold storage companies may entice you by offering ultra cheap storage, sometimes below the actual vaulting costs for the precious metals.

Why would anyone do that? Only if the low storage fees you are being charged are subsidized by some other revenue stream. All other possible revenue streams (such as interest on currency deposits or speculation profits) suggest that your bullion may be at risk, so be careful with ultra cheap storage facilities.

With all these concerns in mind, investors should look to reputable companies for coin and bullion purchases, and for storage facilities that will hold your bullion outside of the banking system. Three entities that are commonly cited for physical bullion purchase and storage include:

- GoldMoney.com – founded by James Turk
- GoldSwitzerland.com – managed by Egon Greyerz

All in all, gold and silver investing is a lengthy topic with many whys and wherefores. Our short recap of the history for you to consider, in analyzing whether you should become a buyer, is as follows. All fiat currencies eventually collapse. That will also eventually be the same fate for the USD one day. Reserve currencies also change and financial systems often must be retooled. Financial systems collapse from too much debt and money printing, and this repeatable cycle has gone on for thousands of years.

No one knows whether any of this will happen to any of us in the next six months, next year, or in the next decade but macro events in the world definitely suggest that a tipping point may be near at hand for some of these potentialities. Because of these risks, you probably should devote some portion of your portfolio not just to income producing passive assets, but to tangible, real, hard assets simply because they represent wealth insurance. In today's world they especially represent insurance against the wealth destructive policies of central bankers like the Fed.

Gold and silver are *real tangible assets* that have represented wealth for thousands of years, and they have been shown to be able to hold your purchasing power during difficult times. They have often been a "safe port" whenever there has been a financial storm of monetary messiness. They are a form of wealth preservation.

They are real assets that have no counterparty risk (though only if you actually own them free of any encumbrances and *hold them yourself by taking delivery*) and they can serve as insurance for various types of financial crises that periodically happen in the world. The fact that various fundamental forces may soon move their prices dramatically upwards is just icing on the cake beyond these basic reasons for holding them in your portfolio regardless of the naysayers.

Right now, old financial systems have reached critical points because of massive amounts of government (and private) debts and are breaking down. Never before have so many major nations run massive government deficits that have created debts in the trillions of dollars. The banking systems of countless nations, undercapitalized in the extreme, are extremely vulnerable to bankruptcy worldwide. No amount of tax dollars can pay off these debts as they are over-leveraged in the extreme. For some countries, even the total wealth of the entire nation cannot be used to pay off the debt of that country!

International markets are also over-burdened with unfathomably complex SWAP and derivative liabilities that also dwarf the size of world GNP many times over. They represent a potential domino effect of interlinked banking defaults that could collapse the entire world's banking system should one big or even small bank go bad.

At the same time we face all these other risks, various countries are quietly moving ahead to reduce the importance of the U.S. dollar in world trade, which could somewhat harm its reputation, credibility or even damage its role as the global reserve currency. If people lose confidence in the dollar for any reason whatsoever, then because of supply and demand factors the gold and silver markets could skyrocket.

As investors we need to understand these current trends as well as the lessons of financial history. You cannot just ignore history and say that fiat currencies will never fail, reserve currencies will never change and financial systems will never have to be retooled. You cannot say that countries never change their global status of predominance as leaders are constantly being replaced all the time.

All these things commonly happen and will do so in the future. No one can say that the time for anything specific to happen is *now*, but we should all heed the warning that we better be prepared with insurance for some high probability calamities that might happen in the world's financial system. Gold and silver are the means to protect ourselves.

At the end of a fiat currency system, countries typically experience one of either two fates:

(1) either a deflationary collapse with debt defaults, or
(2) an inflationary collapse with subsequent currency reform.

In both of these possibilities, gold and silver are some of the most important assets you can hold to protect yourself. They enable you to preserve your wealth during hard times and often protect it from a government hell-bent on confiscating your money through any means it has.

Gold and silver are highly portable. You can take them anywhere in the world and they will still hold their value. You can also easily store them away and then exchange them for money, goods or services whenever you need it. They enable you to store some of your assets in a better way than in a paper currency that is declining in value.

Ultimately when you are saving your money you want to protect it as much as possible. Gold and silver coins and bars are one of the best ways to achieve this objective during a financial crisis. If history does in fact repeat itself, the cost of this insurance will be tremendously cheap in relation to the wealth it would conserve in the future.

If we go into a period of hyperinflation due to excessive money printing that grows vertically - because we cannot possibly fund our debt obligations yet must still satisfy those obligations by money printing or the system will implode - then the nominal value of gold and silver will probably go up very much as they went up in the 1970s. A similar situation happened in France during the French Revolution when gold increased 288 times in value in just five years, 1790 to 1795.

When money printing grows at a vertical rate that it isn't sustainable, the infinite rate of increase never makes what is around worth more than it was worth in earlier times. Thus at some point NOW, *in our current times,* the value of the dollar (and its fiat counterparts) will have to decline and at that time the precious metals, since they have an independent international pricing, will shine as the best store of value through that process.

Billionaire resource investor Eric Sprott (of Sprott Asset Management) wrote on his blog: "If, by contrast, quantitative easing, also known as counterfeiting works and the world goes back into a boom, then natural resources will again do well because demand recovers and supply is still constrained because of two or three decades of underinvesting. Right now I feel like I'm sitting in a situation where I flip the coin and as I said it is 'heads I win, tails I win.' That's a wonderful place for natural resource investors around the world." In other words, he feels that gold and silver will go higher no matter what happens in the future. If crisis strikes, a shortage of precious metals might be so acute that you might not be able to easily source them in the marketplace at that time. Prudence therefore requires one to think about acting now.

Conclusion

My final conclusion to all this is the following. Many times the people who lost the most money during difficult financial times such as during the retooling of a financial system were those who did not make provisions to survive the maelstrom. They didn't see anything coming so they didn't prepare with adequate financial insurance because they were trapped within an outdated worldview. Gold and silver holdings serve as the proper form of insurance for our present era of black swan financial events. As financial stability decreases faith in precious metals increases. They are insurance against errant financial policies, the follies of international central bankers, and unexpected financial catastrophes caused by a world overstocked with unpayable debts.

Time and again one of the best protections for financial times that shook the fate of nations was to hold precious metals. Holding gold and silver has been one of the few dependable ways to protect and preserve your wealth throughout all sorts of financial crises, and in particular the possible financial changes that *are* probably coming.

Of course, this has always been dependent on the fact that you actually *own* the gold and silver rather than that someone *owes* you gold and silver. If your ownership is not in your complete control, there is always the possibility that the other party might not satisfy its obligations to you in a crisis.

If a bank owes you gold and silver, for instance, that won't do you any good during a crisis if that counterparty bank becomes insolvent or the government changes the laws and tries to confiscate it from the banks. That's why most people try to hold precious metals in their own hands or in some safe location outside the fragile banking system.

Whenever any nation runs into financial troubles, people ordinarily rush to safety by either exchanging their cash for a safer, stronger currency or by buying precious metals. First, they run from their domestic fiat currency to other currencies because that is the easiest and most familiar option. This is why we talked about opening a foreign bank account in last month's issue. Typically they try to exchange their own currency for the world's reserve currency since it is usually considered the safest currency around.

For most people this has been the easiest option to financially protect themselves during domestic troubles. *When the reserve currency itself is in financial danger, however, then your next best option is to turn to gold and silver.* They have no debt attached to them and no counterparty risk that they will fail, but they can easily serve as readily exchangeable money. They have stood as an emergency store of value for thousands of years.

This is where the value of precious metals shines. *They enable you to store your savings in an alternative, better way than paper currencies during a financial crisis. In difficult times, owning gold and silver often represents the best type of financial insurance.*

Fiat paper currencies, reserve currencies and financial systems may come and go, but gold and silver have survived them all.

Hundreds of fiat currencies in the world have passed away into the realm of non-existence, but this has never happened for gold and silver. They have been money for thousands of years and you can bet for sure that they will retain their value into the future no matter what happens to King Dollar.

Gold and silver have maintained their purchasing power throughout history, especially when monetary systems collapse, precisely because they cannot be printed into existence. The world has seen many instances of wars, dictatorships, political collapse and collapsing currencies, hyperinflation, depressions and more ... and throughout them all gold and silver have continued to hold their value.

No one knows when our own fiat currency system will eventually collapse but indeed it one day will. It is not a question of *if* but of *when*. Gold and silver are the insurance policy one holds against that event and other calamities that might one day severely shake the financial system. They are what you buy and store away for your household and children.

When the dust all clears after a period of severe financial trouble, then at the end of the day gold and silver have always survived. They have always retained some sort of value in the new world while other assets have been thoroughly destroyed. They even enable you to buy up assets on the cheap whenever a crisis reaches its end.

Remember that people commonly buy insurance policies, even though the probability of accidents is low, because the benefits of having insurance *far outweigh the costs.* This is a common thing to do and no one generally thinks much about it.

Holding gold and silver in your portfolio, instead of just holding paper assets, is like having an insurance policy for troubles in the financial system. In particular, you should especially think of them as a form of insurance *against central bank imprudence since central bankers,* with their unlimited money printing policies, are the root seeds behind financial destruction.

Basically, gold and silver are a protection against monetary recklessness and fiscal foolishness. They have always been the premier investments when governments were acting fiscally or monetarily bizarre.

If history does in fact repeat itself, the cost of this form of financial insurance may one day be tremendously cheap in relation to the wealth it could preserve.

Hence, while gold and silver are often a "great investment" for reasons of supply and demand imbalances, you should also think of holding some precious metals not because they will go up in value but because they are a basic protection against the possibility of extreme financial outcomes. They are insurance against central bank risk.

Right now there are negative real yields on bank deposits, T-bonds and T-bills which makes the opportunity cost of owning gold and silver essentially nil. Because of legal changes in the U.S. banking system, now even holding cash in a bank subjects you to financial risks that never existed previously. That's because you have now become an "unsecured creditor" to the bank and your funds can be taken if the bank goes under. In other countries your bank deposits entail the risks of bail-ins that might also result in your cash disappearing.

Because people all over are finally waking up and clearly recognizing these risks, this is a major reason why we are seeing fresh money – especially from Asia - buy physical gold and silver as a safety hedge and safe haven investment that represents financial insurance. This Russian, Chinese, Indian and southeast Asian demand cumulatively far outstrips all available mine supply already!

I believe that we are near one of those historical inflection points that will eventually require a re-juggling of the world's financial system. I also believe that China, Russia and other nations are trying to replace the predominance of the dollar in world trade, which may ultimately threaten its reserve currency status in time. Excessive government debts and QE monetary policies by central banks, overleveraged and undercapitalized banks, and excessive derivative trades and swap agreements have reached levels that now threaten the world's financial system in total.

Because many nations are starting to trade oil using other currencies, they are abandoning the use of the dollar (Petrodollar), and hence trillions in oil derivative contracts are presently being unwound around the world. This unwinding requires a temporary upwards demand for the dollar to settle those trades. For instance, if you want to pay off a loan (like a derivatives contract) you have to have a large sum of money to dissolve the loan. Therefore, entities across the world need to locate trillions of dollars to unwind, dissolve and settle oil contracts denominated in the USD.

As demand for the Petrodollar is fractured due to moves by China and Russia, the Saudis and other nations will no doubt dump their dollars and T-bonds and buy gold and other stable currencies instead. King Dollar will no longer sit on the throne. It therefore seems prudent to be a gold and silver investor in some measure to prevent the loss of its reserve status or importance in world trade. You must prepare yourself for this because the replacement of a reserve currency has happened in the past and it is actually happening this very moment. It is not theory. Events are unfolding exactly along the lines that show the dollar will lose its dominance in world trade and its reserve status may be imperiled.

Furthermore, the odds clearly and strongly favor something going badly wrong in the world's economic, financial and banking conditions – an unforeseen "black swan" event that cannot be contained - and precious metals are the one form of insurance that could protect you against these unforeseen calamities. Faith in gold usually rises as instability increases, and thus summarizing it all it is prudent for investors to consider holding some gold and silver in their portfolios.

CHAPTER 14:
DIRECT REGISTRATION TO PROTECT YOUR STOCKS

Let's talk about something shocking that might help you protect your stock investments. The topic is disturbing because it concerns a legal security breach you might want to patch in order to protect your stock portfolio. Please understand that this is not legal advice even though it brings up legal maters.

Let us start out with a simple question: Do you legally own the stocks in your brokerage account? If you answered "yes" then I must break some unfortunate news to you. You are wrong. The true *legal ownership* of all the stocks in your brokerage account does not reside in your name!

The truth is that you don't *legally* own the stocks or any of the bonds in your brokerage account but are a beneficiary owner. A company called the Depository Trust & Clearing Corporation legally owns them. Unless you have "direct registration" of your stocks, the true legal owner of all your shares is the DTCC (Depository Trust & Clearing Corporation, also known as the DTC or Depository Trust Company), which goes under the name of CEDE and Company.

The DTCC is the world's largest securities depository and holds trillions in assets for its participants and their customer. The public remains largely in the dark about its existence because it is a privately owned depository bank for institutional and brokerage firms only. It processes all of their book entry settlement transactions.

Here is how this works. When someone buys a share of stock the transaction must be cleared before it becomes finalized. People trade stock shares with each other via their brokers, and these trades must eventually be cleared to make sure that those who bought shares get them legally transferred from those who sold the same shares. A clearance of accounting must always be conducted. Buyers and sellers must be matched. Accounts must be settled.

Many years ago, owning stocks meant that you would have the stock certificates lying in your safe or safety deposit box. If and when you wanted to trade them mean that you then had to get them shipped off to a broker to conduct the transaction. This became very cumbersome as time went on and therefore a shortcut was invented. Your broker would now hold your stocks (instead of you) and your broker would handle all the relevant paper transfers. In order for your broker to legally be able to hold stocks for you, the stocks were placed under the broker's "street name." This meant that your shares were then held in the name of the brokerage company, which was just holding them in trust so that it could efficiently trade them for you. In reality you became the beneficiary rather than the owner of the shares, which was all fine and dandy if everything went right.

Over time the rules were again changed so that the brokers no longer put the stocks in their own name. Instead, what is typically done now is that shares are held under the name of "Cede and Company" or "Cede & Co" or some such variation. In other words, decades ago shares were usually registered in your broker's street name, but this is no longer allowed. Because broker names are used no longer and your own name is not used, the DTCC is now the standard Registered Owner (holder) of your stocks and bonds through "Cede and Company."

The DTCC is therefore the legal property-holder, share-holder, stock-holder or direct owner of your stocks and bonds. Your name appears nowhere on the book entry or certificate itself as the actual owner of any stock shares you purchase. Your shares are held in "street name" because the DTCC holds them in the name of the broker-dealer or the custodian bank you use. You do not appear as the underlying shareholder.

Where does your name appear in all of this? Technically you have been designated by the legal registered owner, the DTCC, as the *Beneficial Owner* of your transactions. This means that your lawful rights in any stock or bond are confined to that of a successor or heir.

Beneficial shareholders, which include individuals as well as institutional investors, do not maintain physical possession of their certificates; third-party broker-dealers or custodian banks hold their securities on their behalf or they are simply held by electronic book keeping.

Here is how this all now works. When you buy stock, the transaction is usually cleared within a 3-day settlement period. The company that does this is the DTCC, which has private owners. Through its subsidiaries the DTCC provides clearing, settlement and information services for equities, corporate and municipal bonds, government and mortgage-backed securities, money market instruments and over-the-counter derivatives. The DTCC basically handles the clearing process for all sorts of financial instruments, including your stocks and bonds.

In other words, the clearing and settlement of most all stock and bond transactions occurs within the DTCC, which is the central counter party risk-taker. It processes the vast majority of all stock transactions in the United States as well as for many other countries.

Rather than rely on the physical delivery of certificates, the DTCC uses electronic book-entry to facilitate the custody and settlement of shares and share transactions. To facilitate this, stock and bond certificates are technically held in the name of DTCC's private holding company, Cede and Company.

The problem in all this with that is that "Cede" isn't just some dummy name, but an actual corporation that the DTCC controls. If you ask anybody who actually knows about it they will naturally tell you that it is all a formality to serve you better, of course. No one can argue with that because it should be that way and usually is that way. You *should* expect it to be that way into the future. The key word is "should."

If DTCC and Cede stick to their job and just keep your stock and bond transactions flowing smoothly then things work fine. They have until now and probably will continue that way into the future. Personally, I really don't have any worries about this myself. However, if somebody at some point should decide otherwise, *or there's some national U.S. or international financial emergency of some type that interferes with share transference*, it is always possible that the DTCC just might not give you your stocks back because legally it owns them. Approximately 99% of all stocks in the U.S. appear to be legally owned by them.

There is always the strange, rare, almost impossible possibility that some cyber mishap might destroy all evidence of your shares in the system, including all the electronic backups that would make this nearly impossible. Perhaps the government decides that it will convert your bond holdings into something else by fiat decree because of some financial emergency. I cannot foresee anything myself, but you cannot foresee the fat tail, six sigma black swan events called the "unexpected."

Nevertheless, let's be clear about this so far. The DTCC is the legal owner of that bond or stock listed on your brokerage account, not you. You are a beneficiary owner. Rather than in your name, your shares are legally registered in the DTCC's "street name," Cede & Company. Cede & Company is the legal registered owner or agent and represents the aggregate position of the Depository Trust Company that is the primary safekeeping, clearing, and settlement organization for securities traded in the United States.

For legal or safety purposes some people want to be the direct registered owner of their stocks and bonds rather than have their brokerage firm or the DTCC (or Cede & Company) serve in that capacity. A "Registered Holder" literally possesses, owns, and holds his stocks or bonds with his name appearing on the face of the certificate. Being a registered holder means that the company that issued the stock or bond certificate has registered the owner's (holder's) name on their official books.

This is not the most convenient way, but is actually *the safest way to own a paper asset*. You literally possess the fully registered certificate and only you can transfer or sell it. You have complete control over it. By all rights and definitions of law, you are the actual owner rather than the beneficial owner. You have it, you hold it, you possess it, and it's yours.

How can you become the legal owner of your shares rather than just the beneficial owner? The answer is that you must get your share assets out of the name of Cede and Company. Ok, so how? And what are the pros and cons?

Direct Registration

In order to regain the direct legal ownership in your name for your share certificates you must ask for transfer out of DTCC into what is called "direct registration." Direct registration, or DRS (direct registration system), is the means to directly own your stock and bond holdings without any intermediary such as Cede and Company (or your brokerage firm). With direct registration, your name is put on the ownership accounting books of the transfer agent used by the stock or bond company that has issued shares. This totally eliminates your broker and the DTCC clearing agent as proxy owners for your shares.

The shares that you hold in direct registration are evidenced by a statement from the transfer agent (a company such as American Stock Transfer & Trust Company) sent directly to you. This is what you put in your safety deposit box, namely a statement from the transfer agent of the direct registration of stock certificates in your name. This is called the DRS Transaction Advice Form, which you receive following each transaction involving your shares held with DRS, and it contains your DRS account information.

The information that you are the owner of shares is also kept electronically by the transfer agent, as you would naturally expect, but you want to keep any notifications as a backup. In life it is always smart to play things safe by keeping paper copies of any notifications that are important like this. The transfer agent maintains evidence of your share ownership through electronic book-entry without issuing you paper stock certificates precisely because it avoids the need for issuing physical share certificates. It will issue paper stock certificates if you ask for them, but since that's a hassle you must request this service and pay for it. You always have that option and also the right to do so.

Some firms charge a small fee for direct registration, which should never exceed $50. Some brokerage firms decide to serve their customers and even charge nothing to move something to DRS. In any case, the typical DRS process at a brokerage is as follows:

1. To get shares to the brokerage from a transfer agent you must fill out a special brokerage form that they submit to the transfer agent.

2. The transfer agents vary greatly as to the time it takes them to deliver the shares. This could take a few days up to two weeks, but they transfer the owner to your name.

Normally a broker wants to control your shares in order to guarantee them the sell order. It wants that commission. In controlling your shares it can also make them available for short selling. Therefore there is a lot of motivation for brokers to resist your request for direct registration. There are many reasons why brokers don't want you to use direct registration and none of those reasons assists you except the reason of convenience.

Why You Should Not Keep Shares With Your Broker

Jim Sinclair once said: "So far 4 out of every 5 investors who speak to their brokers and/or banks are talked out of direct registration by ignorance or lies. Direct registration takes you out of the system. Direct registration takes you off the balance sheet of the broker and/or clearinghouse. Direct registration can increase protection for tax favored accounts. However, how can I help people who will not help themselves and who fully know that they are rolling the dice on the integrity of their financial agent for theirs and their families' financial survival?"

Here are the actual risks that apply when your shares are held with a brokerage:

- In the event of a systemic crisis you will likely have no access to you brokerage account.

- If your brokerage account is a margin account it might be possible for your broker to loan your shares to other entities who are short selling your stock.

- Because of the Sentinel case and the MF Global legal cases it is possible that your shares can potentially be used as collateral for a brokerage's own speculative positions. This is a big risk because it just might be the one that precipitates a financial crisis.

- Your shares are exposed to counterparty risk in regards to the clearing house and potentially the parent company of the brokerage.

You can see that direct registration is not an investment decision but an issue of security and protection. They are your shares - not the broker's or DTCC's - and if you want them in direct registration or in certificate form then that is your right. Doing so only makes a buy or sell transaction more costly, less timely and thus more inefficient, but that is your right if you want to do that. The ownership of your shares via certificates (available through direct registration) means:

- Your shares cannot be lent out by a broker for short selling.

- There is zero counterparty risk.

- You have *physical possession* of your shares, meaning that the shares cannot be seized or confiscated digitally or somehow digitally disappear due to cyber attacks of any sort. Holding stocks or bonds as certificates also makes it hard for governments to confiscate your funds.

- The certificates (your shares) can easily be moved to any location in the world at will.

As a stockholder who holds certificates you have a direct relationship with the company (the company whose stock or bond you buy) in question. This means that they must pay any dividends directly to you rather than to a third party (as is the case when your shares are held at a brokerage via a street name).

The Steps

Now if the direct registration and certificate process sounds good to you, let's go through the steps on how to do this.

You must first inform your broker (usually through written instructions so that there is a legal trail) that you want direct registration of your shares. Most of the large brokerages, such as Fidelity, will tell you how long it normally takes but if you are using a small brokerage and expect sluggishness, specify a time frame within which to have this executed. If your broker does not want to carry out your instructions for direct registration then find a new broker who will.

Most U.S. stocks offer direct registration. If your company does not offer direct registration then you can just ask for paper certificates to be issued to you in your name. Obtaining paper certificates is very easy. You simply ask your broker to tell the company's transfer agent about your request and then the transfer agent will print the share certificates and send them to you in the mail. The fee for this service is usually about $20 per company. If your shares are currently held via direct registration then you bypass your broker. They are out of the loop so you don't ask your broker to do anything. Rather, you ask the company's transfer agent directly.

Now comes the time for selling your shares. To sell shares that are in direct registration you must instruct the company's transfer agent to transfer the shares back to your broker; your broker needs to have them in its possession before it can sell them. After this request to the transfer agent, usually within 24 hours your shares will be available for liquidation. If you hold paper certificates in your hands, however, you need to first deliver the certificates back to the transfer agent with the instructions to then transfer the shares to your broker. Once again, generally your shares would be available for sale within about a day or so of being received by the broker.

Usually there is no fee for the selling side of the process - from either direct registration or paper certificates - but you must confirm this with your transfer agent and broker. Situations and policies change, but that's the normal process at the present.

Summary

Here's the whole story of direct registration in short.

Basically, if you purchase any stock or bond through a broker then it is being held for you under a "street name" of the DTCC (usually Cede & Company) unless you have specifically requested to elect direct registration. Whenever you purchase stocks or bonds without becoming the registered holder you simply become a "beneficial owner" and not the direct legal owner of those instruments.

There is a big difference between being the *actual owner* and *beneficial owner* of any asset. In most cases you will never experience any problems, but if there should ever be a calamity of some type in the financial system – as many advisors are expecting because of rising global debts, excessive money printing by the central banks and an expected decline of the U.S. dollar - then you should understand that there are some risks as to the difference.

Directly registering shares in your name is a relatively simple task, but brokers do not actively promote direct registration because it is in the brokerage firm's best interests that you leave your shares in the street name. Nonetheless, here's how to do it.

First, tell your broker (brokerage firm) to transfer the stock shares to the relevant transfer agent. The cost of a transfer should be minimal and not exceed $50 per company. Once that process is complete, your stock shares are then digitally registered with the transfer agent via electronic book-keeping. The direction registration process is then completed. You will then have an internet account with the transfer agent (who registers that you own the shares) where you can view your holdings. You can see that you own them by just logging in and checking your account.

If you just have a book entry for stocks or bonds through DRS then you won't be issued share certificates, but if you want absolute ownership protection then obtaining actual paper certificates is the one extra step you can take. This is the step of obtaining an actual physical paper share certificate and holding it in your own hands.

While direct registration offers protection, personally possessing your stock share certificates provides the highest level of insurance. Of course, you mustn't lose the certificates! When you hold the shares in your hand with your own name on them it is easy to prove who the owner is. The brokerage house cannot loan them out and dividends are paid to you directly. The problem is that you can lose the certificates and it is troublesome to deliver them back to the broker when you want to sell them. That's the deficiency in the process.

Nonetheless, once the transfer agent has you in their records as the owner of some company's shares you can direct the transfer agent to issue certificates to you in your name. Direct registration is the first part of the process, and afterwards you can have certificates issued by the transfer agent. After those certificates are issued and mailed to you, possession of those stock certificates will give you the total protection of getting your investments "out of the financial system."

Certification (holding paper certificates) offers the absolute highest level of protection for your assets. That is, as long as you hold your shares in a safe place. In terms of the task of safekeeping certificates, this is something that most people are quite capable of doing since it is the same as guarding a passport, insurance policy, some gold coins or other important documents.

Certificates are of no real value to any thief as they cannot be simply exchanged for cash. Insurance companies also allow you to take out an insurance policy covering your shares for loss or theft. For instance, when you are mailing your certificates to a transfer agent, it is recommended that you insure your package for two percent (2%) of the current market value of the shares, which is the cost of a bond to have your certificates replaced if they are lost or stolen. If you were to lose your certificates usually there would be a fee ranging between 1.5% – 3% of the total value of the shares in question to have them reissued.

For most people, just keeping shares in direct registration is easier than keeping them in certificate form. I personally favor DRS over holding certificates simply because of the factors of convenience. It reduces the time, costs and risks associated with storing the paper share certificates and eliminates the bother of having to replace them if they are lost or stolen. It's just cheaper, quicker and overall more efficient. Nevertheless you now know how to go to the highest form of protection and security if you wish to maximize the financial security of your assets. It is hard to find information on this technique, but now you have an explanatory guide to help you.

CHAPTER 15:
FOREIGN BANK ACCOUNTS

Many people question the wisdom of opening up a foreign bank account. Their biggest question is, "Should I have one? Is this a smart thing to do and a safe thing to do? Which country is best?"

In today's world of potentially gigantic black swan events that can destroy your wealth, if you can open up an offshore bank account then you should certainly consider doing so in a safe country with strong economic and financial situations. Here's why.

I could tell you multiple stories about various friends who had to abandon their home countries in an emergency and totally give up all the assets they had accumulated in life. Sometimes they left because of war or persecution, but they had to find opportunity elsewhere and a means to stay alive. You can read the biography of billionaire investor-trader George Soros to see what he had to do to stay alive in Hungary before he finally escaped the country. What prevented most of my own friends from being totally penniless was their friends and family in their new foreign locations, or having stored some money away in a foreign bank account where their government could not reach it.

There are many reasons you should open an offshore bank account but none of these reasons should ever be for illegal activities such as money laundering or tax evasion. For any foreign account you open you must still pay tax on your offshore earnings and disclose to the U.S. Treasury and IRS the details of your account. You cannot hide this information even if you tried because FATCA requires that nearly every single bank on the planet enter into an information-sharing agreement with the IRS.

Why then should you open an offshore bank account? Let's go into the reasons you might consider. A foreign bank account means that some of your money is held outside of your country and that is a great means of asset protection. By being located overseas this can one day help prevent you from having your assets frozen, seized or confiscated by a wrongful domestic government agency. It can help protect you in case of a frivolous lawsuit. It is also another way to protect your life savings against all sorts of domestic "black swan" events that could imperil a national banking system and cripple your savings.

Governments also sometimes institute policies harmful to your financial health such as bail-ins, capital controls, asset seizures, nationalizations of retirement savings, bank deposit taxes and negative interest rates. You also might be able to partially escape these events with a foreign bank account.

The benefits of having a foreign bank account include insurance in case of an domestic emergency, so building some international diversification with an offshore bank account *if you can open one* is highly recommended. Wherever you live, other countries may offer sounder banking systems than those within your own nation. Right now, the beauty is that those banks might even offer higher interest rates. And of course, a foreign bank account can help protect you against political risks so that your money is out of the reach of greedy government bureaucrats.

It doesn't hurt when a foreign bank account might pay significantly higher interest rates than a domestic U.S. account. If the account is denominated in a strong foreign currency, there might be foreign exchange benefits to a foreign account as well. Basically, when you internationalize some of your savings, holding your money in foreign currencies can sometimes protect your purchasing power if and when your own domestic currency declines in value. If you think that the dollar may lose its reserve currency status, or decline in value for some other reason, foreign currencies are therefore a must.

Many analysts currently consider both the U.S. banking system and the U.S. government insolvent. American banks are certainly under-capitalized and have trillions in dangerous, over-leveraged derivatives and swap exposure, but we can say that about many other countries as well.

The U.S. Depositor is Now an Unsecured Lender

What many people have not closely considered, however, is that U.S. laws have also changed so that they now classify your bank CDs and passbook savings accounts as "unsecured credit" provided to the banks. In other words, bank account depositors are now classified as *unsecured lenders (creditors) to the banks*. This leaves you without standing if your bank goes into failure or gets liquidated.

You might be thinking of FDIC insurance when you read that, but you cannot count on FIDC insurance to protect all your savings if a U.S. bank goes bad. You could still lose your savings if a bank gets liquidated because now those savings are no longer considered yours since you gave them to the bank (with what is now classified) as unsecured credit. Which creditor stands in line before you? Get ready to see who they put in front of you in the line.

The 2005 bankruptcy reforms made the counter-parties to derivatives contracts senior to unsecured lenders! In other words, your bank's hefty derivative exposure is now considered "secured credit." Basically, your deposited funds are being used to manage your bank's derivatives exposure, which is being secured by your savings, but those savings themselves are unsecured credit.

Why did they make those illogical and unethical changes? You will have to come to the conclusion for yourself. It means danger is at hand and they are setting things up just in case the dam breaks.

As an American, if that doesn't frighten you enough to consider a foreign bank account then I don't know what will. Every shred of objective evidence along these lines suggests that it doesn't make sense to hold 100% of your savings solely in the U.S. anymore. In today's world a foreign bank account is a wise means of asset protection. There are many countries, such as in Asia, offering sounder banking systems and banks.

From an investment perspective, non-U.S. accounts certainly add substantial diversification to overall asset allocation. An offshore account helps diversify your sovereign risk so that you can protect your wealth and financial freedom. For all these reasons you really should consider holding some money offshore.

Obamacare Fears – The Medical Rationale

If you are an American, another factor you should take into account for this decision are some possible future implications of Obamacare. Some forward-looking analysts have voiced the concern that seniors, for economic reasons that a cash-constrained government may one day face in the future be denied care under the Affordable Care Act that we call "Obamacare." In the future, unless it explodes or is done away with by law it is *very conceivable* that health care might in some way or to some degree be rationed and denied to those who have the shortest life expectancy or whose "treatment" may cost too much. This seems to be a trend we have seen in other nations. Consider that if you were a government and didn't have cash but promised all these expensive services, wouldn't that be the logical thing to do as well? If you have to put a cap on costs to balance your budget what are you going to do?

Analysts are painting this possible picture for situations such as expensive heart surgery or cancer treatments for an eighty-year old individual who, because of his or her age, isn't expected to live long. Another option is for expensive operations like knee and hip replacements to be mostly denied. Any such denial might force seniors to seek medical attention overseas, and thus the benefits of having an offshore bank account as you will soon see.

No one can foresee the future implications of Obamacare, so this worry is probably overblown at present. However, many analysts feel that Obamacare can and will lead to the eventual rationing (or delay) of medical services for the elderly because otherwise its numbers just don't add up. If the elderly in the future are regularly denied medical care because of their age, a lot of Americans will have to go offshore for treatments being denied or delayed.

You will certainly need money for a foreign medical procedure and this is where the critical potential complication comes in. Because of the state of U.S. government finances, many are forecasting the possibility of currency controls in the future. If there one day might be restrictions in transferring your funds from your bank account to a medical facility in another country, this means you might have to already have some of your money outside the country if you wanted to use it in this way.

What some analysts are asking us to imagine is the following scenario: you need a medical procedure that has been denied by Obamacare. You find an out-of-country medical facility that will perform the procedure, but when you attempt to wire funds to the medical facility the U.S. government blocks the transfer. This scenario is why placing some assets offshore could be the most important *healthcare* decision a person can make. It may not be a financial decision but a medical decision that prompts this course of action. While this scenario may seem entirely fictitious, it exposes yet another reason for opening a foreign bank account. An offshore bank account can protect you against capital controls so that you will always have access to medical treatments abroad.

A foreign bank account will certainly help you diversify away from the risks of the American banking system and holding U.S. dollars. Common banking options are found by looking to Asia, Europe, the Mid-East, Caribbean or South America. If you are European, an account outside of the European banking system will help insulate you from Euro woes. On the domestic side, it will also protect you against European bail-ins, asset confiscations, and currency controls if they should happen. Any savings you have denominated in a foreign currency will also help to insulate you from your domestic government's policy of making their currency less valuable each year because of excessive money printing and the resulting inflation this causes.

People typically try to protect themselves from these risks by purchasing hard assets such as farmland, oil wells, gold and silver, lumber and so on. If the asset produces income you can live off of during an emergency then that is a priority. However, holding your money overseas in a strong currency is another way to accomplish similar aims to some degree. It is yet another type of financial insurance policy that will not just protect you but also provide you with some peace of mind.

The question now is: "Which countries in the world would be safest for foreign accounts? Where can you go for the world's safest banks?"

The "holy grail" of an offshore bank account would be an account in a country with an extremely safe banking system, where your deposits are insured, where there is an appreciating foreign currency, where the account pays a higher interest rate than domestic U.S. deposits, and where the funds are easily accessed in times of need. This is why many individuals immediately think of Singapore, Hong Kong, Australia, Canada and Switzerland as potential foreign banks. Other countries are popular too so how can you decide which country is best?

There is no one way and no definitive answer as to which foreign country or banking system is best. No one can claim that. However, after completing a "deep dive analysis" we can come to some conclusions that might help to guide you to some conclusions. The type of analysis I'm about to show you can be done for any year of interest simply by referencing some Wikipedia pages and some other financial rankings.

The Safest Banks in the World

Every year *Global Finance* magazine publishes a report called the "50 Safest Banks" in the world. The ranking is produced after evaluating the total assets of the 500 largest banks in the world along with their long-term credit ratings from Moody's, Standard & Poor's and Fitch. According to *Global Finance*, the "World's 50 Safest Banks" in 2014 were:

1. KfW - Germany

2. Zu☐rcher Kantonalbank - Switzerland
3. Landwirtschaftliche Rentenbank - Germany
4. L-Bank - Germany
5. Bank Nederlandse Gemeenten - Netherlands
6. Nederlandse Waterschapsbank - Netherlands
7. NRW.BANK - Germany
8. Caisse des Dépo☐ts et Consignations - France
9. Banque et Caisse d'Epargne de l'Etat - Luxembourg
10. Société de Financement Local (SFIL) - France
11. TD Bank Group - Canada
12. DBS Bank - Singapore
13. Oversea-Chinese Banking Corporation - Singapore
14. United Overseas Bank - Singapore
15. Rabobank - Netherlands
16. Royal Bank of Canada - Canada
17. National Australia Bank - Australia
18. Commonwealth Bank of Australia - Australia
19. ANZ Group - Australia
20. Westpac - Australia
21. Nordea - Sweden
22. Bank of Nova Scotia - Canada
23. Svenska Handelsbanken - Sweden
24. Hang Seng Bank – Hong Kong
25. National Bank Of Abu Dhabi - UAE
26. Caisse centrale Desjardins - Canada
27. HSBC – United Kingdom
28. Sparkassen-Finanzgruppe (Sparkasse) – Germany
29. China Development Bank - China
30. Bank of Montreal - Canada
31. CIBC - Canada
32. Agricultural Development Bank of China - China
33. Export-Import Bank of China - China
34. HSBC France - France
35. Korea Finance Corporation – South Korea
36. Industrial Bank of Korea – South Korea
37. Korea Development Bank – South Korea
38. Pohjola - Finland
39. CoBank – United States
40. AgriBank – United States
41. National Bank of Kuwait - Kuwait
42. Export-Import Bank of Korea (KEXIM) – South Korea
43. BancoEstado - Chile
44. Banque Cantonale Vaudoise - Switzerland
45. Agfirst – United States
46. DZ Bank - Germany

47. BNY Mellon – United States
48. U.S. Bancorp – United States
49. Qatar National Bank - Qatar
50. Samba Financial Group – Saudi Arabia

I'm not entirely satisfied with its system for determining "safe" banks since it primarily takes into account assets and credit ratings. I believe no one, including *Global Finance* and the big three credit ratings agencies (Moody's, Standard&Poor's and Fitch) *adequately take into account the excessive swap and derivatives exposure of these banks that could send many of them into bankruptcy*, and which could quickly take down their interlinked partners in a domino series of events.

If we factor in the potential disastrous effects that could happen because of "black swan" events related to derivatives, swaps, excessive money printing, interest rate increases, unexpected QE effects gone haywire and so on, these lists are misleading as to a bank's "safety." Nonetheless, these lists provide extremely useful insights because if we count the number of banks in each country for the world rankings, we find that the following countries show the largest concentration of "safe banks."

1. Germany
2. United States
3. Canada
4. Australia
5. Singapore
6. Netherlands

European banks generally dominate the top spots in this list, but of course these positions would be threatened should there be a breakdown in the Euro. Singapore banks remain the strongest in Asia and Chile comes out as the top contender for South America.

If we were to look at the "safest banks" for just the emerging markets alone, the lists would be heavily weighted toward banks in countries like South Korea, Saudi Arabia, China, UAE and Chile, but many of these regional banks are still not "strong enough" to make it into the larger list of the world's safest banks. Nevertheless we should make note of these countries in our mind because the emerging markets are the wave of the future.

After examining 86 countries, the Standard&Poors rating agency also came up with its own list of the five countries with the least-risky banking systems. Those countries, in no particular order, were reported to be Australia, Switzerland, Canada, Germany, and Hong Kong.

Now *Global Finance* broke down its macro rating of the world's safest banks into safest banks by world sector. It said that the following were the safest banks in Asia which are also ranked in order of descending safety:

DBS Bank – Singapore

Oversea-Chinese Banking Corporation – Singapore
United Overseas Bank – Singapore
Hang Seng Bank – Hong Kong
China Development Bank – China
Agricultural Development Bank of China – China
Export-Import Bank of China – China
Korea Finance Corporation – South Korea
Industrial Bank of Korea – South Korea
Korea Development Bank – South Korea
Export-Import Bank of Korea (KEXIM) – South Korea

It reported the following banks as the safest emerging market banks in the Middle East and Africa:

National Bank Of Abu Dhabi – UAE
National Bank of Kuwait – Kuwait
Qatar National Bank – Qatar
Samba Financial Group – Saudi Arabia
National Commercial Bank - Saudi Arabia
Al Rajhi Bank - Saudi Arabia
Riyadh Bank - Saudi Arabia
Abu Dhabi Commercial Bank – UAE
SABB - Saudi Arabia
Banque Saudi Fransi - Saudi Arabia
Union National Bank - UAE

Here are *Global Finance's* 2014 rankings for the safest banks in Latin America:

BancoEstado – Chile
Banco de Chile – Chile
Banco Santander Chile – Chile
Banco de Crédito e Inversiones – Chile
HSBC Mexico – Mexico
Banobras – Mexico
Banco de Crédito BCP – Peru
Banco Santander Mexico – Mexico
BBVA Continental – Peru
Scotiabank Inverlat – Mexico

You can search through the rankings to find non-U.S. banks but if you wanted to determine the safest banks or credit unions in the United States then you should start by turning to the financial safety rankings put out by Weiss Research, namely its WeissRatings.com and FinancialRatingsSeries.com publications. The Weiss financial strength ratings take into account a bank's profitability, asset quality, liquidity, capitalization and stability. This is the first place where I would start.

Before you run out to open up a foreign account, you cannot just use lists like this without doing some thinking. You should perform some rudimentary analysis to get a feel for the financially strongest, and thus safest countries of the world that might have the fewest potential problems with their banking systems. Since most people wouldn't know where to even start with this task, I want to lead you through a little bit of analysis that you can do on your own every year to get a rough feel for the health of nations. You can draw some inferences about banking systems from there.

The Financially Strongest Countries in the World

There is no guarantee that a financially strong country will have a strong banking system, or that your bank account would be protected in that location from various calamities. Nonetheless, you will get all sorts of valuable insights if you start to analyze countries in terms of various financial parameters, so let's do this using Wikipedia.

First, let's start by trying to determine which countries are the *richest in the world on a relative basis*. Even though the measurement isn't perfect, we are going to look at GDP per capita instead of straight GDP so that we can create a relative measure of economic strength. This will be our first rough proxy for wealth. Nothing is perfect, but that's our first step into this sort of simplified analysis that you can do at home.

If you go to Wikipedia and search for "List of countries by GDP (nominal) per capita" you will find rankings provided by the IMF, World Bank, CIA and United Nations. We will keep our analysis simple by focusing on just the top twenty five countries on the IMF list: Luxembourg, Norway, Qatar, Switzerland, Australia, Singapore, Denmark, USA, Canada, Sweden, Austria, Kuwait, Netherlands, Finland, Ireland, Iceland, Belgium, Germany, United Arab Emirates, France, Israel, New Zealand, United Kingdom, Brunei, and Japan.

Next, let's consider that a country might be rich in terms of a high GDP or GDP per capita, but of those nations, those who are *net lenders to the world* (with a positive trade balance) would be economically stronger than the others. Think about it … *in general* would this not be so? If the world were to go into a recession, for instance, wouldn't those countries with a positive trade balance (more exports than imports) be the ones most likely to still have goods demanded by the rest of the world, and therefore be the ones best equipped to keep their economies in tact? If the world went into a recession, wouldn't the strongest net exporters most likely still be better off than the largest importers?

Here is how to use that information to pick financially strong countries that you might consider when selecting a jurisdiction for a foreign bank account.

A nation's "current account" is an important indicator about its economic health and is composed of three components. It is defined as the sum of the net income from abroad, net current transfers and a country's balance of trade (exports less imports). The *trade balance* is typically the biggest determinant of a nation's current account surplus or deficit so we will use a country's current account to get an idea of its net exporting position. Because a nation's current account contains the balance of trade as its most major component, it reveals the general pattern of its foreign trade. If a nation's exports exceed its imports, it has a positive trade balance, which is what we want to see to identify a nation as economically strong.

During periods of economic uncertainty, nations with current account deficits often come under speculative attack and their currencies weaken. You would *not* want to have a bank account denominated in the local currency of such countries during difficult times. You want countries with positive current account balances as potential hosts of your foreign bank account simply because that suggests that the nation is economically and thus financially strong. The direct linkage is not necessarily there, but remember we are just trying to arrive at approximates using a simple type of analysis that you can repeat on your own at home using readily available information.

Everything is relative, so we want the current account balance as a proportion of GDP. Going to Wikipedia and looking up "List of countries by current account balance as a percentage of GDP," we have the following list of "strong" countries: Brunei, Kuwait, Tuvalu, Qatar, Azerbaijan, Singapore, Saudi Arabia, United Arab Emirates, Bahrain, Taiwan, Norway, Gabon, Netherlands, Trinidad and Tobago, Oman, Switzerland, Iran, Germany, Luxembourg, Vietnam, Ireland, Denmark, Slovenia, Sweden. You can see that this list is heavily weighted toward oil producing nations. If the world switched from using oil to an alternative source of energy, those countries would probably drop from this list and their strong financial standing in the world would probably decline.

Wikipedia also has a list of "Countries by net international investment position per capita."

The NIIP, or net international investment position, is the value of foreign assets owned by a nation minus the value of domestic assets owned by foreigners. In other words, the NIIP can be regarded as a *nation's balance sheet with the rest of the world*. It is like the net worth of a balance sheet statement because it represents foreign assets minus foreign liabilities.

A positive NIIP figure indicates that a nation's foreign assets exceed its liabilities. Since assets minus liabilities is a measure of a net worth or wealth, we can also use this figure to get a rough feeling for which countries are rich (and therefore possible candidates for safe bank deposits). In other words, if someone owns a lot of assets after all their debt has been subtracted away, ranking individuals along these lines would give us an approximate ranking of their wealth so we will do a similar thing for countries.

Previously we looked at GDP per capita to try to determine which countries were wealthier than others. Using this alternative measure, and even though the Wikipedia figures are outdated, we find that the top eighteen countries with a positive NIIP per capita are Luxembourg, Singapore, Switzerland, Norway, Hong Kong, Taiwan, Mauritius, Japan, Netherlands, Belgium, Saudi Arabia, Denmark, Germany, Finland, Israel, Malta, China and Russia.

If we look for commonalities, we arrive at the following countries that appear on all three lists. I have also provided the international credit ratings for their sovereign bonds: *Luxembourg (AAA), Norway (AAA), Switzerland (AAA), Singapore*

(AAA), Denmark (AAA), Netherlands (AA+), and Germany (AAA).

Note that Germany, who is the financial strength behind the Euro, is on this list. Switzerland, an international private banking capital of the world, is on the list as is Luxembourg, also known for its international banking facilities and special expertise in managing mutual funds and pension funds. Asian banking and financial center powerhouse Singapore is on this list, too, and then come Norway (benefitting from its oil), Denmark and the Netherlands.

The countries that appear on just two of these lists rather than all three include Qatar (AA), Sweden (AAA) Finland (AAA), Belgium (AA), Israel (A+), Japan (AA-), Kuwait (AA), Ireland (A-), United Arab Emirates (AA), Brunei (unavailable), Taiwan (AA-), and Saudi Arabia (AA-). Note the presence of Taiwan and UAE on this list, which we will discuss later.

None of these lists are definitive in any way. However, they do give a rough idea of how "wealthy" or "financially strong" various countries might be considered, relatively speaking, and thus provides us with a prioritized list of those best able to handle shaky financial times. These lists can help guide you to where you might want to open a foreign bank account if it is possible for your situation.

Selecting a Foreign Jurisdiction

To open up a specific type of bank account in a country you must check with your desired bank to get account opening information. The thing to do is to decide if you want a foreign account in the first place, and then come up with a list of the safest international banking options readily available. In making a final decision, you should concentrate on offshore banking jurisdictions with a strong and stable financial sector, low taxes, and which don't have a history of plundering savers or banks in bad times.

You should also consider something other than a dollar-denominated account because the U.S. is actively devaluing its currency at breakneck speed due to ZIRP-related excessive money printing, which over the long run will make the dollar less valuable internationally. Since the dollar-denominated interest rate is already near zero, you should evaluate whether parking your funds overseas in dollars is wise if a stronger currency is available that also offers a higher interest rate.

That being said, which countries look good along these lines?

While I like Swiss banking, it is very expensive. The Swiss have a history of expensive fees and negative interest rates, so any move towards Swiss banking should be because you expect the Swiss Franc to appreciate rather than because you want to secure a higher interest rate. Swiss banking is also not an option if you have privacy concerns. One of the main reasons people favored Swiss bank accounts in the past was because of possible anonymity (which has disappeared due to required FATCA reporting) but that anonymity is no longer possible since the Swiss share banking information with the United States. The biggest draw now is because people want to protect assets using a European option other than the shaky Euro, but there is a possibility of negative interest rates or other penalties when it comes to Swiss banking.

All that aside, Switzerland is not a location we recommend for holding gold either because of massive allocated account improprieties that aren't being reported in the press. All these shenanigans together call its banking system practices and safety of its banking system into question. The fact that the Swiss central bank just recently ditched its peg to the Euro, without warning anyone, is a policy we strongly applauded but its way of having gone about matters suggests unanticipated shocks from the Swiss system that might harm depositors by surprise and we want to avoid that at all costs.

As to Australia, it is a robust exporting nation with strong banks, and it should remain strong in any global financial catastrophe. However, it is not at the top of my list for an offshore account. That's because the country has passed new legislation authorizing depositor bail-ins, like Cyprus, where your funds might be confiscated if there ever were a banking crisis. Canada, which is economically and financially linked to the U.S. at the hip, has also passed similar legislation.

Norway is financially strong and one of the safest countries in the world from that and other angles. I would personally buy Norwegian bonds in an instant because of the nation's financial strength. Unfortunately, it is very difficult for a non-resident American to open up a Norwegian bank account if you don't live in the country, so we must bypass this possibility too.

Since we are looking for dollar and Euro alternatives, the Yen pops into most people's minds, but our deep dive analysis shows that Japanese banks don't appear on any list of financial safety. The debt level of Japanese government is so high that the government has to take 43% of its central tax revenue just to pay the interest on its bonds. Obviously if interest rates were to increase Japan would be bankrupt in a moment's notice.

The potential fate of Japanese bonds is a perfect illustration of the dangers that we are trying to escape through an astute choice of a foreign bank account. Yen bonds face a triple threat of increasing interest rates (since the rates are now nearly zero and can only go up), the Yen's devaluation from excessive money printing (greater than the Fed's), and the fact that Japan is so indebted that the government (country) itself faces default risk.

Most people don't know it, but while the U.S. Federal Reserve reported that it was stepping down QE (quantitative easing), it had actually exported the QE to Japan through an agreement with the Japanese government that it would buy U.S. Treasury Bonds for Japanese government pension funds. In words, while the FED announced it would end QE it actually exported QE to Japan by commandeering its $1.1 trillion pension fund that would now buy the bonds that the FED had been buying itself.

While in a perfect world we would have the net derivatives and swap exposure of a nation's banks to help us define risks even better, and further details on national domestic and government debt levels, those numbers aren't easily available. Nevertheless after much analysis, the numbers suggest that Singapore is near the top of the list of the best places for offshore bank accounts, and Hong Kong is also in that upper tier. Taiwan is also a third possibility for Asia, but the less risky Asian banking systems generally lie in Hong Kong and Singapore.

Nothing is definitive, but these countries keep coming up on lists derived from multiple angles. Gold bug Jim Sinclair also likes the trio of Singapore, Hong Kong and Taiwanese banks but we have arrived at those jurisdictions from our own independent analysis. If we were to add an Arab nation we would turn to the UAE because of its financial strength and potential to become one of the world's gold trading centers in the future. Singapore is also trying to become an Asian gold trading hub as well, and Shanghai (China) has already made inroads in the same direction. In our opinion, this one factor will be very important in the future for a nation's financial stability.

Bank account deposits in both Hong Kong and Singapore have government insurance, and both territories are international financial centers that strongly adhere to the rule of law. Not only are excellent banking services available in both countries, but they are both highly recommended locations for storing precious metals out of the reach of the Western banking system.

Banks commonly offer multi-currency accounts in both countries where you can park your savings in one or more international currencies, and trade in and out of these currencies simply by pushing a few buttons on your computer. *In both countries Americans are still welcome to open up accounts*, which is not the case in many other foreign jurisdictions because of the paperwork burdens of FATCA.

The Singapore dollar has been appreciating nicely over the last few years, which is another reason to consider a Singapore offshore account. What works against Singapore is the fact that the country has one of the highest debt-to-GDP ratios in the world (after Ireland and Japan) despite all the other financial numbers we have considered. On the other hand, financial analyst Marc Faber has pointed out that Singapore is a place where the US government will most likely stay out of domestic affairs (including interference in its banking system) since it needs its Singapore military base for the surveillance of Asia. Singapore is also trying to become one of the gold-trading capitals of Asia, in competition with Shanghai, and this hard money emphasis is another factor in its favor.

Hong Kong is another wonderful banking location besides Singapore. I have lived there for many years myself and can tell you that Hong Kong is wonderful for financial services. The economy is robust and Hong Kong is a play on booming China without its political problems. The Hong Kong government just finished its fiscal year with a surplus of at least HK$60 billion, which was six times more than the finance ministry projected! Tell me what governments in the world at present run their countries with a surplus?

Furthermore, the Hong Kong's Monetary Authority Exchange Fund (the country's central bank) also shows a strong balance sheet where the capital reserves are equal to over 20% of total assets. For a central bank this capitalization ratio equates to a massive margin of safety suggesting one of the safest banking systems in the world. As a comparison, consider that the capital reserve for the U.S. Federal Reserve is around 1.27% whereas it is 0.47% in Canada.

The Hong Kong dollar is currently pegged to the US dollar, which is a good thing for individuals who actually want to have their funds tied to the US dollar. Of course, Hong Kong could easily switch its currency peg to the Chinese renminbi if the dollar's value was to suddenly collapse, and that is actually another benefit in its favor. This also makes Hong Kong, along with Singapore, one of my favorite foreign banking locations.

Hang Seng Bank is considered the safest bank in Hong Kong according to *Global Finance,* although wisdom would also suggest the Bank of China (because it represents Mainland China), which would never be allowed to go bankrupt. China would also be sure to support Hong Kong to insure that nothing ever collapsed its financials or economy whereas Singapore, being independent and small, might have to struggle in that area if international financial difficulties ever arose to grab the world stage and affect every country at the same time. If you wanted you could even look to open up an account of a Singapore bank in Hong Kong such as DBS Bank, Overseas Chinese Banking Corporation and United Overseas Bank.

As to Taiwanese banks, they are a third possibility on our list because those banks are also somewhat outside of the western economic and financial systems. *Global Finance* says that the Bank of Taiwan is the safest in Taiwan whereas the National Bank of Abu Dhabi appears as its safest bank selection for the United Arab Emirates (UAE).

Opening an Account

In previous days you might have opened up a foreign bank account over the internet, but in most cases you will need to show up in person to open any offshore bank account in any foreign jurisdiction. The documents required to open an account will vary by your chosen bank and jurisdiction but they will usually include a passport, proof of your address, a letter of introduction from another bank, and a cash deposit. Before you make a trip overseas to open up any foreign account, please check with your intended bank to see what documents they might require.

The key point is that you should definitely be internationally diversified to some degree if you truly want to protect your wealth. In such an uncertain world, it is wise not just to diversify from active trading into long-term investing and passive high yield income, but to diversify across various asset classes as well as to have the custody of your assets spread out across different jurisdictions.

I have met many dozens of individuals and families who have escaped foreign jurisdictions with little cash in their hands and no assets to their name because they had to leave everything behind. These stories consistently tell me that international diversification is smart, and a deep study history also teaches this lesson as well. However, you don't even need to study history to come to this conclusion. Think about the individuals presently living in the Ukraine (war and currency devaluation), Cyprus (capital controls and bail-ins) or Venezuela (inflation and retirement savings nationalization) who are financially suffering because of the state of their nations and you will realize that those who were smart enough to open foreign bank accounts have shielded themselves to some degree because of their foresight.

No one ever expects problems to strike home but history shows that unexpected financial calamities can and will come. It is prudent to be prepared just as it is prudent to buy insurance in case of unanticipated disasters.

Two of my favorite lines from literature hammer home the point that the world changes in unexpected ways and you best prepare for that instead of counting on constant stability. The first comes from the Chinese novel, *Romance of the Three Kingdoms,* which tells the story of how various feudal lords fought in ancient China over the goal of trying to replace or restore the Han dynasty. The novel starts out with the famous lines, "Empires wax and wane; states cleave asunder and coalesce." In short, everything changes so err on the side of prudence. *A Tale of Two Cities* similarly starts out with, "It was the best of times, it was the worst of times, it was the age of wisdom, it was the age of foolishness." Once again these opening lines remind me to be prudent when it comes to planning for the safety of assets.

History has shown time and again that economic and financial catastrophes happen to every country and most people never expected them. For many of those situations, the act of having located some of your assets outside of your home country, in countries with safer economies and/or banking systems, proved to be very wise.

The basic idea is that if things get domestically crazy, some assets will be protected from catastrophic domestic economic or financial conditions or even the whims of a rapacious government. A foreign account will help you maximize your personal freedom and buy you peace of mind because it will help dilute your political risks, namely the risks to your wealth from your own government. This is what you must consider when pondering the wisdom of holding a foreign bank account.

CHAPTER 16:

THE WAR ON CASH

It is strange to think that central banks are advocating not just negative interest rates but even the abolishment of cash, and have started doing so across the world by abolishing large denomination notes. After former Standard Chartered CEO Peter Sands recently called for withdrawing the € 500 note from circulation, Mario Draghi announced that the European Central Bank would phase out the € 500 note, the second largest denomination in print. Just one day later Harvard economist Larry Summers said it's time to kill the U.S. $100 bill too. There is definitely a war on cash going on. The question is as to why.

Under the feeble excuse of cracking down on crime (with the explanation that only criminals need large denomination bills since they use it to move cash illicitly) or eliminating tax avoidance, several European nations are already forbidding large cash transactions. France already has a € 1,000 limit on cash transactions while in Italy it is also illegal to pay in cash for anything worth more than € 1,000. Spain limits private cash transactions to € 2,500. British merchants accepting more than € 15,0000 in cash for a transaction must first register with the tax authorities. Recently, Germany also proposed a € 5,000 cap on cash transactions while China, India and Sweden are developing plans to eliminate cash.

Politicians like to give the impression that their decisions are designed to help protect the public, and so the war on cash is being billed as deterring its usage in "financing terrorism, money laundering and other illegal activities." How ridiculous. The explanation is utterly preposterous. Organized crime is no doubt laughing on the floor about the claim that eliminating large bills will somehow deter their operations. As many have pointed out, crime pre-dates cash and will still exist long after anyone ever bans it. So where is this actually going? What is this all about?

It is natural that governments would theoretically want as many financial transactions as possible to be made electronically so that they could track absolutely everything with total surveillance and thereby collect more taxes. It is also a way to control citizen purchases, and thus citizens. However, almost everyone with brains would object to these objectives because most people want their transactions to remain private. Hence, why all the fuss now?

The most reasonable and logical conclusion as to the reasons behind this new policy proposal is that the banking system is in deep trouble. Previous attempts to fix both the banking system and kick start the economy have failed, and now the powers in control are preparing the way for bank bail-ins and the possible need to recapitalize entire banking systems that are at risk of failure. If you force people into electronic deposits, you can threaten them with negative interest rates and force them to spend the way you want. You can also deduct whatever you want from accounts without any public recourse. By controlling your cash, the government can make you into a very compliant slave! The very next step would be to chip you so that you had ready access to your electronic cash, and then the government will control you completely.

Several countries have already turned to the crazy non-solution of negative interest rates (NIRP) as a way to "stimulate" their economies, boldly claiming that negative rates would prod bank depositors to remove their cash and spend it, thus stimulating their economies. This crazy policy, of course, has done no such thing. No sane economist could have imagined this policy years ago but now it is taken for granted simply because every other sane measure has failed. However, who in their right mind will lend money to a borrower hoping for a profit but knowing, for certain, that they will be getting less money back at a future date?

You certainly won't spend money you need, and you certainly will be saving every penny possible if you lost your job or you feel your job is in jeopardy. How negative interest rates will cause you to spend in those situations is beyond anyone's idea because it won't. In fact, if banks actually started charging savers interest on their own money, savers who needed that money would have to save even more to offset the additional costs imposed by the banks on their savings. In other words, people would spend even less!

All this talk of stimulating the economy through negative interest rates is therefore just nonsense. It has never happened and never will. It is just another desperate ploy by central bankers who have run out of policy options and are ready to try any wild possible to save banking systems and try to stimulate economies out of recessions. In actuality, since these policies are so transparently foolish and doomed to fail at economic stimulation, they must be part of a bigger plan.

Think for a second. In the real world, rational people know that if they put money in the bank and it gets eaten up by negative interest rates, they will take it out and keep it in cash, gold or silver or anything else. Cash, of course, would be the first option. Anybody can figure this out, so no one proposing negative interest rates and the banning of cash would do so except with a different strategy in mind.

A war on cash is ridiculous. Cash is critical for the smooth functioning of an economy. It allows low-income people to participate in the economy without a bank account, and accounts for a significant proportion of a country's gray market GDP. In fact, cash is the only way that some people can even participate in an economy! God forbid that a cashless economy eventually leads to chipping people in order to control their usage of money.

What is worrying the central bankers must be the fact that holding cash allows you to escape any of the effects desired by negative interest rates, and so there is now the testing of a political move to ban it. After all, as soon as a government announced negative interest rates for its citizens, people would pull their money out of the banking system in response to the threat of losing a percentage of their deposits. Since negative interest rates wouldn't "work" if cash escaped the grips of this system (not that the policy would work anyway), there has to be something else going on.

Governments and/or the banks want to "eat" your money for something – either for on-going profits (since they can't make money under ZIRP loaning it out), to cover their losses from debts or bad derivative plays, or for the eventual re-capitalization of the banking system that has to happen if it indeed fails. In the larger picture, central bankers across the world can no longer effectively stimulate economies by money printing as this policy has reached its limit of effectiveness. They are now at the point of pushing on strings when it comes to any type of Keynesian stimulation. Therefore the real reason we are seeing the beginning of negative interest rate policies and a war on cash is because central bankers are out of ammunition and are desperate.

As long as there is physical cash, people will choose to hold it separately rather than lose it by putting it in banks charging interest. Therefore central bankers would like to take away your ability to hold cash outside the banking system. Ergo, eliminate large denomination bills first, and then go to digital currency entirely that the central banks control. In other words, eliminate cash. By eliminating cash, governments create a system whereby all money is forced into the banks, and then the banks and/or governments can grab it whenever they want. Bankers will essentially control the people since they hold their money and the people cannot rebel. Presto, a system of power over the populace is created that makes the people slaves.

If you leave your money in the bank then both governments and banks will be assured it is where they can confiscate it to bail out or even recapitalize zombie banks. They can then do with your money whatever they like under the guise of "emergency legislation" that makes everything look legitimate and necessary so they cannot be blamed. On the other hand, hoarding cash outside the banking system is easy if you hold large denomination bills that enables you to escape this, hence in the governments' mind they must be phased out of existence.

Put simply, banning cash creates a system whereby the government can confiscate your money at its discretion. It is also a way to prepare for a banking default by making sure the banks will have some cash ready for bail-ins and recapitalization efforts. The amount of money that can be collected this way is trivial compared to the size of banker bad debts and potential derivative losses usually involved in a default, but so goes the thinking of politicians and the leaders of banking.

Here is the bad part about all this as far as liberty concerns go. Banning cash is also a way to establish total surveillance over citizens since all transactions can then be tracked, traced and taxed. This violates privacy concerns, weakens individual liberties and enables governments to gain even greater control over citizens just as one would see in a fascist, communist or totalitarian government state.

In short, banning cash eliminates a citizen's control over their own wealth. If a bank holds all your money and the state controls the banks, then the state can penalize, control or shut off an individual simply because it doesn't like them or disagrees with their behavior. It can silence behavior it does not like.

What then is the solution when you hear negative interest rates are coming? This headline from ZeroHedge.com gives a hint: "Safes Sell Out In Japan, 1,000 Franc Note Demand Soars As NIRP Triggers Cash Hoarding." Japanese officials claimed that negative interest rates would cause citizens to move their funds into riskier but higher-earning assets but being rational, Japanese citizens moved it into pure cash that earns nothing instead by using large 10,000-Yen notes! In Switzerland, circulation of the 1,000 Franc note soared 17% in 2014 just after the SNB's move to a negative interest rate policy.

A sane conclusion to all this is as follows. Be prepared for change. The war on cash is not about drug money or terrorists or any other exotic claim. It is all about capital control and population control. In a cashless economy, you cannot get your money out. In a cashless society, the government can control your obedience.

When it comes to negative interest rate policies and attempts to ban cash or large denomination bills, there are no good intentions here by governments as regards the "public good." A smart course of action – if NIRP is on the horizon or some government is trying to ban cash - is to buy a safe and actually hold more money in cash. Or, one might consider buying gold and silver not just because the war on cash is likely to send precious metals through the roof but because it advertises the desperation of a banking system in peril, and precious metals are financial catastrophe insurance.

CHAPTER 17:
PROTECTION AGAINST HYPERINFLATION

Because money printing has been so rampant, many analysts have been warning about the potential for hyperinflation in not just the United States but across the world. This growing worry is due to the fact that most of the major countries have been practicing debt-laden QE and inflationary money printing policies for years, which sets the stage for hyperinflation if there is ever a loss of confidence in the currencies. To make matters worse, they have also latched their monetary policies together.

What exactly is hyperinflation? What is its ultimate cause? If we suspect it will happen, what should we do to protect ourselves from it?

Hyperinflation is a situation where a country experiences a very high rate of inflation that destroys the economy and the accumulated wealth of savers. Because of the high rate of inflation, the prices of staples and other domestic items increase so much that a national currency, which has usually increased in volume, becomes virtually worthless.

For example, a loaf of bread might originally cost one dollar, but with hyperinflation the price might rise to one hundred dollars, then one thousand dollars and eventually a million dollars or more. Because what previously cost one dollar now costs millions, hyperinflation essentially causes the value of a nation's currency to become virtually worthless. The speed of this inflation is often so rapid that sometimes a nation cannot even print new currency notes as fast as the rate by which the currency is devaluing.

To illustrate, here is a brief timeline of the exchange rate of German marks per one U.S. dollar as historically occurred during Weimar Germany's famous episode of hyperinflation:

April 1919: 12 marks
November 1921: 263 marks
January 1923: 17,000 marks
August 1923: 4.621 million marks
October 1923: 25.26 billion marks
December 1923: 4.2 trillion marks.

There have been numerous cases of hyperinflation in history. During hyperinflation a paper currency loses its function as a store of value, so some economies revert to barter or start using another country's currency as the medium of exchange for transactions. Hyperinflations, once started, typically end only when the fiat currency is finally declared to be backed by tangible assets such as the precious metals. Hyperinflation is rarely ended by a paper currency being backed by another fiat paper currency.

In the last hundred years alone, hyperinflation has occurred on more than twenty occasions around the world including within China, Germany, Russia, Hungary, Yugoslavia, Chile, Greece, Turkey and Zimbabwe. Some of the most famous incidents include the hyperinflation caused by the issuance of assignats in Revolutionary France and of course the hyperinflation of Weimar Germany. One of the interesting facts about hyperinflation is that it is often connected to war.

The reason hyperinflation sometimes occurs during warfare is because the steep cost of continually buying armaments to win the conflict puts nations in deep debt, and they often turn to rampant money printing to pay their deficits. During a war, governments need to do whatever is necessary to continue fighting to survive, which means they must continue buying weapons otherwise the alternative is their defeat. However, the war itself makes it difficult to raise or collect taxes among the citizenry. War also makes it difficult to raise money through bond sales in order to finance the government deficits. During a war the borrowing of money basically becomes costly and/or difficult so the financial authorities typically turn to "monetizing" the ballooning government deficit by simply printing money. This is the chain of causation behind warfare-caused hyperinflation.

If we examine the Chinese hyperinflation from 1939-1945 we find that it is a classic example of a government printing money to pay civil war costs and then suffering as a result. Hyperinflation was also previously seen in the United States on the Confederate side during the Civil War and also during the Revolutionary War. For instance, during George Washington's day Congress had to finance the Revolutionary War so it chose to continually print more and more paper money. As more "Continentals" flooded the countryside, the value of the money dropped dramatically and the prices of goods rose dramatically producing hyperinflation. The crash in the value of a Continental note was spectacular, which gave rise to the phrase "not worth a Continental."

During this time, Congress frantically tried to stop the depreciation of the Continental currency it had created. It passed laws requiring citizens to accept the fiat paper money on par with gold or silver, but its attempts at price control had the effect of eliminating goods from the market. In a pattern seen time and again throughout history, because of price controls farmers and shopkeepers simply stopped offering goods of real value in exchange for the near-valueless paper.

Aside from war, most cases of hyperinflation typically occur when an ordinary (non-wartime) government has financed increasingly larger and larger deficits by massive amounts of fiat money creation until there is so much money in circulation that people lose all faith in the currency. Due to excessive money printing, the amount of money in circulation eventually far exceeds the amount normally required for transactions to match the national output of goods and services, and its surplus everywhere causes people to lose faith in its value. When confidence in the value of a currency is lost, and especially if other factors contribute to reinforce the effect, the value of fiat money can quickly collapse to produce hyperinflation.

In most cases of hyperinflations, the calamity was caused because for some reason a monetary authority simply kept printing money to pay all its expenses, including the interest on its own debt, rather than cut costs or raise revenues. For instance, by the 2020s the United States government will be making annual interest payments on its debt that total more than the combined military budgets of Brazil, Russia, India, China, Japan, South Korea, Canada, Australia, Britain, France, Germany, Saudi Arabia, Spain, Italy, Turkey, and Israel. If interest rates were to rise to 10%, nearly half of U.S. government income would be going toward paying interest on its debt, so the only way out of the problem is through inflation or default.

The history of hyperinflations usually involves a loss of both fiscal and monetary control. In past historical examples, you'll typically find that a government has not only racked up massive internal deficits due to lax fiscal control (ex. to finance the defense industry or large social welfare programs) but has amassed huge external debts too. The debts have become so large that they cannot be covered by taxes and so the government must print money to fund them. In what harkens of a Ponzi scheme, it must even issue new debt to repay its existing debt plus its interest.

An unsustainable debt burden that a government has grown can only be handled in three ways: either by outright default, by the forgiveness of debt (a debt Jubilee) or by money printing. Typically governments choose the third option and therefore print gobs of money. But they print so much money to cover their debts to fulfill their needs that prices in the economy rise exponentially and the value of the currency resultantly falls to near zero. As this loss of confidence in the currency proceeds, similar to a bank run people then try to frantically exchange it for anything of real, tangible value.

The most common ways to protect your wealth during such times is by (1) holding a stable foreign currency instead of the depreciating national currency, or by (2) holding physical gold or silver since they retain their international value during such times of distress. You can also (3) hold functional assets such as commodities, consumable staples, or other tangible assets of lasting value. This includes income producing farmland or real estate that maintains its worldly value regardless of its monetary value.

To understand hyperinflation it pays for us to review some of the most famous cases of its occurrence. The first case we shall review will set the stage for our analysis and involves the history of Revolutionary France.

French Revolution

The case of hyperinflation in Revolutionary France, after the French Revolution in 1789, bears many lessons for today. The National Assembly, once in control of the government, inherited a financial mess from the monarchy but still decided to engage in a military buildup while supporting massive public spending projects. It supported these expensive projects because it wished to do something about the stagnant economy, unemployment and great scarcity of money in the nation.

Essentially bankrupt, to pay its bills the National Assembly confiscated the landed properties of the French Catholic Church and tried to monetize them by printing certificates (assignats) representing the value of the properties. In addition to the problem of counterfeiting, no disciplinary control was exercised over the amount of assignats issued and their value eventually exceeded that of the confiscated properties. Initially they circulated alongside gold at par value but eventually their value against gold began to fall. The overprinting of assignats and their price depreciation caused massive hyperinflation with the result that the assignats eventually lost most of their nominal value.

In the French Revolution, this hyperinflation caused the price of gold to go up 288 times in just the five years from 1790 to 1795 alone, which highlights the potential safety role of the precious metals in such situations. By 1795, the hyperinflation in France was so bad that it was said that the inflation rate was 13,000 percent! At that time, the French people were running from the worthless fiat money seeking some way to hold the value of their wealth through physical items such as gold, jewels and real estate. By redeeming their currency for gold and silver the people ended up owning tangible assets of value, whereas the paper currency only had a value based on promises that were ultimately worth nothing. It was only when Napoleon replaced France's paper money system with a gold-backed money system that stability was restored in the country and the hyperinflation was finally ended.

Weimar Germany

Another classic example of the collapse of a currency was the Weimar hyperinflation of 1922–1923. In that instance, the German government expanded the creation of its currency in the belief that if people had more money they would spend more and the economy would boom. Unfortunately, the money creation only resulted in rising prices rather than greater wealth. After all, if you could just print more money to become wealthier than everyone would do it.

Although printing excess money was itself the problem, the government continued printing because the bankers and political leaders reasoned (similar to the situation in Revolutionary France) that if they could only print *enough* then many problems would be solved. However, no such thing happened. In hyperinflation the politicians and monetary official always point the blame at other parties and rarely stop to think that the money printing itself might be the problem.

The German countryside farmers had no problems growing food during the Weimar Republic, but because of the currency depreciation they refused to bring their produce into the city in return for what they considered worthless paper. Each day that a farmer delayed delivering his produce to the city the prices for his goods also would increase so waiting was a good strategy because he therefore made more money. Whenever he could obtain bartered items for his produce rather than worthless paper there was also no reason to exchange his produce for worthless paper.

Hence, while food was readily available in Germany's countryside, the German farmers kept the harvest of 1923 in their warehouses while city supermarkets were empty. As a result, food riots broke out and starvation spread even though food was available. Civil unrest loomed and gangs of workers even marched into the countryside to loot the farms and dig up vegetables. In addition to the food shortages, businesses started to close down and unemployment soared. The economy started collapsing.

By mid-1923, the hyperinflation was raging with prices often doubling every few hours so it became common for workers to be paid several times a day. Their wives would meet them to take the money and then would rush to the shops to exchange it for goods. However, by this time more and more shops were empty of any products to buy. Merchants could not even obtain goods to replenish their inventories. The net result was that a wild stampede developed to buy real goods and get rid of the worthless money. The hyperinflation was so bad that by late 1923 it took 200 billion marks just to buy a loaf of bread. One can study the modern day example of hyperinflationary Zimbabwe to see a similar rise in prices.

The state of Germany's economy threatened to break the nation apart, but eventually the hyperinflation was stopped by a return to a currency backed by real goods just as in Revolutionary France. One of the general rules of hyperinflations is that the paper currency cannot be replaced by another paper currency in order to end the depreciation. With that in mind, here is how the hyperinflation ended.

On November 9, 1923, Adolf Hitler seized power in Germany. On November 13, Hjalmar Schacht was appointed Commissioner for National Currency and two days later the printing of the rapidly devalued mark ceased. A few days later, the very first Rentenmarks, backed by German land used for agriculture and business, began to emerge. On November 20, the devalued mark was pegged to the Rentenmark at the rate of a trillion to one with an exchange rate of 4.2 Rentenmarks to equal one U.S. dollar. The hyperinflation was thereby halted, but it had destroyed the savings of the middle class.

In this famous instance, the hyperinflation had occurred because the German government had ended up continually printing a flood of new money, thus causing prices to rise astronomically. As the inflation gained momentum, events seemed to demand the printing of larger and larger issues of currency (just as in France) but no one stopped the money printing. Only after the mark was once again tied to a real commodity was order finally restored.

While the German situation probably ranks as the most famous case of hyperinflation, it was not the worst episode in history. For instance, in 1946 the prices for goods in Hungary were doubling every fifteen hours, which equates to an inflation rate of 41.9 quintillion percent. In 2008, the inflation rate in Zimbabwe due to hyperinflation reached 79.6 billion percent. I still have a framed "100 trillion dollar" Zimbabwe currency note hanging on my wall to remind me of what can happen in a nation due to fiscal and monetary mismanagement.

Despite our modern educational system that produces PhDs in business, economics and finance to oversee fiscal and monetary policies, the "wise men" seem to continually make the same mistakes throughout history. Central bankers make the same mistakes again and again to produce hyperinflations that destroy economies and the public.

In the 20th century alone, hyperinflation has happened dozens of times throughout the world with the most recent cases being Venezuela and Zimbabwe, as stated. Chile offers yet another case study that is instructive because of the different way in which the hyperinflation occurred. The Chilean history even provides lessons about how you might position yourself for wealth despite a hyperinflationary crisis.

Chile

The causes of Chile's hyperinflation were quite different than those of the French or German situations. The history is that in 1970 Salvador Allende was elected president of Chile. As part of his policies, land was expropriated and given to Chilean workers. Companies and mines were also nationalized and loyal supporters put in managerial positions of power.

This is something that has also historically been seen in various African nations when newly elected black governments would strip white farmers and business owners of their property and give it to valued supporters. Without the experienced managers in charge, however, production would drop, properties would go to ruin and many of those nations would face economic collapse.

Allende also instituted wage and price controls for the general economy by simultaneously freezing the prices of basic goods and services. For popular support, he also increased wages by decree. Exceedingly popular among the workers, initially Allende's policies seemed great because the workers now had more money to spend while basic goods and services still retained the same low prices. With more money in hand, the workers thus increased their buying so as to rapidly empty stores and warehouses of consumer goods and basic products.

However, just as in French Revolutionary days the private companies quickly went bankrupt because they were forced to maintain the same revenue structures while paying higher worker wages. The bankrupt firms were then taken over by the government and made to continue their operations at a loss in order to satisfy internal demand. Because the bankrupt firms were essentially running at a loss, whenever there was a cash shortfall the Allende government would simply print more money to satisfy the shortfall. It would give the newly printed money to the now State-controlled companies, which would in turn pay the workers. Thus, hyperinflation started in Chile because of disastrous economic policies that led to excessive money printing.

While in Germany there were goods available for purchase during the hyperinflation, the German farmers simply refused to deliver food to the markets. However, in Chile the workers had plenty of cash in hand, but it was essentially useless because there were no goods to buy! Of course the disappearance of marketplace products to buy eventually happened within Germany too because all consumers in this type of situation eventually realize it is better to exchange their cash for goods of value rather than retain it as worthless, depreciating paper. They eventually go on a rush to empty store shelves just as happened in Revolutionary France. Everyone rushes to exchange their cash for items of value.

During a hyperinflation, consumers with any brains at all look at their devaluing currency and say to themselves, "Wait a minute, this piece of paper is worth nothing. It cannot buy me anything at all. Every day it has less and less value and the store shelves are emptying of everything anyway. I'm going to get rid of it as soon as possible. I'm going to exchange it for any goods I can get and buy any items that can hold their value if I can find them."

If they have any opportunity at all, the public in such situations will try to sell their currency for a stronger one, or exchange it for hard assets like gold and silver. When you are worried that your money will become worthless you will certainly spend it faster, which creates and reinforces hyperinflation. The rule is that people don't want to hold cash during hyperinflations so they buy commodities or anything else that seems to store value.

An additional and marked difference to note between the Chilean and German hyperinflationary situations is the following, which seems like a paradox. While in Germany the hyperinflation caused the value of stocks to rise, in Chile the hyperinflation caused the exact opposite, namely a collapse in asset prices! You would think that in a hyperinflationary environment the asset prices – such as the prices of stocks and real estate - should always rise. However, there is a very important caveat affecting affairs that has to do with survival. Since it is had to predict the course of hyperinflation, this is the lesson we must take to heart.

If your basic necessities for living go unmet - such as the availability of food, water, shelter and clothing - any asset that you possess will be willingly sold in order to meet your basic needs.   For instance, those starving of food or dying of thirst will often sell anything they have to get food and water in order to survive. The people of Chile therefore sold anything of value which they had in order to meet the basic needs for their families' survivals.

What happened in Chile along these lines is as follows. As Chile deteriorated in 1972 and 1973, both the stock market and the housing market collapsed. The prices dropped like a rock for every asset class because people were cashing out of their assets in order to buy basic goods or were cashing out so that they could leave the country altogether.

In an important article Gonzalos Lira, who writes of this time, recounts two stories packed with powerful lessons:

> A true story: In '73, at the height of the Allende-created hyperinflation, an uncle of mine, who was then a college student, was offered an apartment in exchange for his car. That's right—an apartment. He owned a crappy little Fiat 147—a POS if ever there was such a thing—but cars in Chile in the middle of that hyperinflation were so scarce, and considered so valuable, that he was offered an apartment in exchange. To this day, my uncle still tells the story—with deep regret, because he didn't follow through on the offer: "That Fiat was in the junkyard by '78, but that apartment still stands! And today it's worth nearly a half a million dollars!" Actually, I think it's worth a bit more than that.
>
> Another true story: A banker friend of mine manages the assets of a

fabulously wealthy 70-something gentleman, whom I'll call Alfredo. In 1973, Don Alfredo was a youngish man, just starting out, with a degree in engineering but no money—until he inherited US$3,000 from a deceased aunt. Alfredo realized that the $3,000 were in a sense worthless: He couldn't buy anything with them, and it wasn't enough for him to leave the country and start over someplace else. After all, even then, $3,000 was not that much money.

So he took those $3,000, went down to the stock exchange, and spent all of it on Chilean blue-chip companies: Mining companies, chemical companies, paper companies, and so on. The stock were selling for nothing—less than penny stock—because of the disastrous policies of the Allende government. His stock broker at the time told him not to buy stocks, as Allende's government, it was thought, would soon nationalize these companies as well.

Alfredo ignored his broker, and went ahead with the stock purchases: He spent all of his $3,000 on buckets of near-worthless equities.

On September 11, 1973, the commanders in chief of the four branches of the Chilean military staged a coup d'état. Within a year, Alfredo's stock had rebounded about ten-fold. Since then, they've multiplied several thousand-fold—yes: Several thousand-fold. Don Alfredo has lived off of that $3,000 investment ever since—it's what made him a multi-millionaire today.

He realized, of course, that either those blue-chip companies would be nationalized by Allende—in which case he would lose all his $3,000 inheritance, which really wouldn't change his fortunes very much—or somehow a new normal would arrive in Chile. Since the $3,000 couldn't buy him anything, he took a gamble—and won.

The lessons from all these various hyperinflation case studies are many, especially those we can access through the writings of Gonzalos Lira, whom you might study.

Hyperinflation, first and foremost, is a currency event that can have different causes. Regardless of its ultimate causes, in days it can take you from the status of being financially set for life to being unable to afford even a loaf of bread. However, on must always remember this. After a hyperinflationary event, *which may last for years*, there is always a new normal. With that in mind, one must prepare for its eventual demise. A common way for the troubles to end is for the currency to finally be pegged to the precious metals, such as the prices of gold and silver (or content of gold and silver in coins), or to be backed by some other type of tangible asset.

One of the reasons that the fiat U.S. dollar has escaped hyperinflation for so long is because Henry Kissinger arranged for Saudi Arabian petroleum to be traded in dollars, and as a result of the worldwide oil trade being conducted solely in dollars we can say that the dollar was de facto pegged to oil! In other words, the United States dollar has escaped hyperinflation only because it has actually been pegged to a hard asset, namely oil. The U.S. dollar is an oil-backed currency.

Now that China and Russia are bit-by-bit chipping away at the dollar's monopoly in worldwide oil trade and reducing the dollar's role in world trade, history suggests that the U.S. dollar will also eventually collapse as the Petrodollar disappears. Strong evidence already exists suggesting that the demand for U.S. Treasury bonds is rapidly shrinking worldwide and can only be propped up artificially by using secretive machinery involving the derivatives markets. This is a recipe for failure that risks the dollar's status as the world's reserve currency. At the same time to make the situation worse, America has also resorted to unsterilized money printing to monetize its debts, which is a common road to Zimbabwe-style hyperinflation. A sure road to hyperinflation is to start counterfeiting money by monetizing a nation's ever burgeoning deficit.

Let's examine the dangers from yet another angle. Right now countless governments across the world have also simultaneously engaged in a common but insane level of debt issuance and money printing (QE quantitative easing) in order to avoid banking defaults, pay government debt interest and increase inflation. They have all linked their ships together via the same insane monetary policy.

The rationale for the money printing is that inflation must be kindled in economies. Bankers believe inflation will stave off a deflationary collapse that would normally occur because of their bad debts going into default. The theory is that inflation *should* cause rising asset prices, and those price increases should counteract some of the bad debts. Inflation might wipe away the prospect of some debt defaults entirely or cause increases in other asset prices that could offset the debt losses.

Unfortunately, bankers aren't the only ones with excessive levels of debt. The debt burden that has been created by governments is now so large that many central banks must maintain zero interest rate policies otherwise defaults will occur because they cannot pay off its interest. Japan, for instance, is a country that faces this situation.

The combination of too much debt, low interest rates and excessive money printing definitely has the potential to ignite into hyperinflation, but no one can say for sure this will happen such as when or where. While the misguided policies to pay off deficits and stave off banking bankruptcies – such as QE, NIRP and ZIRP - have kept the large banks within many countries alive, they certainly haven't helped the common man, which is the main end goal of economic policy.

For instance, the push to ignite inflation has caused poor unemployed people to pay higher prices at the grocery store, thus making their problems even worse. Now they have both unemployment *and* inflation instead of just unemployment alone. That certainly isn't helping the economy.

At present governments are also simultaneously engaged in currency wars of depreciation to stimulate their economies. They want to make their currencies cheaper so that they can continue exporting products and thus keep their economies humming. But everyone is depreciating his currency at the same time in a situation reminiscent of the trade wars prior to the Great Depression.

As fiat currency wars continue to rage on between the central banks, the precious metals will likely hold their value relative to paper currencies. If hyperinflation occurs in the major developed nations, gold and silver may even become money again. Why? Because history shows that declaring a gold-backed currency is one of the dependable ways to end any hyperinflation that may arise. However, this would be opposed by central bankers since it would mean a loss of their powers. Nevertheless this can indeed become a possibility if many nations simultaneously choose to do so and the price of the precious metals rose substantially.

A common question often asked is what items disappear from the store shelves quickest and become most valuable during a hyperinflation. The answer is whatever goods that normally become valuable in a crisis, or which people typically turn to in barter economies. In particular, you must remember that imports will become scarce because import prices will rise and many foreign nations will refuse to sell items to a country that offers worthless currency in return. If any country faces the prospect of hyperinflation it is therefore best to stock up on foreign imports ahead of time to ride out the storm.

Survivalists and preppers often make lists of the best barter items to stockpile for such an emergency, and these are the items that appear most often on these lists: ammunition, garden seeds, candles, batteries, solar battery recharger and solar batteries, soap, bleach, toilet tissue, diapers, condoms, toiletries (toothpaste, dental floss, shampoo), lighters and matches (fire making supplies), tobacco and cigarettes, painkillers, antibiotics, alcohol, screws and nails, tools (saw blades, hatchets, axe heads, hammer heads, hand drills), duct tape, vitamins, blankets, water containers, ammunition, tampons and pads, toilet paper, feminine products, diapers, disposable razors and razor blades, fuel (gas, diesel, propane, kerosene), reading glasses, bags, tie wraps, fishing supplies, knives of various sorts, spices, playing cards, pencils and paper, pepper spray, mylar blankets, tents, sewing and mending supplies, flashlights. The stories of many individuals who have lived through foreign crises repeatedly stress the value of ammunition, which might possibly be used even as a currency if an economic collapse gets ugly.

Price controls won't protect you for any of these items during an emergency. This is because if costs keep rising but companies are only allowed to charge artificially low prices then they won't be able to produce the product at a profit. Facing bankruptcy they will shut down and then the items will disappear from the marketplace.

The following is another important list of food items people often store in fear of an economic crisis: water, canned food, dried beans, white rice, pasta, powdered milk, hazelnuts, chocolate, whole grains, honey, dried soup mix, coffee and tea, peanut butter, cooking oil, salt, sugar, pink salmon, spices, jams and jellies, vinegar, baking soda, baking powder, bouillon cubes, and hard liquor (bourbon, rum, gin, vodka).

Remember that another way to protect yourself during a hyperinflation, however, is to hold some physical gold and silver in your hands because precious metals can be used for barter and always retain their international values. Due to its higher price, gold can serve as a stable store of value while silver's lower price will make it useful for everyday transactions during an emergency.

It is also best to also hold some gold and silver abroad, rather than domestically, due to the risks of government confiscation during a hyperinflation. History shows that during a hyperinflationary event a government may not only institute price controls and capital controls but also try to seize anything of real value. The recurring pattern in currency crises is government coercion of some type such as price controls, property confiscation and investigation (persecution) of citizens.

Because of all these risks, another means of protecting oneself against hyperinflation is to hold a foreign bank account in a currency not likely to be affected by the potential depreciation. You would want a strong and stable currency that is likely to hold its value. Astronomical debts, excessive levels of money printing and failing QE, ZIRP and now NIRP policies endanger most of the major currencies of the world. Therefore the currency to hold during a hyperinflationary crisis is the one that the world deems safest while the safest vehicles are gold or silver since they maintain an international value and have no counterparty risks.

You might also be able to diversify your assets and gain some measure of protection by holding foreign real estate whose value will depend on the economic conditions within that country (Argentina, New Zealand, etc.), hopefully isolated from the hyperinflationary trends. Holding foreign real estate also helps you escape capital controls since the IRS can freeze any bank account in the U.S. without warning. A foreign bank account will protect you from being trapped in such a nightmare.

In summary, time and again in history we have seen fiat paper currencies collapse. Assets have been frozen, gold has been confiscated, and capital controls have been imposed when no one expected such hard times to come. If there is hyperinflation in the future, the countries affected with collapsing currencies will most certainly introduce exchange controls, which is why holding a foreign bank account is ever so important.

Hyperinflation appears when central banks print far too much money for all sorts of reasons (the government spent way too much, too much debt, propping up bankrupt companies, "there isn't enough money in the economy," "the money in the economy isn't moving around fast enough") but of course they always fault something else for the event. The EU, USA, UK, Japan and many other countries have followed this course of insane money printing along with gargantuan debts. The probabilities or odds for a hyperinflationary event have definitely risen over the last decade, and you now have enough information to know how to prepare.

ABOUT THE AUTHOR

Bill Bodri is an ex-Wall Street research analyst, direct investor and popular author of investment and business books including:

- *Bankism: How the Government's Bank-First Policies are Destroying the Nation and How to Survive the Aftermath of a Coming Dollar Collapse*

- *Breakthrough Strategies of Wall Street Traders: 17 Remarkable Traders Reveal Their Top Performing Investment Strategies*

- *Super Investing: 5 Proven Methods for Beating the Market and Retiring Rich*

- *Move Forward: Powerful Strategies for Creating Better Outcomes in Life*

- *Quick, Fast, Done: Simple Time Management Secrets From Some of History's Greatest Leaders*

If you enjoyed this book you would probably enjoy *Super Investing and Breakthrough Strategies of Wall Street Traders. Breakthrough Strategies of Wall Street Traders* contains the secret proprietary trading and investing methods that several Wall Street millionaires used to make their riches.

The author can be reached for interviews through wbodri@gmail.com.

www.ingramcontent.com/pod-product-compliance
Lightning Source LLC
Chambersburg PA
CBHW081529220326
41598CB00036B/6371